SIR BONE FUNK

Praise for *Sir Bone Funk* from musicians
who have used Eddie Tebbe's lyrics

There are a few people that write with real passion -- Eddie has that passion. I have been happy to have used two of his works as lyrics in my music. Great work Eddie.
--- George Porter, Jr.

Eddie's writing is so varied and surprising, irreverent, open hearted, frank and clever. Above all, his love of music and love of life (in all its joys and deep sorrows) comes through in every word. Our band are not the first musicians who have found inspiration in Eddie's writing, and we certainly won't be the last.
--- Michael Cerveris, the band Loose Cattle

Eddie Tebbe is an inspiration to me. His indomitable will to live every moment has been a lifeline to me since the flood. He has reminded me by example to embrace every moment of time with friends, music and life.
--- Paul Sanchez, musician

Sir Bone Funk

Living Life in the Key of Triumph

by

Eddie Tebbe

DVille Press

Donaldsonville, Louisiana
www.DvillePress.com

DEDICATION

But I Want Them to Know

The most important thing in a person's life is their parents
and I have the best.

I have not always agreed with what they have done but the
love was always there.

People always say that they want a healthy child but I was not.

At that moment when I'm most mad at my parents I start
to think of the love they must have for me.

It was hard but they never gave up on me.

Each had their own style

And both were right

It is easy to give a child what they want

But easy isn't always best.

I am lucky to have parents who pushed me against the odds
with love and strength

I am lucky to have parents who have fought for me

Through all the pain.

Whatever I achieve

It's because of them

They have made me strong

They have not done everything right all the time

But I want them to know

Lynette Jerry and Henry Tebbe

I thank you for being my parents

And if I had other parents, I wouldn't be me.

I love you.
Edward Gabriel Tebbe

ACKNOWLEGEMENTS

This is to thank anybody who worked on the book, and family, friends, musicians and all those who have used my lyrics or sung them.

Eileen West is the reason I am a writer. Married to the late musician Franko "Washboard" Jackson – my favorite man – she suggested years ago that I try my hand at writing lyrics. I did and loved it, which inspired future writings that make up this book.

In deep gratitude to my doctors and caretakers.

CONTENTS

N.O. musicians sang and/or recorded the following lyrics in this book:

Michael Cerveris "Eddie Time"
George Porter, Jr. "Bone Funk", "Da Medicine Man", "Let's Get It"
Paul Sanchez "This Is All I Have to Say" and "Hitting the Road"
Paul Sanchez and Shamar Allen "Laugh While You're Dying"
Porter Batiste Stoltz "It's Me"
Chris Mulé "The Crossroads of My Life"

FOREWORD

I've always been a determined person. My mom was tenacious and she raised me to be independent, fostering that determination. It got me through a lot of challenges in life. Challenges like being born with cerebral palsy or later being diagnosed with Huntington's Disease. My determination was tested again at the age of nine when I fell from a loft and landed on my head resulting in my developing epilepsy. Determination also enabled me to get a driver's license, graduate high school and college, it allowed me to write and to travel.

My challenges started on day one in the delivery room of the hospital when the doctors saw that my umbilical cord was wrapped around my neck which had cut off oxygen to my brain and I was born with cerebral palsy, a neurological disease that can affect both cognitive and motor functions. In my case, my movements are spastic and my motor functions such as speaking and walking are affected. The doctors suggested that I be put in an institution for the rest of my life which my parents refused to do (yea!)

Growing up, I was raised mostly by my mom. I am the youngest of three children; my brother and my sister were not born with CP but Huntington's is hereditary and unfortunately they both also developed the disease later in life. My parents divorced after I was born and my dad would remain my security blanket -- he always took care of the financial needs that my condition called for. It was my mom who did the day to day parenting. Mom was a very hands-off type of parent. She gave me room to make my own mistakes and learn from them. She never treated me like a kid with CP, and it was assumed that I would do everything other kids my age did, including household chores. Mom always encouraged me to do all I could in spite of my challenges. She had a great laugh, a commitment to justice and freedom, and a love for hitting the road that have all stayed with me through my life.

From an early age I was always a storyteller. I made up and entertained anybody who would listen, with stories about anything and everything. The first time I actually tried writing was when a friend asked me to write lyrics. I was 19 or 20 years old at the time. I began writing my stories on computer when I started attending college at the University of New Orleans where I earned a degree in Secondary Social Studies. I was always a one-handed typist, but I was pretty good with that one hand, and the stories began to collect, stories I mostly showed to friends. The writing bug had taken hold.

I was always thought of as an "old soul" and I was funny, even thought about being a comedian at one point. I think it's why I have so many friends. People are comfortable around me because I was always comfortable with myself. Again, I credit my mother because she never treated me as if I were other-abled. Things like being part of household chores taught me that everybody has to work to get through life, and while to others I may have had to work harder than most, to me it was simply life as I knew it.

I've loved music since I was a kid. My mom took me to Tipitina's, the iconic music club in uptown New Orleans, when I was still just a boy. I don't remember who was playing but I remember being there, music filling up both the room and me. I can remember attending the New Orleans Jazz and Heritage Festival, or Jazz Fest if you're from New Orleans, when I was only six years old. Music gives me a smile, I can sit and listen in a club for hours. Listening to music in a crowded room, is something I can do that's "normal," where I'm just another audience member like everyone else. Before the Huntington's I would make five or six shows a night, driving myself all over town to different clubs, staying out late because the music just made me feel good. It still does, though as the disease has progressed I tire easily and can no longer drive myself to five or six shows a night, but a friend or a friendly Uber driver can still get me to three shows in an evening.

I became such a fixture on the New Orleans music scene that I started making friends with some of the musicians and began writing songs with them. The first one that got released was "Bone Funk on Funk" written with the legendary George Porter Jr. I wrote three more songs with George that got released, "Da Medicine Man on Get You a Healin", "Let's Get It on Funk 'n' Go Nuts" and "It's Me on Expanding the Funkin Universe".

I've written two songs with New Orleans songwriter Paul Sanchez that have also been released: "Laugh While You're Dying" which appeared on a duet release with Shamarr Allen and Paul Sanchez, and "All I Have To Say" from Paul's 2017 release *Heart Renovations.*

I get asked about my prognosis and it is what it is for someone diagnosed with Huntington's Disease, inevitable decline of my ability to speak, walk and care for myself, and death. But as I said to Paul when he asked why I wanted to write a song called "Laugh While You're Dying", you can't choose what happens to you in this life but you can choose how you deal with it, and I think you can laugh, even if you know you're dying. I've also been asked since I was a kid, and even more since the Huntington's diagnosis, what is that keeps me going. I love music, I love my friends, I love writing. But what keeps me going every day is simple: I love life.

Eddie Tebbe

New Orleans, LA

February 2020

Summer's Day at Lou's

It was that kind of day, the kind of summer day in New Orleans that nobody liked, so hot everything moved in slow motion. A midday shower cooled the city down for about five minutes, but now it was over and the heat was worse. The water had turned into steam almost in an instant once it hit the ground. The humidity, which was 100%, seemed like two. In other words, it was hot.

The inside of Lou's was not much to look at. The walls had ten years of grime and dirt on them. The ceiling fans, which moved slower than a snail and were missing one blade from each, had so much dust on them that every once in a while clumps would fall, hopefully not landing in someone's beer. People had to be careful when sitting on a stool, or in the two booths. The stools could have fallen apart at any minute, and they always wobbled. The two booths were sticky with unknown gook and gave splinters very easily. The bar was out of place with beautiful marble, polished brass figures, and an antique cash register. There was no dirt anywhere within a foot of the bar, and the mirror behind it gave the clearest reflection imaginable.

The ceiling fans moved at their slow pace, and the little red ribbon tied to the air conditioner's vent was waving, a little. It was cool in Lou's if you had just entered, but that didn't last long. Paul opened the door and stepped in thinking he had found a place to cool off. The bartender didn't look up at him, said nothing, and kept to his task of drying the glasses. Paul looked around but saw no one else. The whole place was in full view. It wasn't very big. The bar was on the left side wall with the entrance to it being on the other end of the room. The bathroom, one for everybody, was just on the other side of the bar. The two booths were in the right-hand corner. Along the right-side wall there was a pool table and jukebox. It took Paul a few minutes for his eyes to adjust to dim lighting in the place. Not only was the light dim, but it was also different, strange, and it took him a second to notice why.

There were no lights in the establishment and no windows. The illumination came from the bar.

Paul's first instinct was to leave, but this was the kind of place he was looking for, quiet with no one there, and out of the heat. There probably wasn't another bar in the city with no one in it, so he decided to stay. He walked over and sat down, almost falling off the stool, then ordered a White Russian.

"You don't want that," said the bartender without looking at Paul.

"That's my drink."

"So, really think about it. What do you want?"

The bartender took a sparkling clean glass and started to fill it with draft beer.

"You're right, I'll take draft."

Right as the word draft came out of Paul's mouth the bartender placed a full pint glass in front of him. He was a little confused but thanked the bartender anyway. He took a sip of the beer. He had never had that kind before. Too bad because it was the best tasting beer he had ever had.

"What kind of beer is this?"

"My own." The bartender was now wiping down the bar.

"Really? I've never had beer this good." Paul wiped the sweat off his face with some napkins.

His eyes were now adjusted to the light. He stood up to take a closer look at the place. First, he looked at himself in the mirror. Paul wasn't much more than average. He was five feet seven inches tall, one hundred fifty-five pounds, a pretty good build, with a hint of pudge around the waist. Nice facial look, but there was nothing distinguishing about it. He was glad to still have all his hair. At thirty-five most of his friends had thinning. He wore clothes that were once nice, but heavy use had taken its toll. His shoes were nicer than his clothes.

Turning away from the mirror Paul noticed that the wall was covered with pictures. It wasn't only photographs. Some were paint-ings. Very realistic looking, but they had to be paintings. They de-picted things that were before cameras. Paul studied them for a while. All the pictures looked as if they were taken in this place. They were mesmerizing to him. There was something about them, but he couldn't put his finger on it. Did every picture have the bartender in it? He turned to look at the bartender, but he couldn't get a good look. He hadn't gotten a good look since he entered the place. The bartender kept his head down or away and he kept himself busy. Paul tried to get a better look without being obvious but couldn't. The bartender was older. He could be anywhere between fifty and seventy. He was at least six-six with a young muscular body. His hair was gray and balding just enough to make him look dignified. Paul could not tell what his face looked like, but his nose was the eye-catching feature. Paul was pretty sure he was in most of the pictures, or his father, grandfather, great grandfather, and beyond.

Without taking his eyes off the pictures Paul asked the bartender if all the people in the pictures were in his family.
"You could say that."
"They're very fascinating."

Paul touched one of them slightly, moving it from place. As he replaced the picture, he noticed that the part of the wall that was covered by it was just as dirty as the uncovered part. He took his last sip of beer. He turned to walk back to the bar. The place was not cool anymore, and he thought about leaving, but he needed another beer and the quiet to think. He sat at the bar, ordered another beer, and tried to get a good look at the bartender. Which he still could not? Maybe if he talked to him.

"Is this your place?"
"Sure is."
"So, you're Lou?"
"Some people call me that."
"Well, I'm Paul Peters. How long have you had this bar?"
This guy just refused to look him straight on.
"Well...no...let me see...let's just say a long time." The bartender answered without looking up from his account book.
"I never remember seeing this place."
"It's easy to miss."
"I'm not in the habit of going to bars in the middle of the day. I'm usually working at this time. I've just been laid off. They said they like my work, but the company is in trouble. There was good news. If I'm available in the future they would like me back."
"You would go back to work after they treated you like this?"
"It isn't their fault. Stuff like this just happens."

Paul ordered another beer. He was not much of a drinker, but this beer was so good.

"Somebody is to blame. Somebody didn't do what they needed to do to keep the money coming in. Did they give you any indication this might happen?"

"No, but I think you're getting the wrong idea. They didn't want to let me go."

"But they did. Somebody did something wrong. Now you don't have a job. Did they tell you how long before they might want you back?"

The bartender was now cleaning the mirror, but Paul still couldn't get a good look at his face. He decided to give up.

"Not really. Could be a month or never."

"Did you like working there? Did they treat you right?" The bartender talked in a plain tone.

"Normally I guess, and it was okay."

"If it wasn't a great job, and they laid you off without notice, then why aren't you mad? You have the right to be mad. They treated you like dirt, and if they give you another job, they may do it again. Get mad."

With a little emotion Paul said, "You're right. I'll find a better job. If they ask me back, I'll say no. Give me another beer."

The bartender had one already on the way.

Paul knew the company did all they could to keep him, but things like this just happen sometimes. He was a good person. He worked hard, had a wife and two children, and supported his mother. He had a decent income but had not been able to save much money. The next day he would be looking in the classifieds and hitting the pavement. For now, he would indulge in a little self-pity and anger which was against his nature.

It was only twenty minutes since Paul entered the place, and he was now on his fourth beer. The coolness of the place had long been gone. He took off his tie, unbuttoned a few buttons, and rolled up his sleeves. The door swung open. The brightness of the sunlight made him squint. A few seconds later a rush of hot air blew by. He was glad to see someone else. He felt odd in there by himself. The man was dressed in a suit. He looked as if he just got off work. As he walked up to the bar the bartender ignored him.

The man spoke very politely. "Pardon me, may I use your phone?"

"Why?" griped the bartender.

"My wallet is gone. I don't know if I lost it, or it was stolen, but all my keys and money are in my wallet. I would like to call my wife so she can come pick me up."

"I don't let anyone use my phone."

The man was extremely annoyed but kept his composure. "I understand." Turning to Paul, "Sir, would you be so kind as to lend me a quarter for the pay phone?"

"Sure," Paul started reaching in his pocket.

"Get out of my place now," said the bartender in a low angry voice.

"One moment please, sir?" asked the man.

"Now." Paul could have sworn he heard the bartender hiss.

The man walked out not understanding why he was treated that way. Paul froze with his hand in his pocket and fingers around his quarter. His first instinct was to leave as well, but he wanted to know why the bartender acted like that.

The conversation that followed confused Paul. Two minutes after it was over he couldn't remember the details. Something about treating people how they treat others, and even though that guy was well spoken and polite he had never stopped to help anyone. How did the bartender know this? That wasn't all. People didn't have the responsibility to help others. That idea came from the early church to make people give them more money. The people of that time didn't have much money, and the church didn't use the money to help people. They used it to gain more power, but Paul was not fooled that was still the church's goal. He was not a weekly church goer, but his wife was. He was religious, he just found it was hard to go to church every week. He usually went once a mouth. He did participate in many church related fund-raisers. This subject was important to Paul. This bartender had a lot of weird ideas, but on this subject Paul intended to put him in his place. It didn't happen. Maybe it was the beer (he was on his sixth), maybe it was Paul's state of mind, or maybe the bartender was right? Paul did not know himself, but by the end of the debate he agreed with the bartender.

If Paul didn't have the responsibility to help strangers, then did he have the responsibility to help his own family? For the last seven years Paul had been the sole caretaker of his mother. His father died seven years ago, leaving his mother with very little. The first few years were not hard, but she started having major health problems. Even with the help of Medicare and Medicaid the bills were adding up. He could still make ends meet and was happy he could take care of his mother. His mother had two other children, but there was bad blood. All he had thought was that he would need a little help from them. Now he was thinking he had done enough. He would ship mother off to one of the others. The bartender agreed. He pushed the idea further.

"How else can you make life easier on yourself?" asked the bartender.

Paul hesitated, "Well, I guess a lot of ways, but I'd rather not have this conversation. You have had a weird effect on me."

"All I'm trying to do is empower you." The bartender's voice got low. "You would do well by following my rules."

They kept talking. Subject after subject the bartender was changing Paul's views on life. The bartender was true to his underlying belief in individualism, sometimes to the point of anarchy. He was a great convincer. Paul started to believe that the bartender could change anybody's mind on any subject, maybe even making the devil believe in God.

It was 9:00 p.m. and Paul lost count of his beer consumption three hours ago. He had not eaten dinner and, more importantly, he had not called home for the first time in his fifteen-year marriage.

Up to this point Paul could have walked out of the bar and still have been himself. He could go back to work for his former employee if they asked. He could give a quarter to someone if they needed one. He could raise money for the church. He could believe that self-sacrifices can be good. He could have walked out of the bar and been free.

"I have to call my wife," Paul said as he dug in his pocket for a quarter.

"If you must," the bartender replied a little annoyed.

Paul walked over to the pay phone, "Believe me, I must."

As he started dialing the number the door slowly opened like the parting of a curtain. A woman entered. Paul turned to check out who was coming in because for six hours only one other person had entered the bar. It was dark outside so inside the bar Paul did not expect to see the person clearly, but he did. It was as if she had a magical spotlight on her. She was five feet seven inches tall, and one hundred fifty pounds. Every muscle was toned. Even from across the room her face captured his attention. She strolled over to the bar and gracefully sat down. He hung up the phone, did not get his quarter out of the change return, and walked back to his seat. She was wearing snug faded blue jeans with a white T-shirt tucked in. She ordered a beer and gave Paul a smile. The bartender looked her straight in the eye when he served her beer. That distracted Paul's attention for a moment, but he was mesmerized by her. She had blue-green eyes, a color he had never seen. Her smile brightened up the room. Her nose, eyebrows, bone structure, even her ears had a beauty all their own, and together they made a perfect face. Paul continued checking her out from head to toe. He would have been happy with any one part of her. How could any woman be so beautiful?

She got up and walked over to the jukebox. Paul followed her every move, and with every move was more attracted. She only played one song. Eddie Time. She turned and made direct eye contact with Paul who was staring at her.

Paul realized he was staring. "I'm sorry," he said, turning back towards the bar.

"That's okay," she said as she gently took his hand. "Would you like to dance?"

Paul was taken aback. He had forgotten that he needed to go home. The offer to slow dance with this woman was overpowering. They didn't say anything to each other. He just stood up and they started dancing. Paul had enjoyed dancing all his life, and had danced with a lot of partners, but with this woman it was different. They moved together like one. Their bodies fit together perfectly. Nothing in Paul's life every felt that good, that right. Nothing was ever that pleasurable. The emotion was so strong tears were running down their faces. Paul suddenly pulled away from her and ran in the restroom.

He turned on the cold water and splashed his face then looked up into the mirror. What was he doing? He didn't even recognize himself. Could one afternoon change him that much? He was going to put an end to this dream like day. He was going to go home, explain to the woman he loved what happened, make love to her, and then wake up in the morning and find a job. He was never coming to this place again.

When Paul came out of the restroom the bartender and the woman were laughing. He threw some money on the bar, hoping it was enough, and walked towards the door.

"Where do you think you're going?" the bartender asked.

"Home," Paul answered without turning around.

"You can't," the bartender said in a forceful voice.

Paul turned and got a little angry. "What?"

"You better come back."

Paul rarely lost control but he did. "Don't talk to me like that. This place, and you, can go to hell."

"Actually, you can go to hell," the bartender said looking Paul straight in the eyes.

Right than Paul realized the horror and lost consciousness. When he started to wake up, he felt funny. He couldn't move his body. He opened his eyes and saw the bar from a weird perspective. It was as if he was standing against the wall, but he couldn't feel his body. Then he saw the reflection in the mirror. It was hard to tell, but yes, it was true. Paul was in a picture on the wall.

Eddie Time

by Eddie Tebbe and Michael Cerveris

Anytime is sometimes sometimes
Sometimes is sometimes anytime
Sometimes is always sometimes
But only anytime is always
 sometimes
And Eddie time is all the time

You gotta know what to do
You gotta know how to get
 through
You gotta know right from wrong
You gotta know good from bad
You gotta know when to be sad
You gotta know when
 you're done

Anytime is sometimes sometimes
Sometimes is sometimes anytime
Sometimes is always sometimes
But only anytime is always
 sometimes
And Eddie time is all the time

You gotta know night from day
You gotta know just what to say
You gotta know the truth from
 a lie

You gotta know how to get it all
You gotta know how to stand tall
You gotta know hello from
 good-bye

(whistle solo)

You gotta know, yes you do
You gotta know who's in you
You gotta know, you gotta know

You gotta know, yes you do
You gotta know who's in you
You gotta know, you gotta know,
you gotta know

Anytime is sometimes sometimes
Sometimes is sometimes anytime
Sometimes is always sometimes
But only anytime is always
 sometimes
And Eddie time is all the time
Eddie time is all the time
Eddie time is all the time

Eddie Tebbe

Funky White Boy

Chorus:
I'm just a little white boy, but I want to be funky
I want to be a funky white boy
I'm just a little white boy, but I want to be funky
I want to be a funky white boy

Came down here from Kalamazoo
I didn't know what to do
Went one night to see George
Never seen the funk before
Man, that beat changed my life
Got all his tapes in sight
Bought a bass, learned to play
Now I just want to say
Chorus
I love the groove more than most
Like my childhood favorite peanut butter toast
I eat it up all I can
Then come back again
I want more, more, more
The funk thrills to the core
If I may let me play
If you'll listen let me say
Chorus
What I've learned what I've done
Nothing could be as fun
Funky grooving is more than you think
Black, white, yellow, pink
Funk is more than a beat
It teaches us to be complete
So listen closely to what I play
And listen closely to what I say
Chorus

Laugh While You're Dying

You got to breathe or keep trying
laugh while you're dying
your life shouldn't end before it begins
you are who you are get comfortable in your own skin
Don't waste a day
by letting sad get in the way
you can be angry inside, spend your time crying
or you can laugh while you're dying

hearts open wide
when you live on the positive side
you got nothing to lose but those nasty old blues
life is for living but you still got to choose
you ought not pass up a chance to listen to the music and dance
you can keep wondering why but life's still going by and you can laugh
while you're dying

Eddie Tebbe

I Had as Much Fun As I Could Stand

Chorus:
I had as much fun as
I could stand
Down in New Orleans
I had as much fun as
I could stand
I couldn't stay on the scene
I had to go to bed
Just to rest my head
The others would scream and
shout
All I wanted was out

Verse 1:
Let me tell you a story
I've been all around the world
I've been to every party
With every type of girl
But I never had as much fun
As down in the Big Easy
Where the people are hot, the
weather humid
And food is really greasy

Verse 2:
It wasn't even Mardi Gras
Just a regular week
It's hard to imagine
A million people stomping their
feet
I had sensory overload
My emotions went wild
Like being in a candy store
When I was a child

Verse 3:
My friends wanted to stay
But I had to go
My friends wanted to play
Dance to the end of the show
They asked why I wasn't having
fun
I said I was
They asked what could be done
I said my body was out of fun

The History of Unadulterated Funk

This is the history of unadulterated funk.

Change / reform
Back to the norm
Just kiss my baby
Baby I don't mean maybe
Sophisticated cissy
Oldies but goodies
Chug chug a lug
To the one you love
Ride your pony
Makes me horny
People say-hay
Things don't go away
A message from the Meters
We want things better
The same old thing
What did you bring
Dragon he bites me
Why don't you write me
Africa
You are my brah
Cissy strut
Girl rub you butt
I need more time
I need a good rhyme

This song has been a lesson in unadulterated funk.
I have one more thing to say.

Ain't no use
Funk is no abuse

Eddie Tebbe

Fate's View, Story One

My work takes me all over the world, and there are many places I really love, but today I am in one of my all-time favorites, New Orleans. It is late September. Everybody is happy because the first cool front has hit, with temperatures in the high seventies, and the heat has finally broken. The heat will be back in a few days, but not the killer heat that makes people drag around wondering why they live here. That is gone, at least they hope, until March, maybe April. For today people are a little more alive, with a bounce in their step. They are driving around with their air conditioners off, and their windows open for the first time in six months. They are opening all the windows in their homes to air them out. All the bars have their doors open. They like days like this because not having to run the air conditioners saves money, and that is where I am now, sitting at a bar in uptown New Orleans called "Le Bon Temps." It's been a slow day, so I was able to get here early and enjoy myself for a while, but this is not a story about me. Whether I enjoy myself or not is not important. This story is about Jerry, but he isn't here yet. So, let me set the scene.

The bar sits on the corner of Magazine and Bordeaux St. The front door is on the corner of the building directly on the street corner. Standing at the door looking to the right is the jukebox, followed by metal, followed by a booth. To the left is a video poker machine, followed by a table, a booth, another video poker machine, another metal, and a third video poker machine. In the middle of the bar are two pool tables. There's barely enough room for the tables and people, but it works. The bar runs along the right-hand wall and has a fire hydrant in the middle. The bathrooms are catty corner from the front door. Along the left wall there are stools, a pinball machine, and a photo booth. There is a giant mirror taking up half of the wall to make the room feel bigger. Directly across from the bar there is a window that gives a wonderful view of Magazine St. The decorum of the place is interesting. There's stuff everywhere. I have been here hundreds of times, and I still find stuff I haven't seen. Old beer bottles line high up ledges. Beer logo painted mirrors hang on the walls. There is a huge old "Dixie Beer" sign over the front door. One of the most noticeable things is a pair of skis, stuffed legs and all, protruding from the ceiling. The bar, booths, floor, walls, stools, and mantles are all made of unpainted wood. Every local bar has its own distinct feel, but as a group all New Orleans' bars have a similar feel. Le Bon Temps is definitely a local uptown New Orleans bar.

There's Jerry now, stepping up the two steps to get into the place. He is looking pretty good today. Usually he looks tired, and messy, with worn out clothes. Today was an unexpected day off for Jerry. He got a good night's sleep last night and awoke in a great mood, so he spent the morning treating himself, to a nice breakfast, to some new clothes (that he is wearing now), and to a movie. He made a deal with himself that if he spent the morning and early afternoon playing, then by two he was going to be productive. It was out of character for Jerry to play all day, but after the movie he decided he was enjoying the day too much to stop playing. He drove around a while loving the weather. He made a couple of unannounced visits to friends who were working. It was now three-thirty, and he finds himself at Le Bon Temps. When he goes out, which is mostly only on the weekend, he mainly comes to this bar, but he had never been here during the day. He didn't even know for sure if it was opened during the day.

The bar looks different during the day to Jerry. As he looks around, he sees about fifteen people in the place. Four businessmen with their jackets off, ties loosened, and sleeves rolled up, are playing pool. Playing on the other table is a young wanna-be-hippie couple kissing more than playing pool. Each poker machine has a person attached to it, totally unaware of anything but the machine, feeding it more money than they can afford. The rest of the people are at the bar or in the booths. Jerry doesn't see anyone he knows and starts to leave, but he looks me straight in the eyes. I hold his stare for a moment. He then turns around, sits at the bar, and orders a St. Pauli Girl. Good thing I was here.

While sitting at the bar Jerry turns and looks out of the window. He catches a glimpse of a woman driving by.

Jerry is a very nice guy. He works as a salesperson at a computer store for the moment, but sales is not in his blood. For sales a person needs to have confidence and be pushy. Jerry is neither. He is also going to school. He just started and hasn't chosen a major. Teaching and sociology seem interesting to him. In high school he was an average student. He was smart and a hard worker. Good grades just didn't come easily for him. After high school he did some traveling for a year, thinking afterwards he would start college. This happened, that happened, and at twenty-five he was finally starting.

The second person in this story is not here yet, so I will tell you more about Jerry. He had a fairly simple childhood. He grew up in a family neighborhood in Mid City. His parents had a good marriage. They both worked. His father was a realtor and his mother a social worker, and they still are. Jerry had a five-year older sister, but when she was twenty, she was hit by a car and died. That was the roughest thing the family went through, and it was pretty rough. He and his sister were very close. It took a long time for him to forgive his sister for leaving him. He finally did though.

For the last two years Jerry has been trying to get over an emotional break-up. He and his girlfriend Lisa had been going out for three years, living with each other for six months. Jerry had been preparing to ask Lisa to marry him. He thought everything was going well. She hadn't expressed any dissatisfaction with the relationship. Then, three days before he popped the question, she left him. She said it just was not working out, but two weeks later she was living with his best friend. To complicate things even more, they all worked together. So, in the course of three weeks Jerry lost his love, his best friend, and his job. It is two years later now, and he is finally moving on. (He did feel a little bit better when Lisa broke his friend's heart after six months.) He still has not been on any dates. He just has not had the strength to deal with the whole ordeal of getting to know, getting to like or even love, getting to trust and depending on someone. I think he's scared. I think he's ready. That's why I'm here.

There she is, beautiful as ever. It isn't as much her physical beauty as it is her inner beauty that radiates. She has a boyish figure, not helped by her blue jeans and untucked T-shirt, flat chested. Her hair is short, blond, and straight. Her face is nothing special. If you look up plain Jane in the dictionary her picture might be there, but she is beautiful. Her smile is the purest I've ever seen. Her energy draws people to her. Everybody who meets her loves her. Her name is Melissa. As she walks through the bar everyone, men and women, are checking her out. She orders a beer, sits in the booth by the window, and starts to read her book.

Even though Melissa turns most people's heads she has never been confident about her looks. Smart, intelligent, independent, capable, funny, and many other superlatives are things Melissa knows about herself, but she is not confident. But the older she gets the more confident she gets. She is not arrogant or overbearing. She has a great balance of faults and attributes. Melissa works in the local theater scene. Earlier in her career she concentrated on behind the scenes, but she is now doing more acting.

Jerry takes a long and hard look at Melissa. He thinks he knows her from somewhere, but just cannot put it into place. He notices that she is reading the book that he has just finished. It's against his nature, but with a little help, he decides this opening is too big. As he thinks of what he is going to say I think I will play some music. The first song I play does not matter, and neither does the third, but the second will be "Sweet Melissa" by The Allman Brothers.

Right on schedule Jerry walks up to Melissa and asks if he knows her from somewhere. It is not inventive, but it works. They both have the feeling that they know each other. I know that they have never even seen each other before. Jerry asks Melissa her name. She says Melissa at the very same time as the song. They talk for a little about books, theater, movies, themselves. Even though their conversation is far from over Melissa gives Jerry her number.

Both of their drinks are empty, so Jerry comes over to the bar and orders two beers.

"I wonder if I should call this girl?" Jerry says almost to himself.

I get up, put on my jacket, and start to leave. I walk really close to Jerry. I say in a whisper, "I would."

Jerry turns around to see who said that but doesn't see anyone.

"You're right. I will," Jerry says to the air.

Their conversation will go on into the night. They will feel like old friends, and there will be a strong attraction. It was meant to be, but even that needs help sometimes.

Chance Meeting

Verse one:
"Hey there," she said in her sweet voice
"Funny seeing you here" was all I could reply
"Do you mind if I join you?"
"Please do," I said with emotions welling in my eyes
"You look good. You've kept in shape
"You look as good as ever," I sighed

Chorus:
Could this really happen? I ask myself
As I write these words
Is it just my imagination
Can there be understanding
A reconciliation
A new beginning
A new beginning

Verse two:
We stared at each other in silence
"I've never been here before." She broke her stare
"Funny," I said, "It's my first time too."
"You know," she grabbed my hand, "I always cared."
We squeezed each other's hands not letting go
"The pain you caused me was more than I could bear"

Verse three:
"I'd love to talk things over," she said. "If we can?"
"I know I hurt you too, but it was unavoidable."
"I didn't see that for a long time, but now I do."
"I hope," she continued, "your life is more manageable."
I said with a smile, "Yes, it's been a long time."
"A lot has happened. Some of it unbelievable."

Eddie Tebbe

Verse four:
So, the conversation continued for hours
Everything laid out, the animosity dead
We laughed at our many good times
And new hopes where generosity fed
"Well I have to go." She looked at her watch
"I miss you in my life. Can I call you?" We both said

Whirlwind

What I'm trying to tell you
It's out of my control
Forces are pushing me
In your direction
Even if my mind warns stop
It's for my protection

Chorus:
I'm coming after you
With all my might
You're in my sights
I'm in love with you
Nothing I can do
I'm in love with you

The odds aren't good
But I'll take a chance
When fate steps in
The stars will show
Our bodies embracing
Shining bright in the sky
                              Chorus

What makes love happen
This I ask myself
Why with one look
Are you in my heart
What makes me believe
We will never part
                              Chorus

Some things we'll never know
No matter how hard we try
I'm going with my feelings
Throwing caution to the wind
Mystical forces are at play
Come ride with me on the whirlwind

Eddie Tebbe

And You Can Bring Peace Out of Confusion

Darkness blocks the light from your eyes
High pitch noises pierce your ears
You yell but no sound comes out
Touching hands, you feel nothing
The smell's so strong it knocks you down
Your whole life rests on one decision
Isn't that how it feels
What to do, what way to go
And nobody knows but you
Everything seems out-of-whack
Concentrate on your soul
Hard times are a part of life
There's always a light at the end
And you can bring peace out of confusion

A Message of The East

(Inspired by and Dedicated to Sequoyah)

It's the time of day
That most people never see
Never think about, never understand
It comes from the east
It's the sunrise
Its power is immense
It can heal

A bird flies in the night sky
In a flock it must work in a group
It is beautiful
As an individual it must fly alone
And the beauty is magnified

A double edge blade is life
One side hurts, causes pain, causes death
Cuts deep, cuts hard
The other side is magical
Causes life, causes happiness
Doesn't cut, it heals

Without a sunset there can't be a sunrise
Without a group there can't be an individual
Without one side of a blade there can't be the other side
Without death there can't be life
Without the north, south, and west there can't be the east

Eddie Tebbe

Emily

Emily
Your sweetness gives to me
What's needed the most in my life
That's hope for what's to come
But you're so far away
And how should I say
Circumstances aren't what I'd like them to be
Between you and me

Remember when we danced together baby
I twirled you across the floor baby
Your smile stole my soul
I want you to know
I will never forget
But how will you know

On the night we met I felt a stir
I took too long to make my move
But before I knew there was another guy
I hoped the chance hadn't passed me by
Our friendship grew
As well as my wanting you
I said good-bye when you moved away
My eyes held the tears at bay

I thought my chance had come again
When you came back in town
But love was in your eyes for him
The sparkle in my eyes went dim
Still we had our moments
Moments that keep me going
Maybe the future holds something
I hope for what the future brings

Sharon

Verse one:
I've known her all my life
She has the sweetest soul I know
All she wants is to be kind
Have fun and do what's right
So, I thought we'd be perfect together
Where the usual things aren't important
To achieve something better than ourselves
When souls really meet no light is brighter

Chorus:
Was it wrong for me to broach the subject
Was it wrong to think things could be different
Sharon, what are the answers
Sharon, why do you object
Sharon, Sharon, Sharon

Verse two:
Why must she feel so weak
When all I see is strength
Her kind heart causes doubt
Her inner peace she still seeks
All I've never want is to help her there
To ease her doubt by holding her tight
I'm still searching but can't find it alone
Maybe we could give each other the best care

Verse three:
We could complement each other
Our faults and virtues in balance
We could live and grow beyond ourselves
It's worth a shot to be together
But as things are, we must go separate ways
Not knowing where our paths will lead
A friendship lost to nonsense
Like so many in my day

Eddie Tebbe

The Tambourine

Bill poked his head outside the band room then looked at the clock. It was 4:15. Sara and Glenn were supposed to be there by now. Bill paced. He would wait five more minutes then go without them. "Why did he make the bet with Sara anyway?" he asked himself, but he knew. He was trying to impress Sara. He felt he had to do a lot to impress Sara. She was seventeen and he was only fifteen. He was the new kid in the performing arts school, and after three months he was still adjusting, with a juvenile delinquent past, and she was the most talented person in school with a beautiful voice and body.

The door swung open. Bill felt his heart stopped beating. He couldn't be caught. He had a lot of natural talent on the trumpet but was only in the school because a deal was struck. He was being raised by a single father because his mother couldn't handle motherhood and disappeared when he was seven. His father worked six days a week until seven, eight, or nine giving Bill time to run the streets. His father made a decent living and gave him everything he needed except attention. In classic form Bill started getting in trouble when he was eight. Just attention-grabbing stuff at first, but by eleven things started getting serious. At thirteen he was involved in a carjacking. He was sent to juvenile delinquent boot camp for three years. While there it was discovered that he had an affinity for the trumpet. That's when the deal was struck. He would live at home under home watch care and would be able to go to the performing arts school only if he stayed out of trouble.

Bill's heart started again when he saw that it was Sara and Glenn.

"Good. It's about time," Bill said trying to take control. "Sit down and listen closely. Here's the plan. The janitor cleans the third floor first, so when he's done, we'll sneak up the back steps, into Mr. Merl's room, and I'll get us in the closet."

"Are you sure you can get in the closet?" Sara asked.

"I haven't found a lock I can't pick." Bill was trying to show off.

"Are you sure we should do this?" Glenn asked Sara. Being the youngest, only ten, and most musically talented kid in school caused Glenn not to have many friends. Sara had taken him under her wing like a baby brother.

"What, are you scared pee-wee?" Bill said with a little push on Glenn's shoulder.

Sara pushed Bill back, "Leave him alone." She pulled Glenn close to her. "We won't get caught. Don't worry. We're only doing this to make sure he doesn't mess with Mr. Merl's stuff."

"Why do you like Mr. Merl so much?" Bill asked.

"Because he understands that I may not want to rely on my looks and voice, that I'm more interested in my mind."

Even though Bill asked the question he didn't pay much attention to the answer.

"Okay, okay, the janitor should be done with the third floor soon. Let's wait five more minutes," Bill said.

As they waited Glenn sat on Sara's lap. He looked like a ventriloquist's dummy. His body was small, but he had big hands and a big head. His face was round, his skin tanned easily and was bronzed, and his hair was straight, blond, and fell evenly around his head as if his mother put a bowl on his head while cutting it.

Bill sat backwards in a chair halfway across the room trying not to stare. He had liked Sara since the first day he saw her. She was a young-looking seventeen. She had beautiful dark brown skin and an amazingly clear complexion. Her black hair was very short, which was good because it didn't distract attention from her face. Big brown eyes that were always opened wide were entrancing and told of an understanding about life that was beyond her age. A lean bone structure made her smile bigger than life. Many people thought that she could become a model with her looks and slim body.

"Who's your favorite musician?" Glenn asked Bill out of the blue. Glenn made it a mission to know everybody's favorite musician. Sara loved Aretha Franklin and Aaron Neville, Mr. Merl loved Professor Longhair and George Porter Jr. Glenn kept track of all of them in a composition notebook. His own favorite was Louis Armstrong.

"Guns N' Roses. Why do you want to know, pee wee?"

"Don't call me that."

They had waited long enough. Bill took charge. He relayed his plan, and Sara and Glenn took their orders. Neither of them had done anything like this, but Bill had experience. Glenn was going to be the front man. If anyone saw him he could easily explain his presence. Glenn had to check each hallway and stairwell before the other two would move on. The signal was a simple whistle. If Glenn was caught the other two would backtrack and leave school. Everything went as planned and they were in front of Mr. Merl's classroom in minutes.

Bill looked at ease sneaking around. He had an interesting look. Sometimes an evil one. He was five feet seven inches tall with a bony frame, which was deceiving because he was fairly strong. His hair was dark and skin was pale white with freckles. He had a pointy chin and nose, and dark rings around his light blue eyes.

It took Bill only seconds to get them in the classroom. All three stood staring at the reason they were there, Mr. Merl's walk-in closet.

Mr. Merl was their New Orleans music history teacher. All the students loved his class. He knew more than any book. He was always telling stories as if he was there himself to see historic events happen. He was funny, sensitive, easy going, sometimes strict, and treated his students like people. Even other teachers would sit in to watch him teach. Bill was put in his class so that he would make a connection, but it hadn't happened. Bill resisted Mr. Merl at every turn.

For every class Mr. Merl would go into his walk-in closet, and would come out with an artifact, or so he said. He had instruments that were supposed to be played by Louis Armstrong, Buddy Bolden, Sam Cook, or whoever the class was studying. Nobody was allowed to see more than one artifact at a time, and nobody had ever been in the closet. Rumor had it that even the principal was denied access.

"Are you sure you can pick those locks?" Sara asked Bill.

"No problem." Bill took some small tools out of his pocket. "In fact, that is one of the reasons I think your Mr. Merl is a phony."

"He's not a phony," Glenn proclaimed with Sara's agreement.

Bill was in the process of picking the first lock. "If he has all that stuff in this closet it would be locked up a lot better. I mean this old door lock and just one padlock. Don't you think that if the stuff was real then it'd be locked up better?"

Eddie Tebbe

Bill was already finished picking the door lock and was working on the padlock.

"He's not a phony," Sara said. "Just wait and see."

The padlock was taking more time and effort to pick. The anticipation built in each of them. All of them were there for different reasons, but all of them wanted to get in fast and leave. The quietness of the room made it easy to hear each person's breathing. Sara and Glenn got more nervous the longer Bill took. As Bill finished with the lock Sara's heart was in her throat. Glenn jumped with excitement. Bill was pleased with himself, but tried to play it cool, not wanting to let on that he had never picked locks that well.

They rushed in the closet, then all three stopped in their tracks. Each of them had different expectations, but none of them expected what they saw. Nothing.

"Where is everything?" Glenn asked.

"I told you he was a phony," Bill said while looking in the drawers and cabinets.

"No. In fact, it proves that his stuff is real, and he keeps it in a safer place," Sara said.

"That doesn't make sense either. I've seen Mr. Merl come and go and he never has anything with him."

"Well, there's nothing here is there?"

"There's this tambourine," Glenn said.

The tambourine was the only thing in the room. Bill grabbed it from Glenn.

"A stupid tambourine," Bill said as he hit it against his other hand, causing it to jingle.

All of a sudden everything went dark and started moving. Bill dropped the tambourine. Glenn jumped towards Sara, dropping his notebook. She picked him up and held on tight. There was a flash of bright light, then they found themselves outside somewhere. They were all disoriented.

"Where are we?" Bill asked looking at Sara with a scared look.

"I don't know. How'd we get here?" Sara was holding Glenn tight. He still had his eyes closed.

Glenn opened his eyes. "How did we get outside? Sara, Sara." Glenn started to cry.

"It's okay," Sara rubbed Glenn's hair. "Everything will be all right."

Bill leaned up against a wall. He was shaking. Nothing looked right. They were outside, but where? He slid down the wall and put his face in his hands.

"Bill, we have to keep it together. We have to figure out what's going on," Sara said sternly. Bill got up and tried to pull himself together. The feeling of being out of control held on deep inside.

"First thing we need to do is find out where we are," Sara said still holding Glenn.

"Where are we and what's going on?" Glenn asked softly.

Sara whispered in his ear. "I don't know, baby, but we'll be okay."

"Let's find someone who can help," Sara said to Bill.

They walked to the nearest corner. It was Magazine and Nashville.

"I walk by this corner every day on the way home from school," Bill said, "but it looks different. The coffee house is no longer a coffee house. The audio store is just a regular residence. Everything looks less used then normal. Look at the streets. They're clean with no potholes."

Sara looked at the cars slowly going by. "All of these cars are from the sixties. What in the world is going on?"

"I'm hungry," said Glenn.

"I only have three dollars," Sara said. "What about you, Bill?"

"Two."

"That gives us five. That's not much, but let's find a store and maybe a phone."

They walked a couple of blocks down Magazine and found a 'Time Saver.' 'Time Saver's' were usually pretty busy, but this one wasn't. They were the only customers there. The woman behind the counter took a great interest in the three kids. Then she made a phone call.

After separating to find what they wanted Sara, Glenn, and Bill regrouped in the rear of the store. They couldn't believe how cheap everything was. At these prices five dollars would last forever. Sara walked up to the counter to pay for the food while Glenn and Bill stepped outside to wait. By the side of the door was a stack of newspapers. Bill looked at one. He was horrified by the date on the paper, May 3, 1967.

"What!" Bill yelled.

Sara walked outside at the same moment. "What's wrong?"

"Look at this."

Sara looked, and didn't believe what she saw.

"I want to see," Glenn said.

"Hey, you kids," a loud deep voice came from down the block.

Bill looked up and saw that it was a policeman. He took off running.

"Wait, Bill," Sara said as she ran after Bill with Glenn right behind her.

They ran as fast and as far as they could. When they figured they had gotten away, they stopped. They were in Audubon Park. Glenn was tired so he lay on a bench and put his head in Sara's lap.

Sara was upset. "Why did you run? Maybe he could have helped us."

"It's kinda a reflex." Bill didn't like being jumped on. "What do you think that date on the newspaper was about?"

"I think we've gone back in time."

"Back in time? That's crazy."

"Do you have a better explanation?"

"Back in time." Bill was bewildered.

They sat there for a while in silence. When Glenn woke up Sara tried to explain the situation.

"Back in time, cool," reacted Glenn.

Sara laughed.

"It's going to be getting dark soon," Bill said. "What do we do?"

"I say we find someone to help us," Sara answered.

"What are we supposed to say? We haven't even been born yet. Nobody will believe our story."

"Well, what then?"

"For tonight we should sleep in the park."

"Sleep in the park?"

"Yeah, let's do that," Glenn said.

"Look, I've spent the night in this park before, and if this is 1967, then we'd be even safer."

"I don't know. Maybe, but tomorrow we get help."

"Okay."

Bill laid awake most of the night trying to get a handle on the situation and making sure nothing happened to Sara or Glenn. The quietness of the park was different from what he was used to. If he could handle this situation then Sara would be impressed, but just getting home seemed to be the most important thing. He had to figure out what to do.

In the morning food was the immediate problem that needed solving. They walked around until they found somewhere that they could safely eat.

"I have an idea," Bill and Sara said at the same time.

"We need to find someone who will believe us," Sara said.

"Right, that's what I was thinking. We need to find Mr. Merl."

"Right. He has lived here all his life. Maybe he'll know what to do."

They got his address out of the phone book. 721 Valence wasn't that far away from where they were, so they walked to his house. Sara knocked on the front door for five minutes. Nobody was home. The next-door neighbor came out to see what was going on. Bill asked her if she knew where Mr. Merl was or when he would be back. The information came out easily and with detail. Mr. Merl was downtown at the Municipal Auditorium. He wouldn't be back until late. The kids thanked the lady and walked away.

"We can't wait all day," Bill said. "Let's go downtown and try to find him."

They walked down Valence towards St. Charles.

"If you want, something to play with, go and find yourself a toy," a young man softly sang sitting on some front steps. "Cause baby my time, is too expensive, and I'm not a little boy."

Sara stopped. Without thinking she joined in. "If you are serious, don't play with my heart, it makes me furious, but if you want me to love you, baby I will." Then she stopped, realizing who she was singing with.

A young Aaron Neville looked up and smiled. They both sang louder. "Tell it like it is..." They continued to sing the rest of the song together. Bill and Glenn enjoyed the show immensely. A car drove up, and the young man got up to go. Sara just stood there.

As the young man got in the car he said to the driver. "That girl has a great voice. She's something special." The car drove off.

"That was Aaron Neville," Sara said. "He thinks I have a great voice. Do you believe that?"

"The fact that he thinks you have a great voice, the fact that that was Aaron Neville, or the fact that we went back in time?" Bill said. Sara didn't respond.

Bill and Glenn walked ahead while Sara followed. They had to keep making sure she was still following.

The streetcar ride downtown was the nicest Bill had ever taken. The car rocked from side to side making the sounds of a train, the sunlight flickered through the oaks, and Bill got lost in his thoughts. It had now sunk in that this experience was real. His fifteen-year old brain was frantically looking for ways of dealing with this bizarre situation. Bill looked at Sara and Glenn and responsibility for other people crept into his mind for the first time. He got them into this. He would get them out.

They walked down Canal St. to Rampart then turned left. They had been to the Municipal Auditorium many times with their school. About three blocks away from the auditorium Glenn stopped. Bill and Sara didn't notice until a half block later. When they turned around Glenn was gone. They ran back. Sara heard some jazz music coming from inside a club. Bill and Sara looked at each other then walked in. It took a second for their eyes to adjust to the darkness. The place was small and there were only a few people there, leftovers from last night. On stage there was a drummer, a trombone player, a saxophone player, and a trumpet player who were jamming. Bill and Sara only recognized the trumpet player. It was Louis Armstrong.

Glenn made his way towards the stage. There was a piano on the side. Glenn sat on the bench and started playing. The musicians tried to keep playing and see what was going on. The bartender started walking over to get Glenn, but Louis waved him off. "Let the boy play."

"Glenn is really good," Bill said. He and Sara sat in the back. Glenn looked at them with a huge grin.

"Yeah, but we don't have time for this."

"You had your song with Aaron. Let Glenn have his turn."

The band went into another song, and Glenn kept up nicely. Bill got up and walked out of the place.

"Bill, where are you going without Glenn?" Sara got up and followed him.

Outside Bill was sitting on the curb.

"What's wrong?" Sara sat beside him.

Bill was hesitant to answer. Finally, he said. "It's that song. That used to be my favorite song. When I was a kid my mom listened to it all the time. She'd hold me in her arms and dance around. But she left and now I hate it."

"You can be mad at your mom, and still remember the good times. You need to come inside, listen to the music, and enjoy the memories. They're the only thing you have. The music can help heal the pain. I lost someone very close to me and I only listened to their favorite song for a long time. It helped me cry and resolve my feelings. Come back inside."

Sara took Bill's hand and they walked inside. This time they went up front. Bill closed his eyes, and let the music take him back. Tears squeezed out of his closed eyes.

Before they knew it three hours had passed. Glenn didn't want to leave. Luckily the band decided to stop.

"How old are you boy?" Louis asked.

"Ten."

"Ten," Louis said and started laughing. "Hear that guys? Ten."

Their good-byes were said and Glenn gave Louis a hug.

Whatever was going on at the Municipal Auditorium was over. The doors were locked, the lights were off, and nobody was around.

"No, no, no," Sara yelled. "Now what? I want to go home." She looked at Glenn. "We should have never wasted that much time."

Bill got between Sara and Glenn. "Calm down, Sara. It's not the kid's fault. We'll get out of this. We know where he lives. We'll just go back."

"What if he isn't there?"

"Then we'll wait. Maybe that's what we should have done anyway. We'll find him."

Glenn was crying.

"Oh baby," Sara said. "Come here. I'm so sorry. I lost my head." She picked Glenn up.

They trucked their way back uptown.

"Thank you," Sara said to Bill.

"For what?"

"I lost it back there, and you handled the situation right. You've handled this whole thing well. Thank you." Sara rubbed Bill's arm.

"It was my fault anyway."

"No, it wasn't."

"Yes, it was."

"We are going to be in trouble no matter what."

"I know. I've been thinking about that. I'll probably be kicked out of school, and that means back to boot camp. I hate that place but if I can I'll take the blame."

"You don't have to do that," Sara said.

"I want to."

Walking down Valence St. the policeman from the day before came around the corner. All three kids started running. This time the policeman made a better chase. As the three kids turned a corner they ran into a man. Everything happened fast. The man grabbed them all. They heard the jingle of a tambourine, everything went dark and started moving, then there was a bright light. The kids found themselves back in Mr. Merl's closet, and Mr. Merl was there. All three of them hugged him.

"Okay, kids, okay," Mr. Merl said. "Y'all are safe now. Y'all are back."

They left the closet and went into the classroom and sat down.

"Y'all have had an unbelievable experience. We need to talk about what needs to be done now. It's very important that my secret remains one."

"It was my fault..." Bill said.

"It was my fault. I'm sorry," Sara said. "We didn't mean to..."

"Sara, I'm not mad. You're not in trouble. Nobody is in trouble."

"Mr. Merl," Glenn interrupted. "Sara sang with Aaron Neville and I played with Louis Armstrong. It was great."

"Glenn, you can't tell people what happened. They'll think you're lying, and you may get in trouble. All of you need to realize that this was something that only the four of us can talk about. Sleep on it and we'll talk about it tomorrow. I'm interested to hear what happened."

"We've been gone for a day..."

"No, y'all are right back at the same moment y'all left, so go home now."

Sara and Glenn left the room, but Bill stayed behind.

"What do you need to talk about Bill?"

"It was all my idea. I'm very sorry."

"I know you are. I also know this had a positive effect on you."

"How do you know that?"

"A feeling I have. And I know that if you get in trouble over this it wouldn't help."

"Mr. Merl, I'll be a better student, I promise."

"Do your best and I'll be happy. We'll talk tomorrow."

Walking out of the door Bill turned around. "Did you plan this?"

Mr. Merl chuckled.

Bill walked down the street. Sara pulled up beside him in her car.

"Want a ride?"

Bill got in the car. 'Tell It Like It Is' was playing. They rode off singing along.

Eddie Tebbe

Why Not Try

Chorus:
So try, try, try
Why not try
What would it hurt
What could be worse
than wondering
So try, try, try
Why not try

Verse one:
Give it your best effort
That's what your father said
Why not give it a taste
That's what your mother begged
But you dug your heels in
For no good reason
Then later when you tried
You finally realized
Whether right or wrong
You have learned a lot
It's better to try than not

Verse two:
Every boy agonizes
Over asking a girl out
Afraid of her reaction
She might laugh or shout
When he finally does it
It's never that bad
Or even if it is
He will always be glad
Facing up to his fears
Even if you think you'll die
You'll never know until you try

Verse three:
So look at your own life
The decisions that you make
How open minded are you
At trying for trying's sake
Maybe you don't know
Quite what you think
Maybe it's good to go
To places you'd never been
And out of all this
There's one concept I hope you
buy
It's very simple, why not try

Eddie Tebbe

It's in The Air

I was born where the soul meets the blues
I was born where the rock meets the roll
And there's music in my soul from my head to my feet
When I walk these New Orleans streets
When I walk these New Orleans streets

When you hang downtown
There's talk that goes around
I never want to leave this town
Cause when I walk these streets
I can feel the rhythm and beat
I can feel the rhythm in my feet

I go out to see a band
And man, o man
There's something special in the air
You can't get anywhere
I feel pity
For a musician who doesn't come to this city

It all started in Congo Square
The slaves and Indians were told to beware
It was the only place they could play their drums
And that is where the music comes from
You can feel the beat in the air
Breathe it in. It's in the air

The moment you step off the plane
It starts to penetrate your brain
Then moves to your body
You can feel it in your body
Your toes start tapping the street
It's in the air, and you can't stop your feet

Patience, Faith, Love, Hope

The four things in the world
I need most for a good emotional state
Patience, faith, love, hope
These things help me cope

Chorus: you took (these things) away from me
when you broke my heart
you took (these things) away from me
tore my world apart

Patience is something I miss when it's gone
Patience is something I really count on
When the world gets real bad
I can sit back and wait
Wait to see what comes my way
It helps me day by day
                    Chorus: (patience)
Faith is something we all need
I had faith in the world
I had faith in people
I had faith that good could conquer evil
I had faith that you would make it right
I wanted you to stay the night
Imagine my surprise
When I had to walk away
With tears in my eyes
                    Chorus: (faith)

Eddie Tebbe

Love comes in many forms
Love keeps us warm
I've had a friend's love
I've had my family's love
I've had love from up above
The one love I needed
You could have given to me
But you walked away
Now it's hard to get through another day
                              Chorus: (love)
Hope is something different
Different from the other three
Patience, faith, and love
Can be regained internally
Hope has to be given
Or taken away
You had a chance to give
But decided to take
Now every morning when I wake
I wonder if today's the day
That somebody can give me hope
Without hope there's no other way
                              Chorus: (hope)

Sing To Me

Chorus:
Oh jah sing to me
How can the world be
So crazy and ridiculous
Have we forgotten what you taught us

Oh jah please hear my prayer
People just don't care
About letting people live
Didn't you teach us to give
                  Chorus

Oh jah I know you understand
The difficulties of being human
With all the evil and greed
Will you please plant a seed
For friendship and happiness
So we can get through all this
                  Chorus

Oh jah I watch the news
And see your name being used
For evil and destruction
Please send us some direction
                  Chorus

So please sing us a song
We'll wait here all night long
We know that music brings your love
From way up above
So I'll sing this song
And hope I don't go wrong
                  Chorus

Eddie and his mother Lynette

Code Delta

On Bordeaux street, in the residential section of uptown New Orleans, the house in the middle of the block sat empty. The previous owners moved into a bigger house with more bedrooms because they were expecting a new baby. The house on Bordeaux only had two bedrooms. The real-estate agent walked through the house checking one last time to make sure everything was just right. After satisfying herself that everything was perfect, she walked outside to wait for the new owner to arrive. As she waited, she pulled the "For Sale" sign out of the small front yard.

The neighborhood children rode their bikes up and down each driveway on the block racing each other. Their yelling became louder the closer they got then became softer as they passed. On their second go around Dave, a ten-year-old that lived in the house on the corner, came to a sudden stop. The agent was a little startled.

"You sold the house?" Dave asked, out of breath.

"Why, yes, young man, I did." The agent regained her composure. She looked and sounded very prim and proper.

"Do they have kids?"

"There is one child, yes."

"How old?"

"I'm not quite sure. Probably around your age."

"All right," Dave said as he sped off.

The real-estate agent started to say something but put her hand over her mouth. Maybe it was best not to say anything. It wasn't her place.

The moving truck rumbled around the corner. The real-estate agent sighed and looked at her watch. It was six o'clock in the evening. The neighborhood children followed the truck but stayed across the street as it backed into the driveway. Mothers yelled from front doors for their children to come in for dinner. None of the kids wanted to leave. They didn't want to ignore their mothers' calls either, but the excitement of seeing the new people held them in place until the tone of those cries changed. The pack broke up slowly with all of them trying to get one last look.

Dave remained though since his mom had yet to call him. He saw a woman get out of the driver side of the truck. Before doing anything else she went to the other side and helped a boy out. The boy was partially blocked by the woman and it was getting dark, but it was obvious to Dave that there was something wrong with that kid. Before he could investigate further, he heard his mother's voice. Against his desires he went home.

Rosemary shook the real-estate agent's hand, wearing worn-out cut off blue jeans and an old T-shirt; she looked like a person who had worked hard in her life. She introduced her son, Eddie. He stood with both legs bent and knees bending in and his feet pointed inward as he used the side of his feet to balance. His right arm was held rigidly to his chest. He stuck out his unsteady left hand. The agent was a little perplexed but used her left hand to shake his.

"Rosemary," the agent said, still uneasy with using first names, "everything is as it should be. Would you like to take a look?"

"Sure," Rosemary answered.

Eddie ran towards the door. He tripped, fell, hit the ground, bounced up, and continued inside. The real-estate agent didn't take her eyes off the boy and gasped when he fell. His mother seemed to ignore the whole thing. They proceeded into the house.

"Everything looks so nice," Rosemary said to the agent. "Thank you so much. It feels so good to know I own this house." Rosemary had a big smile on her face.

The house wasn't that big. Upon entering, to the left the living room and dining room combination led to a small kitchen which was followed by a storage room. Facing forward, a hallway went straight to the back of the house with the two bedrooms off to the right and the bathroom at the end. Empty of furniture the walls had a fresh coat of cream-colored paint and dark green trim.

"It looks so wonderful," Rosemary said.

"It pleases me to have this house be just what you needed. As we say in the realty business, 'Houses are like true loves. There's one for everybody.'"

Eddie scampered from one bedroom to the next.

"What room do I get?" he asked from the back bedroom.

The agent had to listen closely to understand the boy.

"Whatever one you want dear," Rosemary answered loudly.

"Really?" Eddie said running towards his mom making the agent nervous, "The bigger one?"

"Really."

"I'm taking the back one. It's huge!"

The boy ran back to his new huge room. The mom and agent laughed with amusement at his excitement.

"It touches my heart how you handle your..." the agent said in a normal tone then whispered, "situation."

"What situation is that?" Rosemary asked with a raised voice.

"Well, ah, being a single mother with a crippled child."

Rosemary narrowed her eyes.

"My son is not crippled. He's physically challenged."

"Well, I, I'm sorry that was a bad way to put it," the agent said uncomfortably.

"I appreciate your sentiment," Rosemary said easing her tone. "It's really tough dealing with misunderstandings like this sometimes. It's been a long day. I'd offer you something to drink, but...."

"No, no, I should be going and let you get unpacking. Are you unpacking everything yourself?"

"I have friends coming in the morning. I'll unpack a little tonight."

The two ladies said good-bye at the front door. Eddie stood next to his mother. The agent bent down towards him.

Speaking loudly and slowly she said, "It was nice meeting you. I hope you like your new home."

"I love it."

Rosemary shut the door and sighed. She went to the middle of the living room floor and sat on the brown carpet with a groan. Eddie wriggled into her lap. The mother took the bottom of her T-shirt and wiped the drool off of his chin.

"Do you like this place?" she asked.

"I love it. I love it."

Eddie got up and ran around the living room then tripped right into his mother's arms.

"I'm hungry, Mom."

"Well," Rosemary sighed again, thinking of all the work ahead, "I can't fix you anything so I guess we can..." she paused, "go out!" she yelled as she tickled him.

Eddie tried to talk but couldn't because he was laughing.

"Where would you like to go?" she asked.

After catching his breath Eddie asked, "Anywhere I want?"

"Anywhere you want."

"Bud's Broiler!" Eddie exclaimed.

Dave's house was the biggest on the block. It was three stories tall. His family, the Norths, occupied the top two floors and rented out the apartment on the first floor. The house was well kept and freshly painted every few years in yellow with light blue trim. A large stair-case in the middle of the house ran from the ground to the front porch, which covered the front and the right side of the house. The front door was a single pane of glass with a small wooden frame.

The family sat around the round kitchen table enjoying a home-cooked meal. Mr. and Mrs. North were side by side, Dave to his mom's right was followed by his seven-year old sister, Anne, his five-year old sister, Dawn, and his two-year old little brother, Lou. Every-body was nicely dressed.

Dave gobbled up his food. Mr. North motioned to his wife. She reacted immediately.

"Son, don't eat so fast."

Dave finished his last bite.

"Can I be excused?" Dave asked as he stood up.

"No, you can't," his mother answered. "There was no reason to shovel your food into your mouth like that. Whatever has you in such a hurry can wait. We eat dinner together." She looked at the clock. "Besides your favorite show doesn't start for a half an hour."

"I have a code delta."

"What is that?"

Dave didn't answer.

"I have homework."

"Don't be smart," Mr. North said sternly.

Dave hung his head and sat down again.

"Yes, sir."

He sat there with his shoulders slumped over.

"Seeing you have nothing to do," his mother said, "help clean up your brother."

After finally being released from his parents Dave scurried upstairs so fast that he tripped, but the plush wall-to-wall carpet saved his knees from being hurt. The momentum caused the bedroom door to slam harder than he wanted when he closed it. Dave rushed to the special drawer with his walky-talky.

"Cobra, cobra," he said breathing hard.

The kids on the block had developed a complex system of communicating through electronics and window to window signals. Dave was in touch with his next-door neighbor Brad.

"What is it?" Brad asked.

"Code delta, code delta," was all Dave said before grabbing his backpack and shoving the necessities into it. He looked at the clock. His favorite show was about to start, and his mother usually left him alone until it was over. That gave him an hour. He turned the TV on, crept downstairs, and sneaked out the backdoor.

Brad wrote the message on a piece of paper, grabbed his flashlight, and shined it across the street. John used his binoculars to read the sign and flicked his light. John went to his bathroom window, which was close enough to Matt's window that they could talk. Matt then used a pulley from his other window to send along the message to Adrian. The message was then sent electronically across the rest of the neighborhood. Some kids asked their parents' permission to go to each other's houses, some kids sneaked out, but all of them headed towards the clubhouse in Mike's backyard.

The clubhouse was big and well built by Mike's father who was a carpenter. The yard was also the largest allowing the clubhouse to be secluded. The kids trickled in, everyone asking the same question as they entered. Dave wouldn't tell anybody what was up until all were present. They talked excitedly amongst themselves. Most figured it had to do with the new arrivals. Joey, who was always the last to show because he was the end of the chain, entered making a full complement of eleven.

"Okay, okay," Dave said. He waited. "Quiet!"

Everybody finally calmed down.

"As we all know by now there's a new family that just moved in on the block. Some of us saw the truck pull up. Well, I talked to the agent, remember, and I stayed around to see more. It's a boy our age, but..." Dave paused, he liked having all the kids' attention. "He's a freak."

The clubhouse erupted in noise.

"What do you mean, a freak?"

"There's something wrong with him. I didn't get a close look, but he's not normal."

With great frenzy the kids threw around wild ideas all claiming to know something the others didn't. One thing was for sure. A reconnaissance mission was in order. The next day's activities would be geared to finding out about their new neighbor.

Eddie rolled off of the mattress on the floor. He was a little disoriented at first. Rubbing his curly blond hair, he walked into the living room. There was furniture and boxes everywhere. All the furniture was second hand. His mom and her friends, May and Tim, were unloading the truck. They were trying to maneuver the sofa through the front door.

"Good morning, sleeping beauty," his mother said.

After the grownups put the sofa down Eddie gave Tim a hug and May swooped him up in her arms.

"Well, how do you like your new home?" asked May.

"I love it," Eddie answered.

"I know something else you are going to love."

"What?"

"Guess what I brought you?"

"What?" Eddie could hardly wait.

"An apple..."

"Apple fritter!" he screamed.

May let go as Eddie jumped to the ground and ran into the kitchen. His mother followed him to help him get set up with a plastic cup and straw. While Eddie enjoyed the crisp glazed crust of the fritter the other three got the truck unloaded. May and Tim had to leave with everything still packed. It would take Rosemary a long time to unpack the house.

Eddie disappeared into his room. Rosemary checked on him not long afterwards finding his room completely unpacked and organized.

"This is a great job. I wish I could get things in order as quick and easy as you."

"I'll do the living room bookshelves next," Eddie said.

"Don't you want to go outside and play?"

"But you need help."

"I'll be fine. I want you to go outside. Go meet some of the neighborhood kids."

Eddie looked down and frowned.

"Are you afraid?"

"No, Mom," he said, but he was.

"It might be a little hard at first, but things turn out okay, don't they?" Rosemary said hiding her own nervousness.

With his limits and instructions Eddie ventured into his new land. He did love exploring and the feeling of being independent. First, he checked out his own backyard, and then the front. It was all very exciting as he imagined he was searching his new kingdom. After walking around a short while Eddie wondered where the rest of the kids were.

They were currently in the playhouse planning their surveillance. Feeling everything was covered they headed out. They came through the alleyway between two houses and into the driveway.

Eddie was two houses down, on the other side of the street.

"There he is!" Dave yelled and pointed.

The group rushed towards Eddie, who stood still in fear. The group came to a stop in the middle of the street.

"Hey," Dave said aggressively, "What's your name?"

"Eddie."

Most of the group started laughing and made rude comments about Eddie's speech.

"What?" Dave said. "What's wrong with you, you freak?"

"Nothing," Eddie replied and started walking home.

"Look how he walks."

Some started mimicking Eddie, others rolled on the ground laughing, and a couple picked up and threw some small rocks towards him. When he saw the rocks landing around him Eddie started running, but tripped. He heard a huge roar of laughter. The kids were too busy laughing to make chase, so Eddie made it safely inside.

The group hung around for a while hoping the freak would come back out. They realized that they had probably scared him in for the day. Just in case, they would keep watch from a distance.

Rosemary was taking a nap in her bedroom. Eddie shook, he took a deep breath and went to his room. Tears were running down his face. He fell on his bed crying. A world of emotions rushed through him. He was angry, he was sad, he was frustrated, and he just wanted to know why things were like this. Why did he have to have Cerebral Palsy? Why did kids have to act like that? Eddie got up and started punching the punching bag his mother had given him just for these occasions. After running out of steam he sat in his chair, and wiped his drool, snot, and tears away with the inside of his shirt. It was a good thing there was so much unpacking to do because putting things in order made him feel good.

When Rosemary woke up Eddie had unpacked and arranged the bookshelves and was in the middle of unpacking what he could in the kitchen.

"You've been a busy beaver. I thought I told you to go play," Rosemary said as she grabbed the plates out of Eddie's unsteady hands.

"Neighborhood kids weren't so nice," Eddie said, mad. He told her about the kids chasing him and throwing rocks.

His mother slammed her hands on the table, then caught herself.

"I hate them," Eddie said.

"No, it's not okay what they did, but hating them won't help. They don't know any better."

Rosemary hugged her son.

"You are such a special boy," she said. "It's not fair that you have to deal with so much negative stuff. Every day I'm more proud of you. Did you use your punching bag?"

Eddie nodded his head

"Did it help?"

"A little."

"Do you still feel bad?"

"A little."

"Well, how about I call Diana and see whether or not you can go visit Joan?"

Eddie's eyes lit up. Joan was his best friend.

Dave sat in his room playing Atari and listening to the record player with headphones so his mother couldn't hear. He was supposed to be doing his homework, but it was hard and had frustrated him. His mother opened the door and surprised him. Dave quickly covered up the game, but it was too obvious. He was busted.

"Mom," Dave groaned, "I thought you had to knock."

"This is my house. I will enter any room I want. When you show me I can trust you maybe I'll give you some privacy."

Dave rolled his eyes.

"I thought," his mother continued, "that you were doing your homework."

"Well, I…"

"It's too late now. You'll have to do it tonight, and you can't watch television until it's done."

"I'll do it now. I'll do it now."

"We're going to the mall with Mrs. Green."

"And Mike?" Dave smiled.

"No, he's off with his father."

"Can I stay home?"

"You're not old enough."

"But Mom, I'm home alone sometimes" he whined.

"Plus I need you because you've grown so much."

Dave rolled his eyes.

As Dave and his mother walked over to meet Mrs. Green they passed Rosemary's house as she and her son were getting home. Rosemary was halfway in the back seat of the light blue VW Bug trying to pull out groceries. Dave began staring and laughing at Eddie. His mother whacked Dave across the head.

"Don't stare at that," she said, "It's not polite."

Rosemary heard the comment, backed out of the car, and looked around. She was ready to jump down the throat of whoever said that, but Mrs. North had picked up her pace dragging her son along and was greeting Mrs. Green already.

Eddie could tell his mom was furious by the way she slammed the groceries around and mumbled obscenities under her breath. She was far past him being able to calm her down. He knew to stay quiet.

After dinner Eddie had just settled into the sofa and "The Dukes of Hazzard," his favorite show, had just started when his mom walked into the room.

"Come on," she said, "I need to visit our neighbors."

"Can't I stay here?" Eddie said hopefully.

"Get your shoes on."

Eddie slowly put on his shoes paying more attention to the TV.

"Let's go," Rosemary said as she snapped.

Eddie rolled his eyes as she tied his shoes.

As they waited at the North's door for it to be answered Eddie looked around at how nice everything looked. Mrs. North greeted Rosemary and introductions were made.

"Please come in," Mrs. North said. "Welcome to the neighborhood. I should have stopped by already, but I've been so busy, I apologize. How can I help you?"

They stood in the hallway. Rosemary and her son's dirty blue jeans and wrinkled t-shirts stood in contrast to their current surroundings. Mrs. North secretly found her guests' appearances shabby. Eddie had wandered to the doorway to the living room where Dave sat doing homework. Looking up, Dave saw Eddie. He sat still not knowing what to do.

Rosemary said, "Can I speak to you?"

Mrs. North could tell that her guest had something serious to discuss.

"Well, we can go into my husband's study."

Mrs. North looked at her son.

"Dave, Rosemary and I will be in the study. Keep trying on that homework. If you can't figure it out by the time I'm done, I'll help you. Also, Eddie is a guest in our home. I expect you to treat him as such."

Dave nodded, but with a disgusted look on his face. Rosemary patted Eddie on the head and the mothers walked away. Dave stayed behind the desk severely uncomfortable with the situation.

"Can I get you something to drink?" Dave asked with a tone.

Eddie shook his head.

"Would you like to sit down?"

Eddie walked very slowly trying not to give Dave a reason to laugh. His muscles were even harder to control when he was nervous. Also, he was afraid of breaking something. He wasn't used to so many nice and delicate things. It almost felt like a museum. Sitting on the loveseat he didn't lean back.

The boys sat in silence staring at each other.

"So, your name is Eddie?" Dave asked.

Eddie nodded his head.

"You're not going to talk?"

Eddie didn't react.

"Fine then."

Dave returned to his homework. He kept looking up at Eddie.

Eddie finally spoke trying to speak very clearly, "Having trouble?"

Dave didn't answer.

"What is it?"

Dave looked up. Eddie could tell Dave didn't understand him.

"What are you working on?" Eddie asked again.

"Long division."

"Do you want some help?"

"I'm sure if I can't get it you can't."

"I can do long division in my sleep," Eddie said.

"Prove it," Dave demanded.

Eddie smiled at himself. He walked over to the desk. Dave got up. Eddie sat down, found a clean sheet of paper, looked in the book for the hardest even numbered problem, and started doing it. Dave watched over Eddie's shoulder trying to understand his writing. It was hard following Eddie's hand since there were so many extra movements.

Eddie finished.

"What does that say?" Dave questioned in a high voice. "I can't understand that. You're lying."

"568.3 remainder of 2," Eddie answered. "Look in the back of the book."

Dave took the book and checked. Eddie was right.

Eddie Tebbe

"You must have looked already."

"Fine."

"Okay, do an odd one."

"I'm not here to do your homework, but I'll help you."

"Uh, okay, I guess."

They switched positions. The more Eddie explained, the more relaxed both boys became, and the easier it was for Dave to understand Eddie.

"Oh, I get it," Dave said a few times.

It wasn't long before Dave had completely finished his homework and understood it.

The study was a very dark room. All the furniture and bookshelves were made of dark woods. The blinds on the windows were shut tight. Mrs. North turned on the overhead light and the lamp by the dark green sofa where the two women sat. The room still seemed dark.

"Are you sure I can't get you something to drink?" Mrs. North asked.

"Thanks really, I'm fine."

Rosemary rubbed her hands on her legs.

"Where should I begin?" Rosemary asked herself. "I have to fight for my son's respect. He's not given an equal amount. I can't micromanage his own interaction with kids, and I have to control myself, but when I witness such disrespect from an adult I can't."

"I haven't disrespected your son," Mrs. North said in defense. She became stiff and even more serious. "I'm a little offended."

"Please give me a second to explain. I didn't come here to attack you or insult you. I think if you give me a moment and listen with your mother's heart, you'll appreciate what I have to say."

Mrs. North relaxed a bit, "Go ahead."

"My son is going to have a hard life. One of the reasons is how people perceive him. The more negative that perception is the harder it is to overcome."

"But," Mrs. North defended herself again, "I told my son not to stare at your son."

"I think what you said was 'Don't stare at that.' Did you talk to your son afterwards?"

Mrs. North thought for a moment.

"No."

"When you tell a kid not to stare, they want to stare more. If they don't stare just because it's not polite or to avoid getting in trouble, then they haven't learned the real lesson. My son should not be stared at period. Yes, Eddie's different, but he's just another human being. All your comment does is reinforce your son's natural tendencies to see my son as a freak, something to be stared at, to be made fun of."

"I'm sure my son wouldn't do that."

"He did, and most do to different extents. It's only natural, but with a little open-mindedness it's easily overcome. I'll never be prouder about anything my son does more than how he changes people's minds. Even at his young age he's calmer than I am. If I would have confronted you earlier, I would have been yelling and screaming."

"Well, I'm not in the habit of taking parental advice from strangers," Mrs. North hesitated, "but you are making a good point. I can tell you're fighting for your child. I would hope I could be that strong. I don't know if I agree with everything you've said, but I will have a talk with David. What is it actually that your son has?"

"He has Cerebral Palsy."

"I'm not fully familiar with that."

"It's a birth defect that causes him not to have complete motor control. At some time in the womb the umbilical cord was pinched. His brain didn't get enough oxygen, arresting the development of the Cerebral Cortex."

"Is he, you know, retarded?"

"No, not at all, in fact quite the opposite. His case of CP is mild really. Luckily the oxygen was cut off near delivery. They aren't sure when though."

"Wow." Mrs. North leaned back.

They sat in silence for a few moments.

All the wives had been talking about their new neighbors, wondering what the story was behind the single mother with a handicapped child. Now Mrs. North had detailed information about the child. She wanted some gossip on the mother. Somehow though that stuff seemed less important.

"Do you like your new house?" asked Mrs. North.

They chitchatted for a while. When Rosemary insisted on leaving, they found the boys finishing Dave's homework.

"You're pretty smart," Dave said.

"You're not," Eddie replied with a smile.

Dave cut his eyes at him, but then smiled.

The next day Eddie headed out on his bright yellow three-wheeled bike. It looked like a large tricycle with a basket in-between the back wheels. He was doing donuts in the driveway when Dave, Mike, Brad, and Matt sped by on their dirt-racing bikes. Dave turned and looked at Eddie but kept going and didn't say anything. Eddie rolled down the drive and into the street watching the group loop around and come back. When they saw Eddie, they headed straight at him only putting on the brakes at the last second.

"Hey, look it's the freak," Matt yelled out.

"What, is that a big tricycle, or what?" Mike said.

Three of the boys laughed. Dave hesitated. He and Eddie stared at each other. Dave looked back to his friends and joined in. Eddie looked away in disappointment. He thought he had gotten through to Dave. It really hadn't been that hard before.

"See if I help you with your homework again," Eddie told Dave.

"What did he say?" asked Mike.

"Why does he know you?" Brad asked.

"His mom wanted to talk to my mom yesterday. I had to be nice to him or get in trouble. Come on. Let's go."

The four boys rode off. Dave didn't understand why, but he felt bad about what just happened.

Eddie and his mother sat at the kitchen table. The rain fell hard. There was no thunder and lightning, but the rain sounded loud on the tin awning over the backdoor and the wind was blowing. Rosemary was eating, but her son picked at his food. It was some kind of dish with too many vegetables, looking and smelling funny to Eddie. He wasn't going to eat it.

"Eat your food," Rosemary insisted.

Eddie squinted his face.

"Come on you haven't even tried it."

"I don't like it," Eddie whined.

"How do you know that? You've never had it."

"I know I don't like it."

"Take three good bites then if you don't like it I'll fix you something else."

Eddie pushed his plate away. Rosemary was used to her son's lack of adventure when it came to food, but she could tell there was another problem here.

"What's the matter?" she asked.

"I don't like this yucky food."

"I think there's something that has put you in a bad mood. What is it?"

Eddie easily told his mother what had happened with Dave and the other boys. Usually things went better than this.

Rosemary took a big sigh.

"You know how special you are on the inside, and that's what truly matters. Unfortunately, it takes people a while to get past their first impression. No matter who it is there are certain barriers that people need to get through when dealing with new people. Even if you didn't have CP it still might take some time for you to make friends because we come from a different background. People do get over these things, and you know that. Once people get to know you you make a big impact on them. It might get a little harder though. From about your age through the teenage years until people mature everything that causes your CP to be a barrier will be more difficult to overcome. If allowed, kids can be wide open. As they start maturing it becomes very confusing trying to figure out who they are and what's right and wrong. They make decisions based on very superficial things. Appearances are so important to teenagers." Rosemary fought back her tears of concern for her son. "You'll have to be extremely patient, but if anybody can do it you can. You just have to be strong. I've always talked straight to you about your CP, and I'll never stop no matter how hard it is. All I want to do is wrap you in my arms and protect you from everything, but I have to prepare you for life. I see you not only living a normal life, I see you making a difference. These kids don't know any better than to make fun of you, and you have to show them different. You're my shooting star."

Rosemary grabbed her son and squeezed him tight as tears rolled down her face. Eddie saw the opportunity to get something better to eat.

"Mom, can I have some cheese toast?"

"Sure honey."

Rosemary cleared the table and started making her son's favorite. Eddie sat at the table staring out the window. He loved stormy nights. The way the rain and wind sounded seemed peaceful to him. Eddie walked to the window and looked out on the neighborhood. Getting these kids to accept him was just another challenge. He liked challenges. The bigger one was the more determined Eddie got, and the ideas that his mom instilled in him made him stronger.

Across the street Dave sat on the floor in his room playing Atari. His mom walked in.

"Mom," Dave groaned, "I thought you had to knock."

"This is my house. I will enter any room I want. When you show me I can trust you maybe I'll give you some privacy."

Dave rolled his eyes.

"Are you done with your homework?"

"We didn't have any."

Mrs. North looked at her son with suspicious eyes.

"Well did you get the homework back that you were having so much trouble with?"

"Huh?"

Mrs. North grabbed Dave's book-bag and started looking through it. She finally found the paper. He only had four wrong. That was the best grade he had received in math all year.

"That's great. Why didn't you show us?"

"I don't know?"

"Did someone do this for you?"

"No."

"Eddie was over. Did he do it for you?"

"I said no!"

"Okay, I believe you. Did he help you?"

"Well, yeah, but I…"

"It's okay to get help. In fact, I wanted to talk…"

There was a noise from downstairs.

"I'll talk to you later. Go show your father this homework."

The next day was beautiful. Eddie had to get out. He would be starting in his new school Monday, so he wanted to take advantage of his final four days of his unexpected vacation caused by a scheduling fluke between his old and new schools. That also meant all the neighborhood would be in school.

Around the corner from his block there was a small park. He rode around to it and took the opportunity to practice his tricks on his bike he had been teaching himself knowing his mother would put a stop to them.

The park was part of Dave's view from his window. He looked out of it as he put his backpack on his desk, but the glare from the sun was too strong for him to see anything. Putting on his sunglasses he saw Eddie doing a wheelie. Continuing to watch he saw Eddie stand in the back basket and go up on two wheels on the side, pretty cool stuff. Whatever it was that made Dave look at Eddie differently decreased as the feeling of wanting to get to know Eddie better crept into Dave, so he got on his bike and went around the block.

Dave watched for a few minutes before Eddie noticed him. Eddie kept riding.

"Pretty cool moves," Dave said.

Eddie stopped. They both stared at the other. Eddie wanted to know Dave's motives and Dave wasn't sure what he was doing.

"I like the side wheelie thing you got going," Dave said.

"What can you do?" asked Eddie.

The boys traded bicycle moves for a while. At one point, Eddie's bike tipped over, throwing him across the blacktop. He got up, wiped himself off, and inspected his wounds.

"Are you okay?" Dave asked.

"Sure, just a few more scrapes."

For the first time Dave took a close look at Eddie's knees which were full of scrapes and scars.

Then Eddie let Dave ride his bike and showed him some moves. Dave offered to let Eddie ride his bike, but Eddie couldn't balance on a two-wheeler.

"What, do you think I ride this big trike for fun?" Eddie said.

While Eddie laughed drool flowed out of his mouth. Dave hesitated, watching the drool, before joining in the laughter.

"Would you like to come over for a while?" Dave asked. "My mom won't be home for a while."

"Sure," Eddie replied.

As they rode to his home Dave kept a sharp lookout for his friends. It seemed okay now to be playing with Eddie, but he didn't want to be seen doing so.

The bikes were left in the backyard. As the boys headed inside Eddie ran face first into the doorframe, buckling over, holding his nose. Dave stood there in shock, not knowing what to do.

"Are you okay!?! Are you okay!?!" Dave asked in a frenzy.

Eddie started bawling with laughter. It took Dave a moment to understand it was a joke, but he appreciated it.

"That was great. You have to teach me that one."

The boys headed to Dave's room for a whole afternoon of fun. As they played Atari Dave watched Eddie's whole-body jerk around as he moved the joystick which he held with the top at the bottom so that when he pushed up the character on the screen went down.

"Why do you hold it like that?" Dave asked.

"Because the button is on the right side, but I can't press it correctly with my right hand."

"But don't you get confused?"

"I'm beating the crap out of you, I guess not."

Dave became silent, put his joystick down, and sat on his bed. He had become very impressed by Eddie. All the things that made him different also made him pretty neat. He wanted to know what was wrong but didn't want to make Eddie mad.

Eddie, sensing the mood change, said, "You can ask me anything you want."

It wasn't hard for Eddie to tell when a person wanted to ask him something about his condition.

After some more stalling Dave finally asked, "What's wrong with you?"

"It's called Cerebral Palsy."

Dave repeated it wrong.

"No," Eddie tried to speak clearer, "Cerebral Palsy."

"Cerebral Palsy," Dave replied.

Eddie nodded his head.

"What does it do though?"

Eddie gave Dave the technical answer that he didn't understand.

"You do understand that your brain controls your body, right?"

"Well..."

"Well it does," Eddie continued. "Here's how my uncle explains it. Say this joystick is the part of your brain that controls your movements and Pac-Man is your body. When you move the stick Pac-Man moves the way you want. In my body there is a problem with the process so that I don't have full control over my body. When I move my joystick who knows what's going to happen on the other end? Also, my body moves even when I don't tell it."

"They can't fix it?"

"No. I can get better at doing things, but it will never go away."

That was enough serious talk for the boys and they continued playing. Without the mystery Dave found Eddie being different even less of a big deal. He felt bad about ever making a big deal about it, and he felt bad about making fun of Eddie.

The boys were so busy playing that they didn't hear Mrs. North coming down the hall. She opened the door and walked in.

"Dave, I've been meaning to speak to you about that new kid..." she stopped, noticing Eddie in the room. "Oh..."

"Mom, can Eddie spend the night?" Dave asked.

"Well, I, no," Mrs. North said. "It's a school night."

"But..."

"No sleepovers on a school night."

"Friday then?"

"Well," Mrs. North's mind was racing, she needed time, "if it's okay with his mother we'll see." It took her a moment to adjust. "Have you done your homework?"

Dave didn't answer.

"That's what I thought. Eddie I'm sorry but you'll have to go home. Dave has to do his homework before dinner."

"Okay."

Eddie got up and started leaving.

"Dave," she commanded, "always walk your guest to the door."

Dave got up walking face first into the door. He bent over holding his nose and moaned. Mrs. North looked horrified.

"Oh lord, Dave, are you all right?"

She grabbed her son who fell on the floor laughing.

"Very good," Eddie said joining in.

She looked from one boy to the other.

"That's not funny," she said.

"Yes, it is," Dave said.

At the back door, Eddie was almost down the steps when Dave called him.

"Eddie, I'm sorry."

"For what?"

"Making fun of you."

Eddie smiled.

"It's okay. Just don't do it again."

Dave smiled.

"Ask your mom about Friday," Dave said.

"Don't worry she'll say yes."

Eddie rode home to tell his mother about his breakthrough. The sun was setting, coloring the sky in reds and oranges. Eddie found it very beautiful. His mom was right, the kids would accept him once given a chance. He wondered if his life would always be this up and down. At least today was good. One kid down and the whole neighborhood to go, but maybe the rest would fall like dominos.

The Children's Lives

Chorus:
Something needs to be done
I'm talking about you
Problems are all around
I'm talking to me too
The answers aren't that hard
Let's work together
It's the children's lives now
Let's fix the future

Sometimes it's hard to recognize
What is in your neighbor's eyes
Is it love, is it hate
I just don't know
If we wait will it be too late
To save our souls
Why watch the news anymore
It's all at your front door
The violence, the pain
Does anybody care
What you see are you ashamed
To become aware
                    Chorus

I worry most about the children
And the hatred within them
Baby killing, boy and girls
I ask you why
What's lacking in the world
Causing kids to die
The unbelievable is now frequent
While help is delinquent
People hear, people see
What do we do
Stand by, letting things be
It comes down to you and me.
                    Chorus
People point fingers without aim
Pop culture gets a lot of blame
Things they see, things they read
Confusion all around
Tv doesn't fill a kid's need
Like seeds without water in the
ground
Slogans never solved a thing
Real change takes committing
To what we do not just say
May we all learn
Start again from today
So kids can have their turn
                    Chorus

Eddie Tebbe

Amy

She's sharp as a tack
Fast as a whip
She knows how to attack
So, don't get flip
She knows what she wants
And is not shy about it
She can be direct
Sometimes around-about
She can take care of herself
As long as she please
I don't think she'll ever
Be down on her knees
She's good at things
Some men don't like
She'll beat them in pool
Most any night
She knows where she's going
At least more than some
She knows her body
Knows what's all right
Doesn't need a man
Morning, noon, and night
She's sometimes moody
A real bitch, a real pain
She's like everyone else
She's not to blame
Her name is Amy
That's who this song's about
She's my friend
And that's no doubt

The Ballad of Joe and Mary

Take my hand, and I'll hold you tight
Wrap you in my love day and night
Make you feel safe from the world
I'm your man, and you are my girl
Sunshine or rain
I'll wash away the pain
By this full moon
I pledge my love to you
Gonna get it right, gonna get it right
Gonna get it right, gonna get it right

You accept my love with open arms
We walk through the fields of charm
Everything has beauty and grace
All I need to make it is your smiling face
In any kind of weather
We will always be together
By this full moon
I pledge my love to you
Gonna get it right, gonna get it right
Gonna get it right, gonna get it right

I loved you, but my love grows
Where will it stop, I don't know
It scares me what I'll do for you
Will you do the same thing too
When the winds blow
I'll protect you from the cold
By this half moon
I pledge my love to you
Gonna get it right, gonna get it right
Gonna get it right, gonna get it right

Eddie Tebbe

I'm there for you with all my heart
If it was up to me we'd never part
You need your space I understand
Just don't spend it with another man
The storm's brewing
When I think of what you're doing
By this quarter moon
I pledge my love to you
Gonna get it right, gonna get it right
Gonna get it right, gonna get it right

The nights I spend alone are increasing
While my patience is depleting
I hear the rumors around town
You're having an affair with Dr. Brown
The thunder and lightning
My rage is frightening
By this new moon
I pledge my love to you
Gonna get it right, gonna get it right
Gonna get it right, gonna get it right

My love for you runs so deep
If I can't have you, you must sleep
Life can get complicated
Turns my love to hatred
The twister twists my brain
There's nothing for me to gain
By this bloody moon
I take my love from you
Gonna get it right, gonna get it right
Gonna get it right, gonna get it right

We Ain't Telling

Chorus:
My buddy and me
What did we see?
They want to know
My buddy and me
What did we see?
They want to know
But we ain't telling
We're putting on a show

Playing by the river ----- Saturday night
Got lost --- we were out of sight
We've seen things ---- we shouldn't see
We've been places --- we shouldn't be
Now they want to know -- what we know
That is why ---- we have to go
Both sides ----- want us dead
We'll end up --- with holes in our heads
                                        Chorus
Crooked cops ----- want their cut
They plan --- to keep our mouths shut
They have --- the law on their side
We need ---- to take a long ride
We'll go north ---- or maybe west
We'll go the way --- that feels the best
                                        Chorus

Eddie Tebbe

The mob ----- wants its share
Making sure ---- nothing comes to bear
Running from the mob --- can be hard
Not many people ----- get very far
So we have to run run -- run away
If we want to see see -- another day
We have no idea --- what else to do
We have no idea --- how to get through
Chorus

We were just looking for -- a little fun
When we heard the shots --- from a gun
From on the levee --- we saw the deal go down
We should have ran -- but we stuck around
We waited too long ----- and were seen
New identities ---- are what we need
Chorus

Runnin' Pardners Ride Again

Chorus:
Ride Runnin' Pardners ride
Shooting star across the sky
Runnin' Pardners ride
Ride Runnin' Pardners ride
Shooting star across the sky
Runnin' Pardners ride
Through the night, blazing bright
Let's take that ride some more
times

Verse one:
On the playground was your crew
The world seemed right there
The laughter was true
Free from grownup cares
There is nothing like it again
The connection that is made
They got your back, lost or win
In time it never fades

Verse two:
Where in your world do you go
When your life gets scary
Someplace save you don't show
To the ones that you carry
We all need a reality break
There's nothing wrong with that
Go there for all our sakes
Just don't forget to come back

Verse three:
It has been way too long
Without playing with these guys
Let's break out the old songs
And take them out for a ride
I forgot how good this feels
The music reaches a magical
place
These players are the real deal
Just look at the grin on my face

Eddie Tebbe

Baby Teeth

They want me
I want you
Us, y'all, them
And we two
Running through
Blazing by
Shooting star
Cross the sky
Tiny bites
On my heart
Baby teeth
Bites are sharp
What I want
What I get
Haven't been
The same yet

Chorus:
Love, love, love
What are you waiting for
Love, love, love
Haven't I grown up enough
Love, love, love
Boy, I have to get me some
Love, love, love
If I want to stay around

Open wide
Close it shut
Minds must be
All made up
Memories

Of your youth
Growing old
That's the truth
Baby teeth
Don't come back
Enjoy life
Where you're at
Slip and slide
Jungle gym
Don't forget
Sparks within

                          Chorus
Ancient times
Read and learn
Kings, pharaohs
Nations burned
To the ground
Then rebuilt
Like my heart
Beating still
Hate over
Differences
Skin color
Where you live
Looks vary
Don't get mad
Baby teeth
We've all had

                          Chorus

Thank You Catherine

Waking from the nightmare
(sung by choir) I can feel again
Years of darkness
    i can see again
Hope had left me
    standing alone
Waiting on a miracle
    utterly alone
I had given up
    on happiness
Fate cursed my life
    without happiness

Chorus:
I want to thank you
Thank you so much
Doing what should be done
Doing what's right

The world's the same
but seems different
I'm the same person
but seem different

Everything I thought I'd feel
    i was right
It should've been you
    i was right
My problems aren't gone
    i can deal
My heart's a little broken
    i can deal
    Chorus
I didn't get everything
    that I want
In the end it's you
    that I want
For now I can sleep
    not be afraid
The nightmare can't return
    no longer afraid
    Chorus
I can dream thanks to you
    i can dream
I can dream of you
    i can dream
    Chorus

Eddie Tebbe

Solitaire

Even now, on his deathbed, after a life of contemplating, researching, philosophizing, and soul searching, the question would be his last thought. 'What was she?'

Ten hours ago, Mike Brendor sat down at his computer to play some solitaire. It was Saturday, and there was nothing that had to be done that couldn't wait. He was up until five the night before playing solitaire. Then at nine he woke up, started playing again, and only got up to get food that he ate at the computer, and to go to the bathroom. He sat there like a zombie, his only movement being his hand to move the mouse. His eyes were glossed over and rarely blinked. The stare from his dark brown eyes seemed to go through the computer. Mike never smiled while playing. He didn't smile much at all. Besides working, and doing only what was necessary, he played solitaire. Once he played for three days straight. When he played Solitaire, he didn't have to think. Some people turned to relatives or friends. Some people turned to alcohol or drugs. Some people turned to God, religion, or other spiritual avenues. Some people went crazy or killed themselves. Mike had to lose himself in something, something that would help him forget. Except Mike had to keep a certain level of control. That was part of his personality. He turned to a game he could play alone.

If there was such a thing Mike would be a world class solitaire player. It started when he was twenty-two. He got a new computer, and for the first time had Windows. The regular solitaire game came with the program. He started playing it now and then, and really enjoyed it. He found that playing eased his mind when he had worries.

Playing by the usual rules wasn't hard enough for Mike. The idea of playing the perfect game intrigued him. To Mike a perfect game was one where no cards were moved up to the aces. It cost him a lot of wins. Mike did achieve his goal a few times. Having only one solitaire game became boring, so Mike bought some harder games. Within a pack of games there was Free Cell. In the Free Cell directions, it read that every layout was winnable, and there are thirty-two-thousand layouts. Mike decided to start at one and play five games a day. At that rate it would take eighteen years to play all the layouts. Before Mike knew it, he had fifty different solitaire games. He didn't play them all. At that point playing was still just for fun, something to do right before he went to sleep.

In his mid-twenties Mike's life was going pretty well. He was an up and coming chef, a student of Paul Prudhomme on the road to having his own restaurant. Mike loved cooking since he was a child. At a very young age he was able to recreate the food he had when the family ate out. He worked in the restaurant business from age fourteen, never staying at one job too long. Mike wanted to learn from as many chefs as possible, but he didn't find culinary school useful. Living in New Orleans was a school itself. Good food was on every other corner.

The schedule of a cook also gave Mike an opportunity to take full advantage of New Orleans' nightlife. Any type of live music interested Mike, and with lots of disposable money and low cover charges he saw a lot. On the nights that Mike did not go see a band, or else after a show, he hung out at The Banks Street Bar. Truly only a social drinker it was the people and dart boards that made it his hangout. The bar was a quiet one with plenty of good conversations. The regulars liked Mike because he was an excellent debater. His coworkers liked him too. When he was around, he was the life of the party, but he noticed something weird. He was rarely invited anywhere. Mike was like a bump into buddy that everybody loved but was not thought of if not around. He didn't do anything to change that. He didn't plan group activities. He didn't invite people to his house. He liked his house to be truly his own space, someplace he could go when he was in a sullen or isolated mood.

Family, two close friends, and a girlfriend are where Mike got emotional support. The Brendor family was tight knit and did a lot together. Bar-b-ques, parading, going to festivals, or just eating at the neighborhood diner, it didn't matter. The parents and two children knew each other well. Any combination of them would have long talks, maybe in the kitchen while playing Po-Keen-No, maybe sitting on the porch sipping sweet tea and enjoying the fall weather in December. It was just the four of them in the family, and that made them even closer.

John and Gail were Mike's best friends. When he was eleven a five-year old snotty nose kid named John moved into the neighborhood. Their friendship evolved from dislike to like, to big/little brother to deep friendship. They had a mutual respect for each other's good and bad points. They didn't hang around each other daily, but they didn't need to. Mike met Gail through a classmate in college. She lived in Chicago. They wrote back and forth on a regular basis. Although they had only seen each other a handful of times Mike felt very close to Gail.

When they were both eighteen Jena and Mike met. He loved her from the start, but it took a year for them to go on a date. Slowly Jena fell in love with Mike. They dated for a few years on and off. Finally, when they were twenty-three, Jena committed to the relationship. It started off a little rocky but smoothed out nicely.

At twenty-six Mike felt on top of the world. There was one more step he wanted to make. He planned to ask Jena to marry him. The plan was perfect. They would have dinner at Commander's Palace. Mike knew all the chefs and would be treated right. Hopefully Jena would think something was up, but nothing would happen at dinner. Later at the neighborhood's New Year's Eve party it would all be set up. At midnight when everybody went outside to watch the fireworks and kiss there would be a ten by ten piece of plywood across from the house. After being lit it would read in sparklers "Would you marry me, Jena?"

Everything that night went as planned, but Mike was so wrapped up in his own feelings he didn't notice Jena's nervousness. She relaxed when nothing happened at dinner. At midnight, the moment of the big surprise, Mike expected a yes answer and a great kiss. When Jena ran away Mike didn't know what to think. This was supposed to be the happiest night of his life. Instead it started a sequence of tragic events nobody could have imagined, a sequence of events that would turn Mike into a shell.

The breakup with Jena was more than a heartbreak. Understanding that she didn't love him hurt, but Mike could have dealt with that. Finding out that Jena was seeing another man for two months before they broke up shook Mike. During those last two months he had believed more than ever that Jena loved him. Being led on, being lied

Eddie Tebbe

to, and finding out that a foundation of your life was fake, plus a broken heart, was hard to deal with. People noticed a level of cynicism in Mike that was never there before.

Soon after Mardi Gras Mike's mother got the Brendors together for a wonderful dinner. The mood was upbeat, the snap beans, potatoes, sausage were great, and laughter floated out the windows onto the street. Then the laughter stopped. The mother informed the family that she had terminal liver cancer. The doctors give her a year at most. Assimilation of the information was hard, but after the situation was understood the family was strong behind the person that was strong for them all their lives. Long days and longer nights wore on the whole family, but Mike had the hardest time. He was closest to his mother. As a kid he spent long hours in the kitchen cooking with her. He saw her as a role model, a friend, and a mom. Until this tragedy he had never pictured life without her. Watching her deteriorate eroded the most important part of his life. For her he put on a brave face but emotionally he was in denial. He made himself believe she was going to live. He would sit by his mother's bed holding her hand, reading to her, and talking to her. But he refused to say good-bye, refused to make peace with her death before it happened. Then it happened.

The weather reflected the mood in the car on the way to the funeral. The fog was thick making visibility low. It wasn't raining, but the windshield wipers were on because of the mist. They made a dragging noise. Inside the car Mike's father sat in the passenger seat with his face in his hands quietly sobbing. In the middle of the back seat, Mike's brother was reaching into the front rubbing his father's arm. Nothing was being said. John was sitting directly behind Mike who was driving. The car sat at the red light on Canal St. and Carrollton Ave. They were turning right, but Mike was waiting for a green light because of the low visibility. Mike was staring out the window into the fog. He was still in shock. He hadn't spoken much in the three days since his mother's death. He thought about the past, he thought about the future without his mom, but most of all he thought about the words he'd had time to say but didn't. The green light for the other direction turned yellow, and Mike took his foot off the break and applied it to the gas. The horrible sounds of screaming and horns were followed by metal crushing metal and shattering glass.

The short newspaper article told the tragic story behind the accident. The Brendor family, which consisted of the father and two brothers, and a family friend, were on their way to the funeral of the matriarch of the family when there was an accident at Canal and Carrollton. Details were vague because there were no witnesses. The only survivor was the youngest Brendor, and driver of one of the cars, Mike, and he was unable to talk.

Mike was able to talk he was just not talking. For two months recovery, and three months afterwards he didn't speak a word to anybody. Then he disappeared. He rented a one room apartment in a bad part of town and didn't let anyone know where he was. There was no way to find him. He had no bank account, no accounts with any services, and he stopped filing tax returns. When he had to, he got a job as a night short order cook. Nobody cared about him, and he didn't care about anyone or anything. He ate only to keep from starving. He talked only when talked to. He kept himself clean only enough to avoid mockery. For five years Mike cared about nothing. He played solitaire.

After ten hours of sitting at the computer playing solitaire Mike's mind was numb, and so was his body. It startled him when the manager knocked loudly on the door. For the first time in five years he had a phone call. Many of the tenants of this severely rundown hotel/apartment building received phone calls on the pay phone in the lobby, but never Mike. The manager, who was usually angry when he had to deliver messages, was amused.

"First call in five years," the manager said with a grin as he walked back down to the lobby.

Taking time to stretch to get the blood circulating again, he didn't care to rush really. He figured it was his boss from the greasy spoon. That was the only person who had the phone number.

The receiver was swinging as Mike stepped into the lobby from the stairwell. He caught it and put it to his ear.

"Hello," he said disinterested.

The voice on the other end was bright and chipper, "Hello, Mike. Remember me?" the woman said in her Australian accent.

Mike recognized the voice immediately. The flood of memories and emotions overwhelmed him. His knees turned weak. He had to sit on the filthy floor and lean against the filthy wall. The voice on the other end was an Australian girl named Olivia. Mike had not heard her voice in nine years.

Nine years ago, Mike and Jena met Olivia and Mel. On Olivia and Mel's first night in New Orleans they ate at the restaurant where Mike worked, and they enjoyed the meal so much they thanked him personally. Being impressed by that, Mike insisted on showing them around town the next day. Very quickly they became the fearsome foursome. Almost every day for the three months Olivia and Mel were in town they saw Mike and Jena. They all enjoyed each other's company, and fun was the name of the game.

From the beginning there was an unspoken attraction between Olivia and Mike. Some of his favorite memories were of the nights he and Olivia spent sitting on his porch until sunrise. Something could have easily happened between them, but neither wanted to risk their relationships.

A few nights before Olivia and Mel were to leave Olivia and Mike found themselves out without their mates. They were at the Maple Leaf seeing Walter Wolfman Washington, one of Olivia's favorite local bands, and dancing. It was something they had done many times in the three months Olivia and Mel had been in New Orleans. The difference this night was the feeling that their time together was ending, and Jena and Mel's eyes were not watching.

The dancing that night turned from fun and platonic to emotional and extremely close. Everybody in the bar dripped with sweat, and the band played their bluesy funk with extra flair. The only thing hotter than the bar and band were Mike and Olivia. As they held each other in their arms the desire for things to be different overpowered their thoughts. They were both in relationships with people they loved, but that wasn't the main barrier. They spoke at length about what they wanted in life and knew that to be together one of them would have to give up on their dreams. Mike loved New Orleans and had no plans to live anywhere else. New Orleans was the place for his restaurant. It was his home. He wanted to travel, but not live on the road. Olivia was a wandering spirit, never wanted to settle down, and had no plans to change. Both had to accept that their paths led in different directions. They had to be glad they met, and had this time to be friends, then enjoy the memories for the rest of their lives.

That night after the band ended, they took a walk along the levy holding hands, chit-chatting, trying to avoid the subject both were thinking about. Mike pulled Olivia towards him and was glad she smiled. Then they kissed, long, hard, and passionately. Neither wanted to pull away. Minutes passed by, and the kiss continued. Everything, all their emotions, had to be expressed in this one kiss. Finally, they eased back until their lips barely touched, savoring the feeling one moment longer. Mike thought he would never forget any detail of that moment. Olivia's long blond hair blowing in the breeze coming off the river, her sad blue eyes staring up at him, her baby powder smell, and her soft moist lips that had the sweetest taste Mike had ever known. Nothing else was said or done. Two days later she was gone. Things turned back to normal.

From time to time for years afterwards Mike caught her smell in the breeze, and her taste on his lips. She became a fantasy. Mike wondered if Olivia was ever real. As his love for Jena grew the fantasy began to fade.

For the five years before the phone call he had forgotten. He had no fantasies. Dealing with the emergence of these emotions after five years of being emotionless was almost too much to handle.

The phone conversation was over, but Mike failed to hang up the phone. He just dropped it from his ear causing it to continue swinging.

"Are are youuu aaalll right?" one of the lobby winos said as he stumbled by.

Mike didn't answer. He just sat there on the filthy floor leaning on the filthy wall.

"Hey brah, how 'bout helping out a brah who has problems," the same lobby wino said as he stumbled back by five minutes later.

Again, Mike didn't say a thing. Olivia was in town for four hours only. She really wanted to see Mike, so they planned to meet at Kaldi's coffee house in the French Quarter. It was a ten-minute walk for Mike. He rushed upstairs to change. Maybe he should take a shower, but he didn't want to waste time. He put on the best clothes he owned. Getting dressed, combing his greasy hair, brushing his neglected teeth, Mike was actually excited, until he looked in the mirror, and for the first time cared about what he saw. What he saw he did not like. His skin was almost powder white from lack of sun because of working nights and never going out during the day. He only weighed one hundred and ten pounds when he should weigh one hundred and fifty. He hadn't bought new clothes in years, and his old clothes made him look even skinnier. His hair was shoulder length and always pulled back into a ponytail. Mike looked nothing like he did ten years ago. He thought about not meeting Olivia, not wanting to disappoint her, but the desire to see her was stronger.

A block before the coffee house Mike had to stop and catch his breath. Walking fast he became winded because he didn't get much exercise. None at all. Getting to the door he turned to go back. He was so afraid. For five years he had not felt anything. Now he had to deal with the return of Olivia. Before he could decide what to do, he heard her.

"Mike," Olivia said with her beautiful Australian voice.

He was caught and turned around. Walking inside he hoped he would see something he didn't like. Maybe Olivia wasn't what she used to be. Olivia was walking towards him with open arms, a gigantic smile, and beaming face. Instinct took over, and he ran to meet her. They hugged, squeezing each other tight. This was the first bodily contact he'd had in five years. It felt wonderful. He didn't want to let go. They stood there holding one another. Finally, the hug broke. Mike got a good look at Olivia. She looked exactly the same as she did standing on the levee after they kissed. She still had long blond hair, sad blue eyes, and baby powder smell. They grabbed a table, sat across from each other, and held hands the whole time.

They sat for a few moments just looking. There was something different about Olivia. Although she looked the same, there was an effervescent glow.

Mike spoke first, "How have you been?"

"Life has taken me places I never dreamed about."

"That's great. What happened to Mel?" Mike figured he would try to keep the conversation on Olivia's life, not wanting to talk about his.

"Mel and I had a great relationship. We traveled around the world many times. We're still in love, but we're on different planes of life now."

Olivia spoke of her travels, the places she saw, people she met, and the feelings she felt. She never stayed in one place for more than six months. She had friends in every corner of the world and was proud of that. Mike sat there listening. Ten years ago, they both talked about their dreams. Ten years later Olivia had realized hers. Mike loved sitting, holding hands, listening to her voice. He wanted to ask questions like, Why was she only in town for four hours? Where was she going? and Could he come with her? He was getting a small taste of life again. Olivia then turned the conversation towards his life.

"So, what have you been doing besides not taking care of yourself?" Olivia asked.

Mike took a deep breath and looked away. "My life has not gone as planned."

For the first time he talked about what happened, although leaving out details, trying to get through it quickly.

"Oh, poor baby," Olivia said rubbing her soft hand across his cheek. "You've been killing yourself with guilt."

The first tear welled in his eye. "I let Mom die without telling her how I felt. Then I killed Dad, my brother, and John."

"What do you mean you killed them? You..."

"I was driving, but not paying attention. It was my fault."

"Maybe it was. Maybe it wasn't. I don't know, and don't care. You need to, look at me, you need to forgive yourself. You didn't do anything that should cause you to give up living. Even if it was your fault, you didn't mean to kill them! It was an accident, one you probably couldn't have stopped, and you're alive. That's a gift, not a curse. You have to live."

"Then let me come with you. I have no reason to stay here."

Olivia closed her eyes. "You can't, for many reasons. Mike, you are my one regret. I've never felt about anyone as I do about you. Ten years ago, I thought we would be together someday. Nothing would make me happier than to have you come with me, but..."

"Then stay."

"I can't. You need to deal with yourself. Get yourself back on track. I'm in a place where you can't come. Our time has yet to be."

Olivia put her hand- on Mike's cheeks, leaned over the table, and gave him the lightest kiss, barely touching lips. He felt as if he was kissed by a cloud.

She got up and started walking away.

"Where are you going?"

"I have to go," Olivia said, then turned around, looking directly in his eyes. He could have sworn he saw his mother's eyes.

"She knows," Olivia said then walked away.

Mike didn't know what to think. He sat there going over the events of the day over and over. That led to thinking about his life. That led to thinking about that terrible year. He had avoided thinking for a long time. Now he couldn't stop. As he walked home, he didn't notice anything, not even the rain that was getting him soaking wet. In the middle of Rampart St., and luckily no cars were coming, a thought hit Mike causing him to stop. How did Olivia know his phone number?

When Mike opened his apartment door, he saw the filth, the broken window with cardboard taped over it, the holes in the wall where the plaster had fallen, the mouse hole in the baseboard, and the utter chaos and mess his life was in. He finally broke down. He sat on his bed, cn sheets that hadn't been washed in ages, and started to cry. It wasn't a movie cry where one good cry solves everything, but it was a start. Mike was finally grieving.

Three years later Mike was well on his way back from the living dead. He had put weight back on, and his skin was golden brown again. Although he had to go through a lot of trouble because of reappearing after five years he was now living back in his family's home. He was cooking at a good restaurant again. He figured it would be three more years before opening his own place. He was even dating. The only thing the same as his nightmare years was the fact that he still played solitaire, some.

One day the phone rang. Mike picked it up. To his surprise it was Mel. Mel was in town for a few days and would love to see him. Mike invited Mel to stay with him. Later that night they sat on the porch, enjoying the fall night. Mike wondered if he should tell Mel about Olivia's visit. He may already know, but Olivia mysteriously hadn't come up in the conversation. Mike decided he would ask.

"Olivia saved my life you know."

Mel turned and looked at Mike. "Olivia saved your life? What are you talking about?"

"She pulled me out of my nightmare."

"You said you got your life together three years ago."

"That's right. Three years ago, she came in town, and..."

Mel got a little irritated. "Look, Mike, I don't know what you're talking about, but it isn't funny. Olivia died six years ago."

"Wh-h-h-at," Mike said in disbelief. "I saw her. I touched her. I kissed her."

"She was meeting me in Innsbruck. She was on a small plane that crashed in the Alps."

"Then what happened to me? Who was that? What was she?"

That question baffled Mike from then on. He pondered every possibility from her not really being dead to it being an angel. One answer never sounded any better than the other. Sometimes he wondered if it ever really happened.

Now Mike is a very old man who lived a long good life. In his family's home lying in bed he decides it is time to die. As the last breath is exhaled, and Mike's spirit is released from his body he finally answered the question. She was, in the simplest definition that we can understand, a ghost, a spiritual being taking a physical form.

Eddie Tebbe

Remembering the First Time I Saw You

When I saw your face
From across the floor
Your clear blue eyes
Captured me---
Your glance trapped me
Like a spider's web
Holding me --- pulling me in
That's where it all begins

Chorus: now when I think about you ---- my baby
              day and night, I think about you -- baby
              you warm my heart, soothe my soul, ease my mind
              please don't leave me behind

I was still waiting
Across the room
Wondering what to say
You threw a smile my way
So beautiful and bright
My heart almost stopped
I lost my sight
Could this be the start ---- of love

Chorus

I asked you to dance
We hit the dance floor
When our bodies touched
A wave of love came over me
Holding me --- pulling me in
That's where it all begins

Chorus

Eddie Tebbe

That was the night
The beginning of my life
Every day since
Has been wonderful
Now when I think about you ---- my baby
Day and night, I think about you -- baby
You warm my heart, soothe my soul, ease my mind
Please don't leave me behind
                          Chorus

Praying by your bedside
Knowing you'll make it through
The doctors don't know much
But I know I love you
Then you open
Your clear blue eyes
And throw a smile my way
I knew everything would be okay

                          Chorus

Jennifer's Eyes

Chorus:
Jennifer's eyes shine so bright
Jennifer's eyes brighten up the darkest night
Jennifer's eyes shine so bright
Jennifer's eyes get me through my darkest night

Whatever she'd done I must forgive
Because without her how could I live
She's been there all my life
Without her eyes I wouldn't have sight

It started when we were just four
When she and her mom walked through the door
We became best friends from the moment she was in
We looked so much alike people thought we were twins
From four to thirteen we were inseparable
Her eyes made the world seem so incredible
                                        Chorus
Somewhere deep inside I wish she was mine
But it never seems to be the right time
We stayed best friends, and went our own ways
I could see her eyes through the bad days

It's hard to explain and may sound funny
But at twenty-two she took my honey
And even though that is over now
I can't figure out my feelings any how
It's like walking through a dark haze
Her eyes are like a maze
                                        Chorus

Eddie Tebbe

Gift of Knowledge

Verse one:
What do you think I'd do
What do you think I'd say
Knowing this information
Facing the truth
Wanting things like they were
Back in the good old days

Chorus:
I won't be captured by darkness
I will handle the pain
I'll choose to be happy
I will not go insane
Time is not a friend
Appreciate it now
I have the gift of knowledge
I'll make it somehow

Verse two:
I asked to know
To deal with it straight
The world was on my shoulders
But now it's much worse
Everybody's heart must break
As we sit and wait

Verse three:
When life hits hard
Deal with the feelings
You can't give up
To be positive
Is the only choice
Whatever you are bearing

My Journey

Chorus:
I'm a lost soul
Running from the world
Trying to find my way
Through this hurricane's twirl
Raging inside me
Tearing me apart
Draining my emotions
I don't know where to start
To put my life together
Pieces all around
Why don't they fit
Interlocking pieces won't stay
bound

First verse:
For a long time
I was rolling down a hill
Finally hit bottom
My life was standing still
Positive energy ran out
I was stuck in the muck
Nowhere to turn
I packed up my old truck
On iffy ground I stood
Would a journey provide
Inner strength and peace
I needed inside

Second verse:
For years I wondered
When I would crack
All the pressure on me
Finally broke my back
I wanted to fly free
Away from my life
Receiving nothing from it
With no answers in sight
I wanted to run and hide
Away from all I had
The black hole inside me
Sucked in the light leaving the
sad

Third verse:
Now on my journey
I'm a little let down
It isn't as romantic
As my head made it sound
The road is lonely
Confusion persists
The friends I've visited
Made it worth the trip
It was necessary
If only a first step
To change my life
I have a long road ahead

Eddie Tebbe

Imagination Gets Killed

Chorus:
Has anybody thought
Is this what we want
Where originality dies
As mother-nature cries
Trading in our free-will
Imagination gets killed

Verse one:
Messages falling from the sky
Who to listen to, and just why
A million images 24 hrs. a day
Across the globe, but what do they say
100 channels anything you please
No waiting, there's no need

Verse two:
More products shown late at night
Just this one more will make things right
Buying it will make your life better
They'll give you two together
Pre-made, pre-packaged, size of a bite
Pre-everything equals a pre-life

Verse three:
On the horizon is there not hope
Given any obstacle can we not cope
I have not given up on humanity
I believe in all possibilities
But the consumer society must be checked
Before everything else gets wrecked

If Wishes Came True

"Are you afraid of flying?" the old man asks with a smile. "You seem a little nervous."

The young lady next to him doesn't answer. She stares out the window. The old man wants to talk even if the young lady doesn't.

"Excuse me, Ms.?"

The young lady comes out of the trance. "Sorry did you say something?"

"I just asked if you were afraid of flying because you seem nervous."

Now self-conscious, the young lady stops her feet from tapping, her hands from rubbing. She stops curling her hair.

"No, not at all. I have a situation I have to deal with, and it's making me nervous."

"Tell me about it. Maybe I can help. I've seen a lot in my life. Maybe I can help." The old man smiles his sweetest smile.

The young lady hesitates. "Well, maybe you can. I'm in love with a friend of mine and I'm not sure how to handle it."

"Are y'all close friends?"

"Very close."

"And how does he... is it a he?"

The young lady nods yes.

"You never know. Anyway, how does he feel about you?"

"I think he's very happy with our friendship. We mainly write each other. He has a girlfriend and they're in love. At times I feel there is a vibe coming from him, but it may be me just seeing what I want to."

The old man takes a deep breath and looks at his companion who is already asleep. "I have a story for you. It's not quite the same situation, but similar enough. Where should I start? This is only a two hour flight so the whole story would take too long." The old man thinks. "Since we're on a plane I'll start on a plane."

Dora's muscles relaxed as the plane touched down. Getting out of the plane and away from the annoying man next to her brought a smile across her face. Dora liked sitting out on a clear night dreaming, staring up at the stars, and seeing shooting stars was always a thrill. Hearing every little detail, told in a monotone voice, about an unknown comet for two hours was too much. The annoying man wasn't even finished so Dora let the man enter the aisle getting swept away in the river of exiting passengers, and she sat back down to wait. As she walked out of the plane her fear of seeing the annoying man was forgotten as her excitement for seeing Eric built.

Although they lived in different parts of the country Dora and Eric were as close as friends could be. A connection was made the first time they were introduced. Dora thought about Eric on a daily basis, and Eric thought about Dora on an hourly basis.

Dora was looking forward to this long weekend. She loved visiting Eric and New Orleans, and it would be the first time Eric would be meeting her new love. All of Dora's favorite things at once. What could be better?

As Dora was landing Eric sat in the airport wired. Sleep had eluded him for several days and trying to eat this morning didn't work. The flight was delayed and Eric picked the wrong seat to sit in. From the moment he sat down the woman in the next seat started babbling something about her boyfriend and a comet. The woman proceeded to explain more about this comet than anyone should know. Eric sat and he smiled only when he saw the plane unloading. Eric walked away from the woman while she was in mid-sentence. Not trying to be rude, but he had spent weeks fantasizing what this weekend might bring. He wanted to see Dora and start the weekend as soon as possible.

What seemed like thousands of people walked past him. They met up with loved ones or whatever and moved on. Some of the flight crew walked by, and there still wasn't Dora. Eric's feelings for their friendship were as strong as Dora's, but Eric found himself in love with her. He had, in part, accepted the fact that geography and sexual preference caused their relationship to be as friends, but Eric was good at fantasizing and he could find signs in Dora's actions that supported his fantasies.

Staring down the empty terminal brought on terrible thoughts. What if he had done or said something wrong? What if the big news a few months ago had caused them to slip apart? What if her feelings were different? The non-response after the letter with the big news, the last two phone conversations, and her last letter were all causing Eric to think that this was a relationship changing visit. What if it was for the worse, not the better? Pure happiness overcame him when he saw Dora.

They ran to each other and embraced. Neither wanting to let go, as they hugged Eric realized he had to put his fantasies away and enjoy his time with Dora. They left the airport ready to enjoy their weekend together.

"I have great news," Dora said as they walked holding hands to the car. "Mildred was able to get off work after all. She's going to meet us later tonight, and don't worry we won't have to pick her up. She'll take a cab. I can't wait for y'all to meet."

Any lingering hope for a fantasy to come true this weekend vanished. Eric concentrated on how good Dora's soft hand felt in his.

"That's great, but we can pick her up. It's no problem."

"I knew you'd say that. Thanks, you're so sweet."

They got in the car.

"Well, what do you want to do?" Eric asked.

"I don't know. I'm hungry though so let's eat?"

"I thought you'd say that. I'll take you to one of my favorite places. The Please-U."

"The Please-U!! I love that place."

Eric was shocked. "You've been there?"

"Ya, when I was a kid my family came here for a visit and me and my mom ate there a couple of times. I still remember it clearly."

"Wow, my mom used to take me there sometimes. I think of it as a favorite place even though I haven't been there in years."

"That's so funny," they said at the same time and laughed.

"Maybe we were there at the same time," Dora said.

"Now that would be too much," Eric said.

They laughed about that for a few minutes.

"What else do you want to do this weekend?" asked Eric.

"I'm not sure yet. I'll wait to see what Millie wants to do."

"My sis, Daisy, and her kid Ann, and Sherry with her two kids Joe and Jane, are going to Pontchartrain Beach tomorrow if you wanted to go. I can't guarantee it will be fun."

"Why?"

"Because when you get all of them together you never know what will happen."

"Well it sounds like a great idea. That was one of the things we did on that same visit. Except my only real memory is that on the way back to the hotel the Pontchartrain Beach balloon that I had flew out the car. I was devastated and my parents said the balloon was going to God. I was not relieved by that answer."

They both smiled as Eric drove into town.

They met Mildred in the terminal and the introductions were made.

"I've heard a lot about you," Mildred said.

"Same here," Eric said. "It's nice to meet you finally. I'm glad you could make it."

They walked through the airport. Eric was on one side of Dora and Mildred on the other. Dora looked at one then the other. She smiled. Everything she wanted was there at that moment.

That night Eric took Dora and Mildred to Bourbon Street. It wasn't something he did regularly, not at all, but he made an exception. They walked down Bourbon. Dora and Mildred were amazed by the sights and sounds. Eric was bored but did get some pleasure from Dora's excitement.

Eric studied Mildred. She reminded him of his sister's girlfriend, and he liked her despite not wanting to. He found himself enjoying Mildred's company, but he was so jealous of her it hurt. Every time Dora gave Mildred a rub on her arm, a playful shove, or a sexy look, a sharp pain cut him apart.

The conversation between Dora and Mildred began to cover day to day stuff. As the three walked down the street Eric was a step behind. Dora was so elated with the situation she didn't notice.

Eric sat in his kitchen. Every time he and Dora were together they sat up all night talking. He was looking forward to another talk. There was a lot on his mind that he wanted to talk about. Dora walked in the room.

She went over to Eric and took his hand. "I'm beat. Thanks for the wonderful day. I can't wait for tomorrow. What time should we get up?"

The fact that Dora wasn't going to stay up and talk hit Eric hard. He calmed himself. "If we want to meet them for breakfast, we should leave around nine. How much time do y'all need to get ready?"

"Hour maybe."

"I'll get y'all up around seven thirty," Eric said.

Dora kissed Eric on the cheek. A thought ran through her head, a thought she tried to repress most of the time.

"Goodnight," she whispered in his ear. Then she joined Mildred in the spare bedroom.

Eric didn't move for a long time, lost in his thoughts. When he became aware of his surroundings, he heard voices coming from the spare bedroom. What Dora and Mildred were saying he couldn't make out. He got up, went into the living room, and turned on the television.

"Would either of you like a drink?" the flight attendant says.

The flight attendant breaks the lady's absolute attention towards the old man's story. She thinks for a moment. She and the old man order Cokes. The flight attendant serves them and moves on.

"Please continue," the lady says.

"Okay. Where was I?" The old man pauses for a moment. "The next morning."

"Millie hurry up we're late," Dora yelled to the spare bedroom.

She looked at Eric and rolled her eyes. Dora and Eric had been ready for quite a while. Dora was upset about it, but Eric didn't mind.

"Do you think we should call your sister?" Dora asked.

"Not yet, let's wait until we are walking out the door."

"She always takes forever to get ready. It drives me crazy."

Eric wasn't worried about that. "Do you realize last night was the first time we've been together and didn't stay up talking?"

Dora thought for a moment. "It was, wasn't it?"

"Yep."

"Every all night talk we've had has meant so much to me." Dora grabbed Eric's hand.

Mildred came into the room. She was finally ready. Eric called his sister, and they decided to meet at The Bluebird Cafe for breakfast.

At breakfast Eric wondered what the day would bring. Six grownups and three children, all under the age of six, going to an amusement park, made for an interesting situation. Eric's thoughts then turned to Dora. Dora saw that he was in deep thought and asked him what he was thinking. He didn't know what to say.

Only a very perceptive person could have seen the sign. Eric did. It started very slowly. Everybody entered the park happy, and they stayed that way for a while. Everybody was being nice and trying to accommodate each other. As the heat rose into the high nineties people's tempers shortened.

Dora wanted to spend as much time as she could with Eric. She walked and talked with him for most of the morning. He enjoyed the attention.

"There it is. That's the exact type of balloon I had when I was here as a kid." Dora pointed to it.

Mildred didn't know the story behind the balloon, so Dora explained. Eric slowed his pace. Sherry walked beside him.

"What's up?" she said.

"I'm in love with Dora," Eric said.

"Well, it doesn't look like you have much of a chance."

"My brain knows that, but my imagination does wonders when it comes to making myself believe there's a chance."

The day dragged on. Everybody started getting more aggravated with each other. Eric stayed out of the conflicts. He saw most of the arguing as unnecessary. He sat in the shade of a tree. Dora sat next to him. Everybody else was off doing their own things. She was upset by a tiff with Mildred.

"None of this gets to you?" she asked.

"What?"

"All the bickering. Everybody getting upset. You haven't seemed upset at all."

"They always work themselves into a frenzy. They all need to step back and understand the situation, and how they affect it, better."

"You would be a great boyfriend."

His heart skipped a beat. Maybe that meant something. Before he could say anything, Mildred walked up. The rest of the group showed up shortly and it was off to another ride. Dora walked ahead with Mildred. She gave Eric a look. They both understood that Mildred was getting jealous, and Dora needed to pay attention to her. He wasn't used to sharing Dora's attention. He hated it.

This ate away at Eric the rest of the afternoon. He couldn't wait for the day to be over. The space between him and Dora, and the rest of the group, grew. Dora tried to pull him closer a few times, but he drew back every time. He wondered if she noticed. She did, but she didn't know what to do.

The sun went down and the park was closing. Eric was in agony. He kept closing his eyes to fight back the tears. The whole group was walking towards the exit. Eric had fallen way behind. He walked by a wishing well, paused for a moment, then walked on, but the thought of making a wish wouldn't leave his mind. He found a dime in his pocket and ran back to the well. With all his hope he closed his eyes and tossed the dime into the well. Still with his eyes closed he heard a baritone voice. The voice told him to show Dora his heart.

"Wait, wait," the lady interrupts the story. "A voice? From whom?"

The old man smiles. "I don't know. Eric has never come up with an answer to that."

"Well, okay, please tell me what happened."

Right before the exit Eric saw a shop with the same balloon Dora lost as a child. He stopped and bought it. He hurried to catch up with Dora.

"Here, this is for you." Eric handed the balloon to Dora.

Dora's heart melted. She gave him a big kiss and hug. While they were embracing, he whispered in her ear.

"I'm in love with you."

Dora squeezed Eric tighter. He felt tears drop on to his neck.

"I'm in love with you," she whispered back.

The lady bites her lip. The plane is already on the ground and is taxiing to the gate.

"What happened?" the lady says.

"Well, with some complications at first, Eric and Dora ended up living happily ever after."

"Thank you so much. That was one of the sweetest stories I've ever heard. It just may have given me the courage to go for it."

"I'm glad I could help." The old man pats her hand and smiles.

The plane is unloading, and the lady gathers her things and leaves. The old man turns to wake his companion. He finds tears running from her closed eyes.

"Dora, are you okay?"

The old man shakes her. Dora opens her eyes and looks at Eric. She rubs his cheek.

"Why didn't you really say anything that day?" Dora asks.

"You knew how I felt, and I knew how you felt, but besides my own imagination there was no reason for me to believe that your feelings for me were strong enough to overcome your gayness. Were they?"

"I don't know. But I never felt for anyone like I've felt for you."

"And I feel the same way, and we've had a wonderful relationship."

They are the last people on the plane. Without another word they walk out of the plane and into the terminal. Dora stops and turns towards Eric.

"I'll always love you more," she says.

"I'll always love you more." Eric grabs her hand.

They walk down the terminal holding hands like an old couple.

"I understand why you changed the ending of the story. I don't understand why you added the part about the voice."

"I didn't add it. I really heard a voice."

"You had a mystical voice talk to you and you didn't listen?"

"I don't know what that voice was, but I'm too logical to follow advice from a strange voice.

The Crossroads of My Life

Standing at the crossroads of my
life
Feel blinded I don't have sight
But I know everything will be all
right
Because that's what happens
I said that's what happens
That's what happens
At the crossroads of your life

I've traveled all around the world
I've married quite a few girls
I have a daughter named Pearl
That's what it's about
I said that's what it's about
That's what it's about
At the crossroads of your life

I've always been concerned about
winning
Now I wonder what I've been
missing
But you can't go back to the be-
ginning
You can't go back
I said you can't go back
You can't go back
From the crossroads of your life

Life is funny in some ways
Looking back on all my days
Sometimes I wish I had stayed
Looking back from
I said looking back from
Looking back from
The crossroads of your life

I've done some wrong, I've done
some right
I've had a lot of sleepless nights
Over decisions I've made in my
life
Decisions must be made
I said decisions must be made
Decisions must be made
At the crossroads of your life

Now I'm thinking about what to
do
Will I be able to get through
Will I be able to start anew
Going on
I said going on
Going on
Past the crossroads of my life

Eddie Tebbe

You Gotta Know

You gotta know what to do
You gotta know how to get through
You gotta know right from wrong
You gotta know when you're done
You gotta know good from bad
You gotta know when to be sad

Chorus: you gotta know
      yes you do
        you gotta know
     who's in you
        you gotta know. You gotta know, you gotta know

You want your life to be right
You want to see her tonight
You want to hold her tight
You want to make love tonight
                      Chorus
You gotta know night from day
You gotta know what to say
You gotta know the truth from a lie
You gotta know hello from good-bye
You gotta know how to get it all
You gotta know how to stan tall
                      Chorus
You want a job to pay your bills
You want something to cure your ills
You want to make a little money
You want to spend it on your honey
                      Chorus

Apart (Duet)

Male-   please come to Austin, she said no
Female-   New Orleans is my home, I don't know if I can go
             my feelings are confused, they're hard to figure out
             it isn't just a fight where we can scream and shout
             I love you, but I love my home
             I love my family, I'm not one to roam

             please stay here, he said no
Male-   the road is calling, and I must go
             Austin is the place where I should be
             tears falling from my eyes can't you see
             I love you, but I can't stay
             is Austin really that far away?

Female-   but sometimes the distance is too hard
             sometimes any distance is too far
Male-   life gets in the way, and time goes by
             distance can also make emotion die
Together- we love each other, but it's not enough
             relationships can get awfully rough

             now it's time to say good-bye
             we both agreed, we both cried
             it's the right thing, we both know
             sometimes it's better to let go
             we love each other even now
             the hurt will fade somehow

Eddie Tebbe

In the Park

Children, as I sit and watch them play
I think of what could I possibly say
To teach them all the things I've known
To show them all the things I've been shown

Children, as I sit and watch them play
I remember a time alone passed by day
When worries were so brief
And unicorns existed in my belief

Children, as I sit and watch them play
I wonder about the world today
It goes so fast, what's the cost
A kid's childhood can get lost

Children, as I sit and watch them play
I marvel and wish it had stayed
The pure joy I see in their faces
The pure delight in how ice cream tastes

Children, as I sit and watch them play
I wish wisdom didn't chase innocence away
The ancient questions still remain
The child inside helps keep us sane

Crying and Whining

Crying and whining I don't understand
Bitching and wishing is getting out of hand
I don't care if the food spilled in your trunk
You should have known 'cause we were all drunk
Not to put it in there anyway
So save your whining for another day
There is only one rule around here
Let me make it absolutely clear
I don't stand for all that stuff
You better stop before I get rough
I don't care what happens at any time
There will be no whine unless it is mine

Heeing and hawing why don't you stop
Groping and pissing makes me want to give you a pop
Right across your hard, thick head
Why don't you worry about yourself instead
Of your little brother and what he's done
Because your own problems are hardly none
There is only one rule around here
Let me make it absolutely clear
I don't stand for all that stuff
You better stop before I get rough
I don't care what happens at any time
There will be no whine unless it is mine

Eddie Tebbe

Belly aching at every little thing
Groaning and moaning like you think you're king
Is really starting to get on my nerves
What in the hell do you think you deserve?
Stop sweating the little stuff, things will get better
Then if you shut up, we can be together
Whine, whine, whine is all you want to do
But my rule still stands true
I don't stand for all that stuff
You better stop before I get rough
I don't care what happens at any time
There will be no whine unless it is mine

The Choice

Eddie threw his keys on the table by the front door. He was just getting back from lunch at Liuzza's, one of New Orleans' many neighborhood diners. Before lunch he was in an okay mood. Now he was depressed again. He had to listen to his companion, a female, go on and on about how amazing he was, and how any woman would be lucky to be with him. Eddie tried to take it in stride, but after hearing those words a million times they made him sick. He knew that if he made a move this woman would come up with reason after reason why not to date him, but only one mattered.

Checking the mail Eddie found nothing important. Checking his e-mail though he found what he wanted. He didn't like reading on the computer, so he made a print-out, poured some iced tea, and went to the patio. In his hand he held the latest article on himself. It was going to appear in the next issue of "Wavelength," the monthly magazine about New Orleans' music. He liked to read all the articles about himself before they were published to avoid mistakes, misquotes, and wrong impressions. The title read "The Real Eddie." It brought a painful grin to his face. A lot of people knew him, but very few knew the darkness in his life. He had always gone to great measures to show the public his good side, which was pretty good. The article made his life sound great and as he read, he almost wanted to be himself.

The article started with an explanation of cerebral palsy, and how Eddie had it since birth, but had overcome it. The article continued from there. He started going out in uptown New Orleans when he was sixteen. By the time he was in his early twenties he was a well-known staple of the night scene. Eddie was hard to miss. He was the only person with cerebral palsy who could be seen beating everybody on the pool table one night, and the next night be hanging out backstage with top bands like The Nevilles, The Meters, or George Porter and The Running Pardners. He was also known as a great dancer. Hanging out with Eddie was almost like being with a celebrity. Most people knew him and liked him.

Eddie had always felt, and was told, that he was going to make a difference. As a junior in high school he decided he wanted to teach high school, and that would be making a difference. He graduated from the University of New Orleans as a teacher, but never pursued teaching because sometime in his early twenties he started writing song lyrics. Because he knew the right people, he was able to get some of them made into songs. He also wrote a few screenplays and short stories. To his amazement his writing made an impact, a difference, and unexpectedly he was a pretty well-off man by his mid-thirties. One of his dreams was to own a music bar so as a fortieth birthday present to himself he opened "Eddie's Big Ass Music Bar." Five years later the bar was known worldwide. Eddie was the owner, but other better qualified people ran it per his instructions.

The article ended by asking what the future held for Eddie which he didn't know. The desire to write had left him for now. He was just going to try to enjoy life. This was a statement Eddie ended all his interviews with and found extremely ironic given his mood. The article was well done. It made the impression he wanted except that he did not like the statement that he had overcome cerebral palsy. He had not. He could not. He just dealt with it.

Eddie made three phone calls, one to the magazine to make the change from overcome to dealing with, another to the bar to give them his guest list for tonight, the George Porter Trio "Viscous," and one to check on his mother, who was dying of a degenerative disease. His mother meant a lot to Eddie. He loved her dearly. She was the biggest reason why he was so independent. She had imbued a fight within him. There were times, in the deepest reaches of depression when suicide became an interest, that the thought of her pulled him through. He had decided that suicide was not an option as long as his mother was alive, because it would crush her.

Sitting there staring into space Eddie started to wonder how a slight physical difference can affect peoples' dealings with a person. People who knew him looked up to him, but he felt only on a very superficial level, because most knew only a part of him. Other people who didn't know him, even at forty-five, treated him like he was retarded. He hated having cerebral palsy. To have the chance to live without cerebral palsy he would have given up most anything even though it was a big reason why he was semi-famous, because it was the reason he was alone. Eddie had never had a romantic relationship with a woman. There were some women who were willing, but that was only because he had money and notoriety. No woman had ever been genuinely attracted to him enough to deal with the cerebral palsy. If they were, they didn't want to do anything about it, and until some woman did everything else in his life was for show.

Cooking was a big aggravation for Eddie. Before he had money, he ate mostly frozen dinners. With money he was able to have someone come in, cook, and freeze four meals a week. The other three nights he would eat out. Tonight he was eating at home. He prepared his dinner and ate. After, he took a shower and got dressed. As he stood in front of the mirror, he thought about all the compliments he received on his looks, and when standing still he got a lot of looks and smiles thrown his way. He was five feet eight inches tall with a head full of wavy dirty blond hair. His muscles stayed toned because of the tension caused by cerebral palsy. Eddie was always amused at people complimenting his muscles, especially his legs, because his muscle movement was his most unattractive trait. But it was his face that most people focused on. Eddie's eyes were his best feature, blue-green and very clear. People who looked into them deeply could see the pain. They did not know what they were seeing, but it struck them as interesting. Beyond any one feature his face had character. That caused people to overestimate his age when he was younger.

Eddie was always a blue jeans and T-shirt guy, and that was what he was wearing tonight. He checked himself one more time. Could anything get much better than that? He grabbed his keys and headed out.

Having his own parking space in front of the bar gave Eddie a juvenile thrill. He enjoyed being a local celebrity. He acted like he was nothing special, but deep inside he thought he was, and after years of hearing that from other people it was easy to believe. So many people wanted to chit-chat that it usually took him a long time to get through the bar, because he did not like being rude. There were all the questions from employees too. He finally made it to the backstage area. He took extra care of George. When Eddie was just a fan, he and George became pretty close, and George did Eddie's first song. They gave each other a hug, sat down, and started talking about what was going on in town. Eddie requested a few songs, and, as always, George said no problem. It was time to start before they knew it. Eddie introduced the band, which he did all the time. Anything to be on stage.

The night went well. The band was great, the crowd was big, and there were no major problems to contend with. Eddie spent some of the time socializing, some of the time dancing, some of the time playing tambourine, and some of the time watching the crowd. It was at these times he sometimes felt isolated from everyone. He didn't have control of his negative feelings. They came and went without notice. Sometimes they were triggered by seeing something, like a couple in love kissing, dancing, or just holding hands, or by hearing something, like how wonderful he was, or women complaining about men, or sometimes he just felt isolated. Tonight he felt okay, for the most part, until later in the night.

Towards the end of the show he saw Beatrice. She was one of his few loves. They had had a very interesting relationship and Eddie had truly thought she was going to be the one. He had gotten farther with her than anyone, but at the last minute she backed down. Ten years later he still couldn't look at her. Even worse she was slow dancing with someone. This set him off. He had to leave. He didn't even say good-bye to anyone.

Driving home was the worst part of any day for Eddie. Tonight it was agonizing. Heading home late at night the loneliness set in. Sometimes he would drive around for hours. He never wanted to enter his house without someone. It was at these moments that he would give anything not to have cerebral palsy. As he drove around, he listened to Aaron Neville's version of 'A Change Is Gonna Come' over and over again. On a night like this one, when there was extra sadness, Eddie sat by the lake and watched the sun rise. It was easier to go home after the sun was up because every day was a new beginning. He knew every day he would still have cerebral palsy, but every new day held hope, the hope that he would find his miracle.

Parking the car Eddie noticed that it was a full moon, and the light from it was especially bright. The light reflected off the water. A cool breeze blew across him slightly moving his hair. He sat on a bench wondering when the nightmare of being alone would end. From across the grass a person approached, gliding more than walking. The person was wearing very large wavy clothes, and Eddie couldn't tell whether it was a man or woman. The person sat next to him, and, for some reason, Eddie didn't get nervous. In fact, he felt at peace. He still could not tell the person's gender even when the stranger spoke in a monotone voice.

"I'm here to help you."

"How?" Eddie said with interest.

"At this moment what do you want?"

"Not to have cerebral palsy."

"I can do that for you."

Eddie began to get irritated. "It's not funny. Don't joke about that."

"I know it sounds impossible, but I'm not messing with you. I can help you."

Against his better judgment Eddie went along. "Are you the devil? You're going to make me normal and I have to give you my soul? Please, you think I'm dumb?"

"No, I'm not the devil."

"An angel?"

"No," the stranger said looking straight into his eyes.

Eddie had always believed he could see into people through their eyes. What he saw in this person's eyes was truth. Eddie started believing.

"But you can't get rid of my cerebral palsy."

"Yes, with one condition. You must give up your life."

"Kill myself. I guess that would get rid of my cerebral palsy, and guess what? I've thought about it lots. I don't need help to do it."

"No, no. I'll make you normal, but you need to leave your life. You can take one thousand dollars. You can't tell anyone, and can't leave any sign of where you went, or why you left."

At this point Eddie believed everything this person said.

"Can I say good-bye to my mother? She's dying."

"No."

"I won't tell her anything."

"No. This is not supposed to be easy. If you take the deal you have to leave and no one can ever know what has happened. If anyone sees you normal and thinks it's you, or if you tell anyone what has happened, you'll die right then. Now, do you want the deal?"

"Yes," Eddie said with no hesitation.

* * *

Three months later Eddie sat by the phone. With his right hand he was rolling a coin over and through his fingers. He had been ninety percent left-handed because his right hand had always been tremendously less coordinated than his left, and now that he had control of everything he wanted to be right-handed. He picked up the phone and made the call. The receptionist answered. Could he please have nurse's station number five? Over the last three months Eddie had called his mother's nursing home once a week, just to check, never saying who he was. As the nurse explained her condition Eddie decided he had to see her. She was getting close to death. Most of the time she was unconscious, and of the time she was awake she was incoherent. His disappearing had a bad effect on her.

He drove straight to the nursing home. He did not want to waste time or chance running into anyone. It was late, 2:00 a.m., but sneaking into his mom's room was easy. It was amazing how inconspicuous he was without cerebral palsy. Walking towards the bed he took a step back. Her eyes were open. He thought she was awake, but after a few minutes he realized she was not. Looking into her eyes Eddie saw a pain there he had not seen before. He felt he was the cause, and tears ran down his face. He almost broke down, and he wanted to leave, but he had to explain. He sat in the chair beside the bed and held her hand.

"Mom, it's me, Eddie. I'm okay. In fact, I'm better than ever. I'm sorry I disappeared without explaining, but it was part of the deal. I think you will agree with my choice. I'm finally a whole person, Mom. From head to toe I have total control of my body, and it's everything I thought it would be. I can do anything I want. Nobody looks at me funny when I walk down the street. People give me instant respect. If I give directions to people, they listen. It's an unbelievable feeling. I always knew people treated me different, but Mom, it's unbelievable. The first night I was normal I picked up a woman. It was easy, and I pick them up all the time now. I'm bartending in Key West. Picking up women is easy. I'm trying to make up for lost time. Mom, please understand my decision. Please be happy for me."

Eddie stopped talking to wipe away his tears.

"Mom, it's not all easy. I've had to put my ego in check. I've always been special, both outside and in. Now my outside is normal. I don't get negative attention, but I don't get positive attention either. I think I'll get used to it. It's only been three months. The harder part is building a new life. I don't care about the money, but my relationship with Asher goes back over forty years. Whom will I turn to now? You and the rest of the family. I can't replace y'all."

There was another long pause.

"I made the right choice. I love you. Good-bye."

Kissing his mother on her forehead Eddie wanted to look into her eyes. His mother started waking up. He left quickly without looking into her eyes. He would never know if she understood, but he hoped she did.

* * *

Eddie knew exactly what day it was. He had thought about celebrating, but he didn't know what to do. It was the one-year anniversary of his new life. He sat at the table rolling a coin over and through his fingers. He sat across from a very young, very beautiful woman. She had reddish blond straight hair that came down to her shoulders. Her face had no imperfections, blue eyes, small nose, and moist mouth with white teeth and pink lips. Her small five feet three inches' frame was firm from daily workouts. Her breasts were slightly big, but added to her attraction, and Eddie could not wait for dinner to be over, so he could go home alone. He had no interest in this sexual woman. Two minutes into their conversation he was bored. He had, over the last year, satisfied his urges. He was now looking for a serious relationship. This girl was not it.

"Do you always play with that coin?" the girl asked.

"Yes," he answered not wanting to explain.

"Why?"

He thought about his words very carefully. "It's to remind me of something."

"What?" This girl was not letting go.

"A year ago, I was a different person. Then I was given a chance to change. The change would make me how I wanted to be, but I had to give up a lot, a whole lot. I made the decision quickly, and I made the right decision, but I do this to remind me why I made the decision."

"Would I have liked you before?"

Eddie started laughing, "You may have liked me, but you wouldn't be here with me having those thoughts that are going around your head."

He could not have told anyone a word that was said after that. She talked, he commented, but his mind was on other things. He still greatly missed his family, friends, and fame, and at times he wondered if he had made the right choice.

After dropping the girl off, without making a move on her which she did not understand or like, Eddie found the song 'A Change Is Gonna Come.' He had not listened to it in a year. He had also not driven around all night in a year. So that is what he did ending up on the beach to watch the sunrise. As he sat on the sand, he saw a figure coming towards him, a figure he recognized in a second, and he never thought he would see again.

"Hello Eddie," the stranger said as if he were expected.

Eddie didn't know how to react. Was this the end of life without cerebral palsy? Or was this something good like being able to go home? Eddie did not say anything.

"I'm here to give you another choice."

"What this time?" Eddie said not sure he wanted an answer.

"I can give you your old life back. This past year would have never happened."

"Would I remember it?"

"No."

"Who are you?" Eddie asked trying to delay his answer so he could think about it.

"Not many people get to see me. Even fewer see me twice, and even fewer than that ever get an answer to that question." There was a long pause. "I am Fate."

Eddie once again did not know what to say. They just sat there for a few minutes. Then Fate spoke.

"I need an answer."

"No. I don't want my old life back."

He turned and Fate was gone, and he knew Fate would never appear again. He also knew he would always wonder about his choice. He would always miss parts of his other life.

Inner War

I've been looking at the pain within
Trying to see where it all begins
I'm hoping that when I find the core
I'll stop the pain of my inner war

That has been raging inside of me
Peace seems like an impossibility
Something that's so far and so remote
Sometimes it's hard not to give up hope

Years and years that I have been fighting
Has worn away my understanding
It gets harder to find the strength inside
The hole in my soul is too wide

To cross it I need lots of will power
Without which the taste of life is sour
What will make that taste go away?
How long can I last I cannot say

Eddie Tebbe

Discovery

Verse one:
Back before history
When we lived in caves
The first discovery was made
Maybe by mistake
We'll never know
But things were never the same

Chorus:
Discovery
It's necessary
Discovery
Sometimes big
At times ordinary
Discovery
Who'll be brave enough
To take the chance
That has to be taken

Verse two:
Chris looked over the water
Galileo stared at the stars
Wondering what could be
Despite the risk
Both understood
The greater possibility

Verse three:
We all discover
From time to time
Although we are scared
Embrace the change
Blaze a new path
Like you have no cares

Sister Blue Sky, Brother Rain

Chorus:
Bye bye sister blue sky
Hello brother rain
Thanks for chasing sister
Away today

A bright blue sky isn't what you wanna see
When you're feeling down
You want the rain to keep falling
Pounding on the ground
So, chorus

The thunder and lightning
The wind howling the blues
Somehow always helps
When you're in that mood
So, chorus

Afternoon the sky's so dark
Except for flashes of light
The thunder sounds like a drum
Pounding in the noon night
So, chorus

Now I feel a little better
Sister blue sky please come back
Brother rain has done his job
For today and has gone away
So, chorus

Eddie Tebbe

Back to The Basics

We tried to be fancy
Tried to be cool
Tried to make a hit
Forgot all the rules
But now we're back
With our music
Now we're back
Back to the basics

No computerized drums
No overdubs
We play it live
We play what you love
Back to the basics
The old time beat
Back to the basics
Back to the street

Trying to make it big
We wanted radio play
But the music got lost
So listen to what I say

Play the music straight
Straight from the heart
Don't let other people
Tear you apart

The bass vibrates
The guitar screams
The keyboards and drums
Fill your dreams
With people dancing
The drums come through
That's what it's about
What we try to do

It's not about money
It's not about fame
Playing good music
Nothing's the same
Catching the groove
Feeling the beat
Shaking your body
Stomping your feet

Mother, Oh Why

Chorus:
Oh why, oh why, oh why
Must you be taken away
Any time is too early
Life just isn't fair
Oh why, oh why, oh why
Must you be taken away

Verse one:
You loved me before I was born
The first warmth I felt was in your arms
I couldn't have survived without you
From little to big you knew what to do
Nobody cared about me quite the same
Showing your emotions without shame

Verse two:
I wasn't an easy kid to raise
Taking on the challenge regardless of praise
With all your strength you fought
Never give up is what you taught
I learned from your determination
Never to give in to intimidation

Verse three:
Why did the fates treat you so bad
To inflict you with something so sad
That slowly sucked your strength away
Instead of growing in your later days
Your time cut oh so short
Before you got your brand-new start

Eddie Tebbe

For My Grandma

See the truth
Open your eyes
After living
Everyone dies
In the soul
In the heart
What is left
When we part
Things we owned
What we've shared
What we've built
Who will care
What measures
A life led
Will we know
After we're dead
Just how strong
The spirit becomes
Equals the energy
Created by one
Strength hereafter
Flows from goodness
Evil will lead
To full darkness
The way to tell
Is quite plain
It's the amount
Of the heart's pain
So while we hurt
Remember this
It's a good thing
The greater one's missed

You're My Heart

FADE IN:

INT. A FAST-LUBE MECHANIC SHOP – DAY – 1973

SOUNDTRACK – FATS DOMINO – WALKING TO NEW ORLE-ANS

MRS. DELORIS HEIRS, a conservative middle-class wife in her early thirties, a little worn by a road trip, is with her three-year old daughter JUNE. Deloris is at the counter dealing with the attendant. June has straight blond hair and blue eyes.

MS. LYNN PERRY, a liberal working-class mother in her mid-twenties, is waiting in line with her three-year old son EDDIE. Eddie has a mild case of Cerebral Palsy and is in leg braces. He has curly blond hair and blue-green eyes

The two children start to play. Deloris finishes and pulls June away. Both kids start to fuss.

While Lynn is at the counter Deloris goes outside and through the front window. We see her get into a moving truck. MR. JOHN HEIRS, a conservative middle-class man in his late thirties, gives the car to the attendant and gets in the truck.

EXT. UPTOWN NEW ORLEANS – DAY

SOUNDTRACK – NEVILLE BROTHERS – SHAKE YOUR TAM-BOURINE

Lynn pulls up in a VW van in front of her lower-middle class house, the most run down on the block. Across the street are the Heirs just getting ready to unload the truck. Eddie tries to wiggle out of Lynn's arms and go across the street. Lynn notices the truck and walks over.

Eddie Tebbe

LYNN
Hi there. I'm Lynn Perry. I live right across the
street.

DELORIS
(holding June, stops to talk)
Hi, I'm Deloris Heirs and this is my daughter June, and that's
my husband John.

LYNN
Well, welcome to the neighborhood. This is my
son Eddie.

DELORIS
They look about the same age. How old is he?

CU - THE CHILDREN INTERACTING

LYNN
He just turned three.

DELORIS
Really? So did June. What's his birthday? June's is
March 1ST.

LYNN
Wow! Eddie's birthday is February 28TH.

DELORIS
Isn't that remarkable! They were born one day apart.

LYNN
Except on Leap Year.

DELORIS

Yeah, right. Honey the babies were born
one day apart. Isn't that funny?

JOHN
(working hard.)

Yes, dear.

LYNN

Can I help?

DELORIS

I'm not sure... Can you watch June?

LYNN

I'd love to.

DELORIS
(starts to hand June to Lynn)
She's a little fussy at first.
(June doesn't fuss)
Well, look at that.

LYNN

I'll just be right across the street.

DELORIS

Thank you so much.

LYNN

I'll cook dinner. I'm sure y'all aren't in no mood to
make anything.

DELORIS

That's very nice of you.

                                    LYNN
                    It's no problem. Just come over when
                    you're done.

INT. LYNN'S KITCHEN - NIGHT

SOUNDTRACK – ARLO GUTHRIE – CITY OF NEW ORLEANS

The kitchen (and whole house) is eclectic. Not much matches. There
are lots of liberal political posters on the walls. Lynn, Deloris, and
John are at the table winding down dinner.

The children are playing nearby. June is trying to straighten Eddie's
hands and teach him to play patty cake.

Deloris starts to go to stop her. Lynn stops Deloris.

CU - THE CHILDREN INTERACTING

                                    LYNN
                                    (VO)
                    Are you going to work?

                                  DELORIS
                                    (VO)
                    Oh, no.

                                    JOHN
                                    (VO)
                    That was very good. We probably would have just got-
                    ten some fast food, which would have never satisfied
                    me, or given me the energy to continue unpacking. In
                    fact, I think I'll get back to it now. Thank you very
                    much.

TWO SHOT

>   DELORIS
>   (John kisses Deloris on the head)
>   I'll be home in a while.

>   JOHN
>   Take your time.

John leaves.

TWO SHOT

>   DELORIS
>   That was a very delicious dish. I've never had it before.
>   How do you make it?

>   LYNN
>   It's very simple. All you need are potatoes, snap beans,
>   smoked sausage, an onion, and soy sauce. You cut up
>   the potatoes, sausage, and onion, snap the beans, throw
>   it all in a pot with a cup of soy sauce, and let it cook
>   over a low fire until it's the consistency that you want.

>   DELORIS
>   That's it?

>   LYNN
>   That's it.

>   DELORIS
>   That is easy. And it's so tasty. Let me help you clean
>   up.

>   LYNN
>   I got it, really.

DELORIS

I feel…

LYNN

You've just traveled across the country and you have a house to unpack. These dishes are nothing.

DELORIS

You're a very nice person.

LYNN

If you give, you get.

DELORIS

That's so true.

LYNN

Would you like some coffee?

DELORIS

Sure, that would be great. I have a long night ahead of me. John will be unpacking until it's done so that means I will too.

LYNN

Really. I've been here two and a half years, and I still haven't completely unpacked.

DELORIS

What does Eddie have? I don't mean to be rude.

LYNN

It's okay. More people should ask. He has Cerebral Palsy.

DELORIS

I'm not familiar with that.

LYNN

It's a neurological disorder that affects the Cerebral Cortex. That's the part of the brain that controls the muscles. There are different causes for it and there are wide ranges of levels. Eddie's case was caused by the umbilical cord getting pinched, cutting off the oxygen.

DELORIS

Do they know how bad it is?

LYNN

At first they thought it was more severe. They figured he'd be mentally affected as well as physically, but the doctors are already sure he's not.

DELORIS

Well, that's good that the doctors are sure of that.

LYNN

That's the thing. The doctors have been contradictory at best, and downright stupid at times. Like they don't understand the condition. They've all been condescending, always suggesting I do things in his best interest that I could never do. I don't see how it's in his best interest to be in an institution. I will raise my son. I can see in his eyes he'll make it if given a chance.

DELORIS

I can't imagine. I don't mean to pry but is his father around?

LYNN

No, he died when I was pregnant with Eddie.

DELORIS

Oh my, I'm so sorry.

LYNN

He was a great man. He would have loved Eddie. He would have fought for him. Eddie looks a lot like him. The same wild curly hair, the same smile, and the same deep eyes.

DELORIS

He's so adorable, and I've never seen June take to another kid like that.

(looks at her watch)

I guess I must be going.

INT. DARK ROOM

SOUNDTRACK – VAN MORRISON – INTO THE MYSTIC

Show time passing and the families getting close by having a top view of a table and having pictures slowly fall from behind the camera onto the table.

INT. JUNE'S BEDROOM – STORMY NIGHT - 1977

SOUNDTRACK – CAT STEVENS - MOONSHADOW

Everything in the room is nice, kept well, and matches.

Deloris checks on June only to find an empty bed. She calmly goes to the phone and dials Lynn.

INT. LYNN'S HALLWAY – MOMENTS LATER

SOUNDTRACK – CAT STEVENS – MOONSHADOW (continues)

> LYNN
> (answering the phone)

Hello?

> DELORIS
> (VO)

Lynn, it's Deloris. Sorry to call so late, is June over there?

> LYNN

It's okay. I wasn't in bed yet. Hold on.

Lynn looks in Eddie's bedroom, finds June in bed with Eddie. There are leg braces next to the bed.

TWO SHOT

> EDDIE

You don't have to be scared of the storm. Storms are good things. Have you ever heard the story of why Mother Nature created storms?

> JUNE

No.

> EDDIE

Well, a long time ago the sky was always blue.

INT. HALLWAY – MOMENTS LATER

SOUNDTRACK – CAT STEVENS – MOONSHADOW (continues)

LYNN
(back on the phone smiling)
She's safe.

DELORIS
(VO)
Is she dry?

LYNN
Yes. Do you want me to send her back?

DELORIS
(VO)
No, I guess not. I go to work at nine, so make sure she's over here by eight-thirty?

Eddie Tebbe

EXT. CAMPGROUND – SUNNY FALL DAY – 1979

SOUNDTRACK – THE METERS – OUT IN THE COUNTRY

They arrive at the campsite and start to set up camp.
Eddie's AUNT MAGGIE, is Eddie's father's older sister in her mid-thirties. She is butch.

The kids are not being helpful and want to go explore.

Eddie walks without braces. His knees are bent, his right foot points inward, and his right-hand curls against his side.

> DELORIS
> John, do you think it's okay for them to go off for a bit?

> JOHN
> (looks at his watch)
> I don't know.

> MAGGIE
> Come on, John. Kids love to explore.

> JOHN
> (rolling his eyes)
> Tell them not to be gone too long.

> DELORIS
> Lynn, is it okay for Eddie?
> LYNN
> Sure, you guys be very careful and stay on the paths.

> JUNE
> Okay.

> EDDIE
> Okay.

EXT. AT THE BOTTOM OF A SMALL HILL – LATER

SOUNDTRACK – GEORGE PORTER JR. & RUNNIN' PARDNERS
– BONE FUNK

They look at each other and without saying a word run off the
path. They are getting filthy and wet but loving every minute. All of a
sudden, Eddie screams. A broken branch has stuck in his upper leg.
There is blood everywhere. After a moment of shock June tries to calm
Eddie.

                    JUNE
          I know what to do. Aunt Maggie just showed me the
other day.

                    EDDIE
          I feel so tired.

                    JUNE
          Wake up, you can't go to sleep. Talk to me.

As Eddie talks June puts a tourniquet on Eddie's leg, then gets him up.

                    EDDIE
          Talk about what? You won't understand me. I don't
          think I can concentrate on my enunciation right now.

                    JUNE
          That's good. Concentrate on your enunciation. Tell me
          a story. You make up good stories.

                    EDDIE
          Ahhh, once upon a time there was a crazy kid with a tree
          jabbed through his leg. I can't think right now. I finally
          got rid of my braces, now this.

Eddie Tebbe

                              JUNE
                Come on.

They start back with June dragging Eddie.

                              EDDIE
                Okay. The rain started falling. At first it was a light
spring drizzle…

EXT. THE CAMP –DUSK

SOUNDTRACK – JOHNNY ADAMS W/ AARON NEVILLE –
NEVER ALONE

As they approach camp June yells for the grownups. The grownups
find June dragging Eddie who is almost unconscious. They frantically
rush to the hospital.

INT. IN THE CAR – MOMENT LATER

SOUNDTRACK – JOHNNY ADAMS W/ AARON NEVILLE –
NEVER ALONE (continues)

June continues to try to get Eddie to finish the story.

                              JUNE
                And then what?

INT. HOSPITAL WAITING ROOM – NIGHT

SOUNDTRACK – JOHNNY ADAMS W/ AARON NEVILLE –
NEVER ALONE (continues)

John, Deloris, Maggie, and a cleaned-up June are in the waiting room.

JOHN

I knew something like this could happen. That boy shouldn't be on his own.

DELORIS

Is now the time?

JOHN

They both could have gotten hurt.

MAGGIE

You didn't say anything before.

JOHN

I always get told to shut up.

MAGGIE

Why don't you do that?

JOHN

Your nephew might die.

DELORIS

John, really.

MAGGIE

What's your point?

                    JOHN
I've seen your sister put the boy's life in danger all the
time.

                    DELORIS
John, you're upset. Now you're upsetting June.

CU – JUNE'S FACE CRYING

                    MAGGIE
I've seen kids with more physical ability than Eddie
whose parents shelter them under the thought of safety
first. Those children have nothing to look forward to.
They have no idea of what they can be. My sister has
chosen a harder way, and yes, it is dangerous, but look
at the life Eddie leads.

                    DELORIS
                (picks up June)
We know that. John is just upset.

                    MAGGIE
I know, but I'm not going to sit here and not defend my
family.

                    JOHN
A parent's job is to protect and provide. You don't have
children. You don't know.

                    MAGGIE
I suggest you go somewhere and cool off.

A NURSE comes to the station nearby.

> NURSE
> (to the nurse at the desk)
> Call the blood bank, the hospitals, and anywhere else
> you can think of. We need AB+.

The group inch closer to the station. The nurse turns towards them.

> NURSE
> He'll be fine. He did lose a lot of blood,
> and he has the rarest type, AB+. So we
> are tracking some down. Does anyone
> have that type?

> JUNE
> I do.

> NURSE
> Really?

> DELORIS
> That's right, she does.

> JUNE
> I'll give blood, I will.

> NURSE
> That's very sweet, but it won't be necessary. We don't
> usually take blood from children.

> JUNE
> But I can help. I have to help.

> NURSE
>
> Are you June?
>
> (June nods)
>
> You are a very smart and brave little girl. You've done so much. You saved his life.

INT. EDDIE'S BEDROOM - THREE MONTHS AFTER THE ACCIDENT – DAY

SOUNDTRACK – CRIS WILLIAMSON – WATERFALL

There is a framed news article from the small town with a picture of Eddie and June in the hospital. Eddie is in his room looking out the window. Lynn comes in.

> LYNN
>
> I just talked to the doctor. I have good news and bad news. What one do you want to hear first?

> EDDIE
>
> The good.

> LYNN
>
> The tests came back fine just as we thought.

> EDDIE
>
> The bad?

> LYNN
>
> You have to go back to school on Monday.

> EDDIE
>
> Great!

> LYNN
>
> Great?

EDDIE

Being home from school sounds nice, and for the first
two weeks it was, but I'm ready to go back. Can I go
out to play?

LYNN

I don't know. How about if I call and see
if June can come over.

EDDIE

Mom, it's great to have June come and play, even to do
homework, and the Atari you got me is so much fun, but
I need to get out. I'm white as a ghost. I need to get
outside.

LYNN

Maybe you and June can play out front?

EDDIE

I want to go to the park.

LYNN

I have things to do. I can't go to the park.

EDDIE

So? The park is on the next corner. Even John has let
me and June go down there by ourselves for two
years. Why can't I go?

LYNN

You just had a horrible accident.

EDDIE

Three months ago. I'm fine. If I can go to school, I
should be able to go to the park.

                    LYNN
I don't know…

                    EDDIE
You can't change now, Mom. I need you to be like you
were. I'm used to that. I need that. It's too late to
change. I won't be able to take it.
                    (pause)
I'm not scared.

                    LYNN
            (crying as she hugs Eddie)
I love you. You continue to amaze me. Okay, you can
go, but go with June.

                    EDDIE
Well…

                    JUNE
            (June enters)
Are you ready?

                    EDDIE
Yeah.

Eddie gives his mom a kiss then rushes out the door with June. Lynn
listens as they rumble down the stairs and out the door. She watches
them run off.

EXT. UPTOWN NEW ORLEANS – HOT SUMMER DAY – 1982

SOUNDTRACK – PROFESSOR LONGHAIR – TIPITINA

They are with a diverse group of neighborhood kids riding bikes.
Eddie has a three-wheel bike. They enter a convenience store named
Time Saver.

INT. IN THE STORE – MOMENTS LATER

SOUNDTRACK – PROFESSOR LONGHAIR – TIPITINA (Continues)

The kids attack the candy. While in line June reads a sign asking for donations. She puts the candy back and puts her money in the donation jar.

>   EDDIE
>   What are you doing?

>   JUNE
>   I'm giving my money to these kids.

>   EDDIE
>   But that is your candy money. You've been saving that
>   all week.

>   JUNE
>   I'll get some next time.

>   EDDIE
>   I'm not giving you any candy. You know how I am
>   about candy.

EXT. AUDUBON PARK – LATER THAT DAY

SOUNDTRACK – ROLLING STONES – PAINT IT BLACK

The group climbs the old oak trees with Spanish moss. Eddie can't get up one. He gets upset and rides off.

Eddie Tebbe

EXT. THE LEVEE ON THE BACK SIDE OF THE PARK – DUSK

SOUNDTRACK – SIMON & GARFUNKEL – BRIDGE OVER
TROUBLED WATER

Eddie sits there crying. June comes up and sits beside him.
                                    JUNE
                    I thought I'd find you here. What's wrong?

                              EDDIE
            I don't like not being able to do things
            like everybody else.

                              JUNE
            That must be hard, but you're gaining ability all the
            time. There are so many things you can do now that you
            couldn't do before. In a few years there will be a lot
            more you can do.
                              EDDIE
            But I'll never be normal.

                              JUNE
            Who cares? You're better than nor-
            mal. You're the best.

                              EDDIE
                    (puts his head on June's shoulder)
            You're the best.

He gives her half his candy. June gets up.

                              JUNE
            We need to get home.

                              EDDIE
            Let's watch the sunset.

JUNE
We'll get in trouble.

EDDIE
It will be worth it.

June sits back down.

INT. JUNE'S BEDROOM – WINTER - 1983

SOUNDTRACK – FOREIGNER – I WANT TO KNOW WHAT
LOVE IS

June is in her room at her desk. Eddie comes in and sits on the bed.
EDDIE
Hey, what are you doing?

JUNE
Just adding up my donation. I just finished my tenth
book. Tomorrow's the deadline.

EDDIE
You read ten books?

JUNE
Yeah, how many did you read?

EDDIE
Four. How much did you collect?

JUNE
I collected $300.

EDDIE
Man, you beat me. I only got $220. $300, that has to be
the most. You'll get that book bag.

JUNE

I don't care. I just like helping people.

EDDIE

You sure do. Are you going to read more, or can we watch TV?

JUNE

We can watch TV.

EDDIE

It's so cool that you have a TV in your room.

Eddie stays on the bed. June gets in a chair a little behind him. They watch an episode of "Three's Company" about dating.

This shot has June in the foreground and Eddie in the background, both facing the camera.

JUNE

Do you think Susan is pretty?
(Eddie doesn't answer)
Hey, you. Do you think Susan is pretty?

EDDIE

What?

JUNE

Do you think Susan is pretty?

EDDIE
(pause)

Sure, I guess.

JUNE

Are you okay?

                        EDDIE
Yeah, yeah.
                    (long pause)
June, would you go steady with me?

                        JUNE
        (She has a big grin on her face)
Yes.
                        EDDIE
Good, I was just wondering if it was possible for a girl
to go steady with me.

                        JUNE
                    (frowns)
Oh, well, of course it is.

                        EDDIE
I was just wondering.

INT. JUNE'S BEDROOM - NIGHT

SOUNDTRACK – JOHN LENNON – IMAGINE

June is packing old stuff into a box. Her mother enters.

                        DELORIS
Are you almost finished?

                        JUNE
Yeah.

                        DELORIS
                (looks in the box)
Are you sure you don't want any of this
stuff?

JUNE
I'm sure.

DELORIS
I just don't want you to feel like you have to give up anything you want. You have such a big heart.

JUNE
Why do people end up homeless?

DELORIS
Oh dear, there are lots of reasons. Some of them are
mentally unbalanced. Some are just people who had a
run of bad luck.

JUNE
Could we end up homeless?

DELORIS
That's not going to happen. But that's why we need to
help people who are less fortunate than we are.

INT. HIGH SCHOOL GYM – NIGHT - 1985

SOUNDTRACK – PRINCE – 1999

They are at a dance. June is with GLENN. Eddie is with a friend,
SARA. They just finished dancing. Sara goes to the bathroom. June,
Glenn, and Eddie sit at the table.

JUNE
Wow, this is a great dance.

GLENN
Yep, they did a good job this time. Last time the band
sucked. It was lame.

JUNE

The eighth-grade dance was fun.

EDDIE

That's because your clothes stayed on.

GLENN

What?

EDDIE

The eighth-grade dance was a toga dance. June over here insisted I didn't wear pants under my toga. Then the toga started falling off. I was stuck sitting the whole night.

GLENN

That's funny.

EDDIE

It wasn't then.

Glenn goes to get drinks.

JUNE

Sara is really digging you.

EDDIE

You think?

JUNE

Definitely, you should make a move on her.

EDDIE

I don't know if I could?

JUNE

You need to. You're a great guy, and I know she likes you. You asked her to this dance, so that means something.

EDDIE

We weren't clear about this being a "date."

Sara comes back. She grabs Eddie by the arm and squeezes. June looks at him. Glenn comes back with the drinks. There isn't a straw.

EDDIE

There weren't straws?

GLENN

No.

EDDIE

I might have one in my locker. If not, I'll do the Bic-Pen trick.

SARA

What's that?

EDDIE

If you have a clear Bic you can remove the ink and you have a straw. I need to go find something.

SARA

I'll go with you.

June gives Eddie a wink as he goes. When he and Sara get to the door to leave the gym a TEACHER stops them.

TEACHER
We're not allowing students in the school this
time. They told the students about this on Friday. Last
time there was vandalism, remember?

EDDIE
I need to get a straw out of my locker.

TEACHER
Well, I guess it's okay. You won't do anything stupid.

They are let through.

INT. EMPTY SCHOOL HALLWAY – MOMENTS LATER

SOUNDTRACK – CHEAP TRICK – I WANT YOU TO WANT ME

EDDIE
I love the school at night.

SARA
Really? I don't like anything about school.

EDDIE
Sure, you do.

SARA
No, I don't.

EDDIE
You like your friends.

SARA
That's different.

EDDIE
You like learning.

                    SARA
Well, I hate homework. I'm here all day; I don't want to
take work home.

                    EDDIE
You're enjoying this dance, ain't ya?

                    SARA
Very much, I'm so glad you wanted to come with me.

They get to the locker. Eddie finds a straw. When they are walking
back Sara sits on the stairs. Eddie sits next to her. He gets nervous.
Sara puts her head on his shoulder. Eddie starts laughing.

                    SARA
What's so funny?

                    EDDIE
Nothing.
                    SARA
What is it? Tell me.

                    EDDIE
I'm just a little nervous.

                    SARA
About what?

Eddie kisses her on the lips. Sara looks shocked and backs up.

                    EDDIE
I guess you didn't want me to do that.

                    SARA
Well, I just didn't expect it.

EDDIE
Well, are we going to be more than friends?

SARA
Eddie, I really like you. You're the best guy I know. It's just right now I'm not looking for a boy-friend.

EDDIE
Oh, okay I understand.
(uncomfortable silence)
We should get back.

INT. BACK IN GYM – MOMENTS LATER

SOUNDTRACK – CYNDI LAUPER – CHANGE OF HEART

Eddie sits down and drinks his Coke. June can tell he's not happy. Sara goes off to talk to other friends.

JUNE
What happened?

EDDIE
I tried to kiss her.

JUNE
And?

EDDIE
You should have seen her face. I told her I wanted to be more than friends. She said she wasn't looking for a boyfriend. So I guess it's not completely hopeless.

GLENN
Let's dance.

JUNE
Not right now. I'm kind of tried.

GLENN
Come on, Eddie, let's do that thing.

Eddie and Glenn do a dance routine.

INT. GYM – LATER

SOUNDTRACK – AARON NEVILLE - HERCULES

Glenn is talking to a GIRL and Eddie overhears.

                    EDDIE'S POV – GLENN
          So why not?

                         GIRL
          Because you're here with June.

                        GLENN
          Yeah, well, we aren't married. We aren't even going
          steady, not really.

                         GIRL
          I don't know. I like you and all, but it doesn't seem
          right...

                        GLENN
          If you like me and I like you, what's the problem?

Eddie interrupts. He is shaking and has more trouble speaking.

                        EDDIE
          The problem is it's wrong. If you don't want to go with
          June that's your dumb-ass problem.

The girl leaves.

                        GLENN
          Come on, Eddie, I was getting somewhere.

EDDIE

You go back with June. She's the best thing you'll ever have a chance at, but if you're too stupid to see that break up with her later. Tonight, you act right or else.

GLENN

Or else what?

EDDIE

I'll make you look bad. I'll make you look really bad.

INT. GYM - THE DANCE IS ENDING

SOUNDTRACK – THE SMITHS – GET WHAT I WANT THIS TIME

Eddie overhears another conversation between Sara and HER FRIEND.

> HER FRIEND
> …I really want a boyfriend.

> SARA
> I know, I was thinking last weekend that I really want a boyfriend.

Eddie puts his face in his hands.

INT. LYNN'S CAR – DAY

SOUNDTRACK – FRANK SINATRA – THAT'S LIFE

Lynn is bringing Eddie and June to get their driver's licenses. Eddie is driving. He and June are quizzing each other with a La. Road Handbook.

> EDDIE
> So, what does a Yield sign mean?

> JUNE
> Give me something hard. It means you have to give the other driver the right of way. Okay here's a hard one. What do you do when your car starts to spin?
> EDDIE
> Please, you turn the steering wheel in the direction of the spin and lightly pump your brakes. Bring it on, baby. We are going to ace that test. Oh yeah, oh yeah.

LYNN
Okay, big shots, let's go.

INT. DMV - LATER

SOUNDTRACK – FRANK SINATRA – THAT'S LIFE (continues)

The worker examines the questionnaire. Towards the end a question states, "Do you have any physical condition that will prevent you from operating a vehicle?" Eddie has "NO" marked. The clerk looks him over, smiles, then passes him through.

EXT. OUTSIDE DMV – LATER

SOUNDTRACK – FRANK SINATRA – THAT'S LIFE (continues)

After the two are looking at their new licenses.

JUNE
I'm glad our birthdays are one day apart…

EDDIE
Except on Leap Year.

JUNE
…so that we could get our licenses at the same time.

EDDIE
Maybe I can get a girlfriend now?

EXT. UPTOWN – DAY

SOUNDTRACK – JESSE HILL – OOH POO PAH DOO

Eddie and June are driving around without an adult. The music is blaring, the windows are open, and Eddie is driving too fast doing "Miami Vice" turns. The ground is a little wet and as he turns the car slides. They both scream and close their eyes. Eddie slams on the brakes and holds the wheel tight. The wheels of the car are turned, but the car heads straight towards a light pole. The car stops an inch from the pole. The tape ejects for no reason. They open their eyes.

BOTH

Wow.

EDDIE

I think I was supposed to turn the wheel with the slide.

They burst out laughing.

INT. EDDIE'S BEDROOM – DAY - 1986

SOUNDTRACK – AARON NEVILLE – TELL IT LIKE IT IS

Eddie is sitting at his computer agonizing over the letter he is writing. It's a letter asking June out. He deletes version after version. Finally, he prints it out.

Dear June,

It has gotten to the point where I have to say something. So, here it goes. Would you like to go out with me? I really don't want to make you feel weird or put pressure on you. Just tell it like it is.
Your friend forever.
Love,
Eddie

Eddie Tebbe

Eddie signs it and puts it in an envelope.

INT. EDDIE'S KITCHEN – MOMENTS LATER

SOUNDTRACK – ART NEVILLE – ALL THESE THINGS

Eddie puts the letter on the table as he gets a drink. Lynn is cooking.
She sees the letter.

Lynn twitches a few times during the scene.

> LYNN
>
> Is that it?

> EDDIE
>
> Yep.

> LYNN
>
> Are you sure you don't want to talk to her face to face?

> EDDIE
>
> Mom, we talked about this. I've been trying to for-
> ever. I keep freezing up. You said this was a good idea.

> LYNN
>
> It is.

> EDDIE
>
> Do you think it will work?

LYNN

I don't know dear. Your CP really complicates an already complicated situation. Unfortunately getting a girl to feel that way about you will be extremely hard. You are going to have to be patient and understanding with girls. At your age the simplest thing can seem like such a big deal. It's a tall task for a teenager to be mature enough to accept something big like CP. It's going to be a tough time for you, but as they mature, they'll start realizing what's important.

EDDIE

So you don't think this will work?

LYNN

If any girl has the maturity to go out with you, June does, but she may view you as a brother.

EDDIE

So I shouldn't say anything?

LYNN

No, not at all. You should express your feelings. You can't go through life hiding from your feelings. I have never witnessed any situation where holding feelings back ultimately was better. You don't always get what you want, it hurts a lot, but in the end it's better. And you never know. No matter how much you think you know how another person will react to something you just don't know until you try. How you are about trying things even though by all appearances you shouldn't be able to do them is how you need to approach these situations.

EDDIE

You're really painting such a nice picture.

Eddie Tebbe

LYNN
You understand things. Since you were little you understood. I've been so lucky that I haven't had to shield you from the tough parts of your life.

SERIES OF SHOTS

SOUNDTRACK – PETER GABRIEL – IN YOUR EYES

A. Eddie goes and slides the letter under June's door, then rings the bell and runs home.

B. Deloris opens the door and looks around.

C. She gives the letter to June who's in her room. Deloris leaves.

SOUNDTRACK – ELTON JOHN – SORRY SEEMS TO BE THE HARDEST WORD

D. June opens and reads the letter. She gets very serious. It takes her two days to sit down and hand write a letter.

Dear Eddie,

I guess my first answer is no. I don't want to date you. You are the best, best friend I have. I love you more than anything, but I do not feel "that way" about you.

I'm glad you are not trying to pressure me. Another person was pressuring me, and when I said no he got all weird about our friendship and acted jealous. I hope that doesn't happen with us, but I can only tell it like it is. I don't, I can't lose your friendship.

Best, best friends always,
June

E. June takes her letter across the street and slides it under the door, rings the doorbell, and runs home.

F. Lynn, who loses her balance picking it up, gives the letter to Eddie.

G. He goes to his room and reads it. He closes his eyes and fights back the tears. Then he folds the letter and puts it in a keepsake box in the closet.

END SERIES OF SHOTS

INT. EDDIE'S HALLWAY – DAY

SOUNDTRACK – ELTON JOHN – SORRY SEEMS TO BE THE HARDEST WORD (continues)

Eddie makes a call.

EDDIE
Meet you in the park.

JUNE
(VO)

Okay

EDDIE

Okay

INT. JUNE'S BEDROOM - DAY

SOUNDTRACK – HEART – DOG & BUTTERFLY

June is in her room. The curtains are drawn, and lights are off. The phone rings. She answers the phone. It's Eddie.

> EDDIE
> (VO)
> Do you want to go see Aliens?

> JUNE
> No, I think I'll pass.

> EDDIE
> (VO)
> What are you doing?

> JUNE
> Not much.

> EDDIE
> (VO)
> Well, come on.

> JUNE
> I'm just not into it right now.

> EDDIE
> (VO)
> Are you sick?

> JUNE
> No.

> EDDIE
> (VO)
> Something's wrong.

> JUNE
> I just need some time to think.

EDDIE
(VO)
About?

JUNE
Eddie, go to the movie. I'll talk to you later.

EDDIE
(VO)
As you wish.

She curls up in bed and cries. After a while she pulls a diary from under her mattress, turns her bedside lamp on, and starts to write. She writes, "I just don't feel right."

INT. SMALL BAR ROOM – NIGHT - 1987

SOUNDTRACK – ROBERT PALMER – HA JULIA

Eddie and June are nervous as they try to enter a bar, "Charity's". The DOORMAN looks at Eddie in a wondering way but doesn't card them.

JUNE
See, I told you we'd get in.

EDDIE
(smiles)
Okay, I thought they would card me. That guy was scared to card me.

JUNE
Why would he be scared of you?

EDDIE
Not me, but of carding me.

JUNE
There they are.

Eddie Tebbe

They join a group of people. One of the guys is playing darts. Eddie tries. The first dart misses the board and backboard sticking in the wall not far from someone. Eddie laughs.

> EDDIE
> Hey, you might want to get on the other side of me. I almost gave you a third ear hole.
> (He throws the second dart hitting the backboard)
> Improvement.
> (He hits the board with the third dart)
> All right.

INT. CHARITY'S – LATER THAT NIGHT

SOUNDTRACK – ROBERT PALMER – SAILING SHOES

Eddie, June, BUDDY, and JOAN are sitting in a booth.

Buddy and Joan are seventeen.

> BUDDY
> You don't drink because of your problem?

> EDDIE
> No. In fact, it might help.

> BUDDY
> What?

> JUNE
> You know how drinking makes a person walk funny...

> EDDIE
> For me it might make me walk straight.

> BUDDY
> Really?

> JOAN
> No, he's joking.

Eddie Tebbe

                         BUDDY
          Oh, okay.

                         EDDIE
          I don't like the taste.

                         JOAN
          Nobody likes the taste at first. You have to get used to
          it.

                         EDDIE
          That's what my mom says about vegetables too, and I
          don't eat them either.

                         JOAN
          You don't eat any veggies?

                         EDDIE
          Some, but not the ones I don't like.

Buddy pulls June to the side.

TWO SHOT

                         BUDDY
          Are you having a good time?

                         JUNE
          Yeah.

                         BUDDY
          I really like this place.

JUNE

It's pretty cool.

BUDDY

Would you like to go out with me?

JUNE

Like a date?

BUDDY

Yes, a date.

JUNE

I don't think so.

BUDDY

Wow, I thought we were hitting it off.

JUNE

We are, but I'm not going to have those feelings for you. I'm really sorry if I led you on.

BUDDY

I really like you, June. You're such a great person.

JUNE

You are too. I just know it will never be that way.

BUDDY

Is it someone else?

JUNE

No.

BUDDY

Well, I guess... I think I need to go.

                    JUNE
      Don't leave.

Buddy leaves. June sighs with frustration.

                    EDDIE
      Where's he going? The night's early.

INT. WOMEN'S BATHROOM – MOMENTS LATER

SOUNDTRACK – CAT STEVENS – MORNING HAS BROKEN

June is crying. She goes back out.

INT. CHARITY'S – MOMENTS LATER

SOUNDTRACK – CAT STEVENS – MORNING HAS BROKEN
(continues)

                    EDDIE
      What's going on?

                    JUNE
      He's upset because I rejected him.

                    EDDIE
      Well, I certainly understand that feeling, but why? I
      thought you liked him.

                    JUNE
      Not like that.

                    EDDIE
      You had me fooled. You must have had him fooled big
      time.

                    JUNE
He was pretty shocked.

                    EDDIE
But why?

                    JUNE
I don't know why.

EXT. JUNE'S BACK YARD – CLEAR NIGHT

SOUNDTRACK – NEVILLE BROTHERS – SITTING IN LIMBO

Eddie and June are looking at the stars.

                    EDDIE
You've been extra quiet. What's wrong?

                    JUNE
Nothing.

                    EDDIE
Still upset about Buddy?

                    JUNE
A little.

                    EDDIE
Then what is it? You're more than a little upset.

                    JUNE
It's nothing, really?

                    EDDIE
So there is something. What is it?

                            JUNE
            I don't know if I can tell you.

                            EDDIE
        If not me, who can you tell? You want to tell me.

                            JUNE
                          (pause.)
            I don't have normal feelings.

                            EDDIE
            What does that mean?

                            JUNE
            I'm not attracted to boys.

                            EDDIE
            Any boys?

                            JUNE
            Not really.

                            EDDIE
            So, you would be attracted to…

                            JUNE
            Girls.

                            EDDIE
            You're gay then.

June shakes her head.

CU – EDDIE'S FACE

Eddie closes his eyes and grimaces.

> EDDIE
> Are you sure?

> JUNE
> Fairly positive, but I also know I want a family.

> EDDIE
> So what's the problem?

> JUNE
> Eddie.

> EDDIE
> Have you…

> JUNE
> Been with a girl? I've kissed someone.

> EDDIE
> And it felt good.

> JUNE
> It felt so right.

> EDDIE
> When you kiss a boy?

> JUNE
> It's nice, but….

> EDDIE
> Who have you told?

                         JUNE
Nobody.

                         EDDIE
Except that girl.

                         JUNE
Not even her.

                         EDDIE
You need to talk to Aunt Maggie. She'll have lots to tell
you. It's not wrong. Some people are gay. There's no
difference. The world will look at you differently, and I
know something about that, but it's not wrong. When
are you going to tell your parents?

                         JUNE
I...

                         EDDIE
You have to tell them.

                         JUNE
Why?

                         EDDIE
Don't be ridiculous. This is not something that you can
hide forever. Aunt Maggie explains it better, but you'll
never feel right until you're okay with yourself, and
you'll never be okay with yourself if you hide the truth.

                         JUNE
What? Am I supposed to wear a sign?

                         EDDIE
No.

JUNE

I don't want to have to deal with this.

EDDIE

I hear your pain. We don't get to choose. Things just happen certain ways. You can't get around it. We do have to deal with it.

JUNE

Do you think there's a reason for what happens?

EDDIE

I hope so. I've been wondering about that since we were little. I watch how things go down and try to figure them out. The other day I was driving and I slowed down for no reason. Two seconds later a cat ran into the street. That's weird. And my whole life people have told me that I was meant for something. In history we're taught that humans have been trying to answer that question forever. It's why people believe in God and religious stuff. So I don't think we can reason it tonight. I do think there are reasons behind things. I just haven't figured out what.

JUNE

When you do, will you tell me? I've been reading about Eastern Philosophies. It's very interesting.

EDDIE

So, when are you going to tell your parents?

JUNE

My dad isn't going to take it well.

                              EDDIE
      You're right, but he'll come around. He just needs some
      help sometimes opening up.

                              JUNE
      Ah yes, Eddie and John's famous talks.

                              EDDIE
      And?

                              JUNE
      Maybe I'm a little jealous. You have a closer relation-
      ship with my dad than me.

                              EDDIE
      Your dad being able to talk to me started as a fluke years
      ago. You're his daughter. That's completely different.
      You have a very good relationship with him. So, when
      are you going to tell your parents?

                              JUNE
      Soon. Will you help me?

                              EDDIE
      As you wish.

INT. EDDIE'S KITCHEN – NIGHT

SOUNDTRACK – TOM PETTY – I WON'T BACK DOWN

Eddie is home alone. He's making dinner. He's getting it done, but
with difficulty. When he finishes he's carrying the plate on a tray.
Right as he puts the tray on the table he jerks and drops it. He gets mad
and kicks the tray then sits and cries. After some time, he takes a deep
breath and cleans up. Then makes another plate.

EXT. OUTSIDE A COFFEE SHOP – DAY

SOUNDTRACK – BEATLES – YESTERDAY

LONG SHOT

June and Maggie are having coffee. June is upset. Maggie is talking.

TWO SHOT

MAGGIE
I can't guarantee your father will ever understand, but I know that you can't hide from who you are. If you don't come clean with yourself and then your parents nothing will ever be quite right. It might not even be conscious, but it will be there. I've been through this. I hated myself until I was in my thirties. It was a big waste of time and energy. Tell them now.

JUNE
Thank you.

They hug.

INT. JUNE'S KITCHEN - NIGHT

SOUNDTRACK – SKYLARK – WILDFLOWER

June is about to tell her parents she's gay. She and Eddie are sitting at June's kitchen table as her parents enter. They sit down.

DELORIS
What's so important? Is something wrong?

JOHN
What is it, dear?

>   JUNE
> I've come to a realization about myself and it's some-
> thing that I need to tell you.

>   DELORIS
> You can tell us anything. You know that.

>   JUNE
> Mom, Dad...
>   (pause)
> I'm gay.

Deloris takes a deep breath.

John gets up, starts pacing, and starts yelling. Deloris starts crying.

>   JOHN
> What? I don't think you know what you're talking
> about. You're not gay. I am not...I...I don't accept it.
> You've been around that Maggie too much, that's it,
> she's got you all confused, that's all. I'm not having
> this kind of talk in my house. We are respectable peo-
> ple. We are a respectable family. This is not allowed.
> You can't bring that kind of stuff in this family. It's
> wrong.

June runs out of the room crying. Deloris follows her. John paces
around mumbling to himself.

CU – EDDIE'S DISAPPOINTED FACE

>   JOHN
> What are you staring at?

EDDIE

I'm just wondering how long it will take you to calm down.

JOHN

I'll never calm down.

EDDIE

Sure you will. Then you'll feel bad.

JOHN

What do you know? You're just a kid.

EDDIE

I understand. You know I understand things.

JOHN

It's wrong. It's wrong.

EDDIE

Maybe, but that's your daughter who you love more than anything.

JOHN

Yes I do, and I don't want her like that.

EDDIE

Her being gay won't change that.

JOHN

Well…

                              EDDIE
June just did the hardest thing she'll ever do in her
life. Her biggest fear is that you won't love her anymore. I don't care how you feel about gayness, that will
take a long time to deal with, but if you don't make June
feel that you still love her now, then you've failed her as
a father.

                              JOHN
                         (long pause)
I don't know if I can.

                              EDDIE
It's going to be the hardest thing you've ever done.

                              JOHN
I don't know how.

                              EDDIE
For now just give her a hug.

John pats Eddie on the back as he returns to the other room.

INT. LIVING ROOM – MOMENTS LATER

SOUNDTRACK – SUBDUDES – LAUGHING AT BIRDS

John goes to June on the sofa where Deloris is comforting her. He
gives her a hug.

INT. AUDITORIUM – NIGHT - 1988

SOUNDTRACK – THE METERS – TIPPI TOES

Eddie and June have just graduated high school. They are backstage in
the chaos of graduates and parents. Deloris is taking pictures. Lynn
has lots of tricky movements. The PRINCIPAL comes over.

PRINCIPAL

Ms. Perry I just wanted to say what a delight it was having Eddie at this school. I hope we helped him along in some way. He has really been an inspiration to us all. I have no doubt Eddie is going to make the next leap as easily as he has handled high school. The same goes for this beautiful young lady. Both of you make a hard job a little easier. Unfortunately, I get to know the parents of the problem students more than the others. I just wanted to express what special children you have. Eddie, I'm going to miss our talks. Please come visit anytime. Have the two of you decided on a college?

JUNE

We've both going to UNO.

PRINCIPAL

That's great. Have you decided on a major?

JUNE

Mine is Social Work.

EDDIE

I'm still leaning towards the psychological arena.

PRINCIPAL

I'm not surprised. Excuse me.

He walks off.

Eddie Tebbe

INT. TIPITINA'S – LATE NIGHT

SOUNDTRACK – NEVILLE BROTHERS – DANCING JONES

June is seeing The Neville Brothers. She's dancing and really enjoying it. Eddie comes up with another guy, JIM SMITH.

JIM is a neatly groomed preppie, twenty-five years old, from New York.

                         JUNE
          Hey.

                         EDDIE
          Hey. This is Jim Smith. We were just throwing darts at
          Charity's. He almost had me. Jim, this is my bestest
          friend June.

                         JIM
          Nice to meet you.

                         JUNE
          Same here.

EXT. OUTSIDE TIP'S – LATER

SOUNDTRACK – NEVILLE BROTHERS – HEY POCKY WAY

At the break they go outside and sit on some steps.

                         JIM
          Man, they are really good.

                         JUNE
          You haven't seen them before?

JIM

No.

JUNE

Are you from here?

JIM

No, I'm from New York.

JUNE

Really, what brings you here?

EDDIE

Guess.

JUNE

You're a student at Tulane.

JIM

That's right. Is it that obvious? Eddie pegged it right away also.

EDDIE

It is to locals.

JUNE

What are you studying? Law?

JIM

Nope, medicine.

JUNE

That's not as bad.

EDDIE

We can still hang out.

> JUNE
> If you like the Nevilles, you can't be that bad.

> EDDIE
> He started out like usual, that blank stare and uneasiness about how to act and what to say, but he came around pretty quickly. He's very good at darts.

> JIM
> You walk up funny with all your movements. What am I supposed to think? I'm surely not thinking you can throw. You should hustle people when you get better.

> BOTH
> (Eddie and June.)
> I like him.

INT. GALLERY - NIGHT

SOUNDTRACK – BILL WITHERS – LEAN ON ME

Show a photo exhibit at a gallery with pictures for Eddie and Jim bonding. Some include June.

INT. KATIE'S RESTAURANT – NIGHT – 1990

SOUNDTRACK – TEMPTATIONS – PAPA WAS A ROLLING STONE

Eddie and Jim are at a table.

> EDDIE
> June couldn't be on time if her life depended on it.

> JIM
> How did it go with that girl?

                    EDDIE
Same as always.

                    JIM
She seemed so into you.

                    EDDIE
They all do. It just doesn't mean what it
should. There's some gap there. It's very frustrating.

June and her girlfriend, KELLY, show up. June looks extra sexy. Eddie takes a long look.

                    JUNE
I hope y'all weren't waiting long.

                    EDDIE
We just got seated.

There is a fussy baby at the next table. Eddie makes faces at it and
makes it laugh.

                    JUNE
All babies love him.

                    KELLY
Hey, Eddie, how are you?

                    EDDIE
Doing fine. You haven't met Jim, have you?

                    KELLY
No. Hi, nice to meet you.

                    JIM
Yes, it's nice to finally meet you.

                    KELLY
I have to say it's my fault we're running late.

                    EDDIE
Yeah right.
                    JUNE
Really.

                    EDDIE
I have spent a good chunk of my life waiting for her.

                    JUNE
Hey.

                    EDDIE
The truth shall set you free.

                    KELLY
This time it was all me. I got a call as we were walking
out the door.

Eddie and June start a side conversation.

TWO SHOT

                    JIM
How did you guys meet?

                    KELLY
In class. We were both taking philosophy.

                    JIM
What's your major?

                    KELLY
Elementary Education.

JIM
You're going to be a teacher. Why?

KELLY
Because I still love my fourth-grade teacher.

JIM
Are you from here?

KELLY
I've been here ten years.

Enter Eddie and June's conversation.

TWO SHOT

EDDIE
Have you noticed a difference with my mom?

JUNE
What kind?

EDDIE
Physically.

JUNE
Are you thinking…

EDDIE
Yes.

JIM
Thinking what?

EDDIE
I think my mom is showing signs of Huntington's.

                    JIM
You have Huntington's in your family?

                    EDDIE
My Grandpa had it.

                    JIM
Really, and you think your mom is showing signs?

                    EDDIE
Yes.

                    KELLY
What's that?

                    JIM
I don't know much about it myself.

                    EDDIE
It's a genetic disease. It causes a slow deterioration of,
well, everything.

                    KELLY
Can they do anything?

                    JIM
Not really. They are just starting to learn about it. It
was misunderstood for a long time.

                    JUNE
You really think she has it?

                    EDDIE
I don't know.

The WAITRESS walks up.

> WAITRESS
Are you guys ready to order?
> EDDIE
Yes, and just in time because this table was just about to become a real downer.

INT. CHARITY'S – DAY - 1991

SOUNDTRACK – NEVILLE BROTHERS – LOVE THE ONE YOU'RE WITH/CAN'T ALWAYS GET WHAT YOU WANT

Eddie sits at the bar talking to the BARTENDER. A nice-looking girl, TRINA, comes in. She has a book bag. She sits a few seats away from Eddie and orders a beer. She says something to the bartender. She takes out a Sociology book. The bartender shakes his head. She slams the book down. Eddie smiles.

> EDDIE
Having trouble?

> TRINA
Pardon me?

> EDDIE
Are you having trouble?

> TRINA
With what?

> EDDIE
Sociology.

> TRINA
Oh, yes, I am. Can you help me?

> EDDIE
Can I help? Sure can.

Eddie Tebbe

She moves next to Eddie taking out her book and notebook.

                    TRINA
          How did you know?

                    EDDIE
          Well, the way you slammed the book down for
          one. Also, I've seen you on campus and that's the same
          book Dr. Carter uses. So, given the time of year I fig-
          ured you were having trouble with his term paper.

                    TRINA
          That's right. You're amazing. You've had him then?

                    EDDIE
          Last year.

                    TRINA
          Do you understand this stuff?

                    EDDIE
          Yes, I have a knack for human behavior.

                    TRINA
          You probably got an A in his class.

                    EDDIE
          It was an easy A too. I was the only student to ever ace
          one of his tests.

                    TRINA
          Really, you must be smart. I would love it if you'd help
          me.

                    EDDIE
          Sure. I'm Eddie.

                    TRINA

Andy?

EDDIE

No, Eddie.

TRINA

Eggie.

EDDIE

E. D. D. I. E.

TRINA

Oh, Eddie, I'm sorry. I'm Trina, pleased to meet you. I've actually seen you around myself and wanted to talk to you.

EDDIE

Really.

TRINA

Surprised that I've noticed you?

EDDIE

About being noticed, no, I'm a very noticeable guy. I expect it, but interest is something else.

TRINA

Well, you have my attention. Let's get to work.

They move to a booth. They go through the book as Eddie explains stuff. Trina is very touchy with Eddie. They laugh a lot. The bartender gives Eddie a wink of encouragement. The books are put away and they are still sitting close.

TRINA

I've had a great time this evening. I've never thought Sociology could be so fun.

They are in a perfect position to kiss, but Eddie leans back.

> EDDIE
> Would you like to go out sometime?

> TRINA
> Oh.
>   (pause)
> I'm really not looking for a boyfriend
> right now.

> EDDIE
>   (tries to be cool about it)
> Oh, bad timing, I guess.

> TRINA
> Yeah. I guess. I should go.

She leaves. Eddie goes back to the bar.

> BARTENDER
> Did you get her number?

> EDDIE
> She's not looking for a boyfriend right now.

> BARTENDER
> You're kidding. She told you that. She had me fooled.

> EDDIE
> Yep.

> BARTENDER
> You know that's bullshit.

                    EDDIE
        Yep.

INT. JUNE AND KELLY'S APARTMENT - NIGHT

SOUNDTRACK – NEVILLE BROTHERS – SWEET HONEY DRIP-
PER

June and Kelly are making dinner. Kelly is looking in the refrigerator.

                    KELLY
        Do you want a salad with that spaghetti?

                    JUNE
        What's in there?

                    KELLY
        Let's see, a little lettuce, a tomato, cucumber, some
        sprouts, and…

                    JUNE
        Is there any dressing?

                    KELLY
        Ranch, your favorite.

                    JUNE
        Then that sounds good to me. I'm almost done here.

They finish fixing dinner and serve themselves.

                    KELLY
        How was the clinic today?

                    JUNE
        It's a mess. It's hard seeing how many people need so
        much help.

KELLY

Well, you want to be a social worker?

JUNE

I know. I want to do something to help. Right now, I'm just doing clerical stuff, so I don't feel like I'm helping much. There is a social worker that is really good at it. I hope I get to work with her.

(pause)

There was the cutest baby today.

KELLY

You didn't bring it home, I hope.

JUNE

No, I didn't, but I want to talk about this again.

KELLY

We've been through this too much. You don't seem to realize I'm not changing my mind.

JUNE

I'm not changing my mind either.

KELLY

Well, I guess you have some decisions to make.

JUNE

What?

KELLY

I love you, and I want to be with you, but I don't want a baby and never will.

JUNE

So you're giving up on us.

> KELLY

I'm being practical.

> JUNE

What does practical have to do with anything?

> KELLY

Then what?

> JUNE

I don't know.

INT. UPSCALE BAR - NIGHT

SOUNDTRACK – RUFUS – TELL ME SOMETHING GOOD

Jim is at a bar. He approaches a group of four ladies. They invite him to sit down. He buys them drinks. He holds their attention. Later he shows them how to play darts. As three of the ladies depart one slips him her number. He starts really putting the moves on the lady that stayed, to her delight. They leave together.

INT. DOCTOR'S OFFICE - DAY

SOUNDTRACK – ERIC CLAPTON – BETTER MAKE IT
THROUGH TODAY

Eddie, June, and his mom are in the doctor's office. The doctor is look-ing at Lynn's file.

> DOCTOR

Well, there's definitely a decrease in motor functions. Given your family history that's not good news. I
have already ruled out a number of possible causes. I'd
like to rule out a few long shots, they are obscure, but at
least they have accurate tests. I'm afraid there's a
ninety-nine percent chance you have Huntington's.

Eddie Tebbe

Lynn, June, and Eddie are crying and holding each other.

DOCTOR
I'll give you a moment.

The doctor leaves. Lynn, June, and Eddie cry for a little while longer. They try to compose themselves. Eddie calls Jim.

EDDIE
It's bad...I know...a few
minutes...yes...later...okay ...bye.
(to his mom)
Jim's real sorry to hear. He'll come by
later.

The doctor comes back in with a stack of papers.

DOCTOR
Here's the very latest on Huntington's available. I think they're close to finding the gene, and once they do that the advances in testing and treatment will take off. The progression of the disease is unpredictable, but you have years where your movements will become worse, and you'll see a decline in your abilities. Your emotions may become unpredictable, with most likely depression. These things though won't stop you from leading your life. Most Huntington's patients don't seek medical treatment this early. You have to make the most of the time you have.

INT. SMALL APARTMENT – DAY - 1992

SOUNDTRACK – THE DIRTY DOZEN BRASS BAND – UN-
CLEAR WATER

June, Eddie, and Jim are moving in the last of June's stuff into her new
apartment. It's small and full of stuff. June and Jim are bringing in the
sofa. Eddie is unpacking and arranging things.

                    EDDIE
          Put that over there. Put the side that Jim has about two
          inches from the wall.

                    JIM
          Thanks for your help.

                    EDDIE
          I'm a director, not a strong back.

                    JUNE
          No joke, thanks for both of y'all's help. I'm going to
          order us some pizza. Jim, is there any kind you want?

                    JIM
          Anything is fine.
                    (June orders the pizza)
          Shouldn't you let her do that?

                    EDDIE
          No, see those boxes with the orange markings? Those
          are from her last move. She never unpacked them. Can
          you put that chair over there?

Jim moves the chair.

                    JUNE

Pizza's on its way.

EDDIE

You are going to have to get rid of some stuff. This place isn't big enough.

JUNE

I know, I was thinking I'd put some stuff in storage, but I don't know what.

EDDIE

I'd start with all the boxes you haven't opened in two years. I'm fairly sure you won't be needing them now.

JIM

June, why did you breakup with Kelly so abruptly? When we were over there a few weeks ago you guys seemed happy. We all had a lot of fun.

JUNE

We were happy for the most part, but there was no future for the relationship.

JIM

That's too bad.

JUNE

Yes, it is.

The action speeds up. The pizza comes. They eat and joke around. Jim leaves. Eddie goes back to unpacking.

SOUNDTRACK – CAT STEVENS – WILD WORLD

JUNE
Stop that, I want to talk to you about something.

EDDIE
(sits beside her)
What?

JUNE
Do you want a kid?
EDDIE
You kind of need a girl and sex for that.

JUNE
Ha, Ha. I'm serious.

EDDIE
Yes, I do, but now?

JUNE
What does that mean?

EDDIE
Now that my mom has Huntington's I have a fifty-fifty chance myself. I can't make that decision easily. Luckily, I don't have to. I can't even get to first base. What's all this about?

JUNE
I was thinking of asking you to donate your sperm.

EDDIE
Oh, when?

JUNE
Not now, I'll have to be in a relationship, and you know.

EDDIE
Well, I can't answer that question without the actual situation.

JUNE
I understand.

INT. CHARITY'S - NIGHT

SOUNDTRACK – THE WHO – PINBALL WIZARDS

Eddie, June, and Jim are entering their bar. Eddie shakes most peoples' hands. A guy stops him, Eddie says something in his ear, and they both laugh. June and Jim are greeted by some people also. They get drinks. Jim gets wine, June gets a Dixie beer, and Eddie gets a Coke. June sets the Coke up for Eddie by the dartboard. Eddie and Jim play a game. A cheerleader looking blond distracts Jim. Eddie wins.

> JIM
> Pardon me.

Jim sits with the blond.

> EDDIE
> There he goes. A man after my own heart. I'll bet you he goes home with her.

> JUNE
> I'm not stupid.

Eddie and June play a game of darts as Jim talks to the lady. Jim brings her over.

> JIM
> Eddie, June, I'd like you to meet Claire.

> CLAIRE
> Hi, it's very nice to meet you.

> JUNE
> Hi.

> EDDIE
> Hello.

JIM
Claire is a junior at Tulane.

JUNE
What are you studying?

CLAIRE
Elementary Education.

JUNE
Really, that's great. I considered that myself.

CLAIRE
What did you choose instead?

JUNE
Social Work.

CLAIRE
Are you at Tulane like Jim and myself?

JUNE
No, I'm a senior at UNO.

JIM
Do you play darts?

CLAIRE
A little.

Claire and Jim play darts. She is very good and beats Jim.

JIM
A little my ass. Your turn, June.

> CLAIRE
>
> How about you two play?

> JIM
>
> Okay.

June and Jim play.

SOUNDTRACK – BEATLES – SOMETHING

> CLAIRE
>
> You have Cerebral Palsy, right?

> EDDIE
>
> Yep.

> CLAIRE
>
> You do very well with it.

> EDDIE
>
> I get by.

> CLAIRE
>
> How do you know these guys?

> EDDIE
>
> June and I have been friends since birth, practically. Jim
> I just met a few years ago.

> CLAIRE
>
> Are you in school?

> EDDIE
>
> I'm taking a few courses at a time at UNO.

CLAIRE

What's your major?

EDDIE

Sociology.

CLAIRE

What do you plan to do with that?

EDDIE

I don't know, but at the rate I'm going I'll be retiring
before I graduate.

CLAIRE

Can you take more classes?

EDDIE

No money, honey. I only work part time, and my mom
isn't in a position to help out.

CLAIRE

What about financial aid?

EDDIE

I've looked into it. I'm not trying to make things sound
bad. I'm enjoying how things are going now. I might
try for some grants, but I'd like to do it on my own for
as long as I can.

CLAIRE

Where do you work?

EDDIE

Run About Courier, a friend runs it.

CLAIRE

It must be interesting being you.

EDDIE

It can be.

CLAIRE

It must be ambiguous.

EDDIE

You're good.
(to Jim)
She's a keeper.
(to Claire)
I usually say I'm a walking enigma. Nobody has ever seen the complexity of my life right off. You must know someone with CP.

CLAIRE

Not really.

All four sit and talk for a while. Claire notices Eddie looking longingly at June.

JUNE

I'm going to play the jukebox.

JIM

I'll join you.
(to Claire)
Would you like to pick some songs?

CLAIRE

No thanks.

JIM

Is there anything I can play for you then?

CLAIRE
No, anything is fine.

EDDIE
June, play that one.

JUNE
The one?

EDDIE
No, the other one.

JUNE
Okay.

Jim and June go to the jukebox.

TWO SHOT

CLAIRE
Whether I go out with Jim depends on what songs he
plays.

EDDIE
(laughs)
He has pretty solid taste in music.

CLAIRE
You love June.

EDDIE
Of course I do.

CLAIRE
You're in love with her I meant.

EDDIE

I knew what you meant. Of course, I am. Doesn't make much difference I'm not her type.

CLAIRE

Because of the CP?

EDDIE

Well, that's a whole other issue, but even before that she's a church member.

CLAIRE

What?

EDDIE

She's gay.

CLAIRE

Oh, completely?

EDDIE

I hope so.

CLAIRE

I thought she gave you a look.

EDDIE

She did, but it's simply a look of exceptional caring. It can easily be perceived as something more. I've learned the hard way that it's not.

CLAIRE

Isn't that unrequited love thing hard?

EDDIE

If you truly accept the situation it becomes a positive thing. You stop focusing on wanting that person and focus on loving that person.

Eddie Tebbe

INT. MICHAEL'S MID-CITY GRILL – DAY – 1993

SOUNDTRACK – CAT STEVENS – HARD HEADED WOMAN

Jim and Eddie are having lunch.

                         EDDIE
          So how are things with Claire?

                         JIM
          Things are going well. We've been seeing a lot of each
          other. She's really great.

                         EDDIE
          I know. And?

                         JIM
          And, what?

                         EDDIE
          Are you in love?

                         JIM
          I never felt like this. When she's not there I want
          her. I'm barely dating anybody else.

                         EDDIE
          I guess for you that's a major step. Do you think about
          Claire when you are with these other girls?

                         JIM
          Yes.

                         EDDIE
          You're in love.

JIM

I'm not sure.

EDDIE

Of course, you're not sure. You're scared. You've finally fallen for a real woman with class, charm, and brains. It was a mistake. She's not like these little girls you usually have. Now you're in it though, and the question is what are you going to do? Are you going to become a man or stay a boy?

JIM

I'm not ready to get married.

EDDIE

Hey, hey, who said anything about getting married? You're so simple minded at times. One step at a time, first stop dating other girls. Let the relationship grow from there. Somewhere down the line, move in together, but don't get married until you've lived together at least two years.

JIM

Is that it, Teach?

EDDIE

Until you say something stupid again. How's school going?

Eddie Tebbe

INT. MANDINA'S – DAY - 1994

June, Jim, and Claire are at lunch. Jim and Claire are already eating
onion rings when June enters.

                    JIM
          There's the soon to be graduate.

                    JUNE
          Sorry I'm late. Things are crazy. Dad has been calling
          every five minutes. I wish he had disowned me.
    (she helps herself to onion rings)
          I haven't eaten anything all day.

The WAITRESS II comes over.

                    WAITRESS II
          Would y'all like to order now?

                    JUNE
          Yes. I'll take a large shrimp po-boy, dressed, with fries
          and a large iced tea.

                    CLAIRE
          We'll split a seafood platter.

                    WAITRESS II
          That will be right out.

                    CLAIRE
          So, how are you feeling?

                    JUNE
          Excited, nervous.

                    CLAIRE
          Nervous about what?

JUNE

Well I have to enter the real-world tomorrow. I don't
feel like I've learned enough. I keep expecting them to
tell me I'm not really graduating.

JIM

That's all? We have some news, tell her.

CLAIRE

That can wait, baby. It's June's day.

JUNE

You have to tell me now.

CLAIRE

We're moving in together.

JUNE

That's great. Y'all make such a cute couple.
CLAIRE

So, what are you going to do in the big bad world?

JUNE

I've interviewed with the New Orleans Public School
system. I feel pretty good about that. I'll be working as
a counselor at a summer camp until then.

CLAIRE

You'll be great.

JIM
(to June)

You do everything great.
(to Claire)
The plans are set for tonight, right?

Eddie Tebbe

CLAIRE

Yes, Jim.

JIM

Have you talked to Eddie?

CLAIRE

Many times. We're meeting him at the D ramp at 7pm.

The food comes.

JIM
(holding up a crab.)

A toast.
(June holds up a shrimp and Claire a crawfish)
To June who I have no doubt will save the world.

INT. SECONDARY SCHOOL - DAY

SOUNDTRACK – CAT STEVENS – WILD WORLD

June is at her first day of work. She is in her tiny office trying to get
organized. An older lady stands at the door. She's the other social
worker, ANN.
Ann is an older burnt-out social worker.

> ANN
> You might try to organize now, but it's nearly impossi-
> ble to keep things neat in these closets they call of-
> fices. Hi, I'm Ann, your neighbor.

> JUNE
> Nice to meet you, I've been trying to get in touch with
> you.

> ANN
> Yes, sorry, I just got back in town. First job, right?

> JUNE
> Do I look that young?

> ANN
> Yes, but I knew it when I listened to your messages last
> night, so optimistic. I didn't realize Mr. Porter was
> leaving.

> JUNE
> They said he gave his resignation at the end of last
> school year.

> ANN
> Well, we tried to stay out of each other's way.

> JUNE
> I have some great ideas I would like to talk to you about.

> ANN
> Of course, you do. Look I have two more years until I retire from this hell. I'd like to do it in peace. Then another bright-eyed newbie will be in here with hope, but by that time you'll be like me.

> JUNE
> With all due respect, I'll never be cynical.

> ANN
> I'm trying to help you out. You don't want to be in the Orleans Parish School System. They don't respect us. I have to fight for my paycheck all the time, and then they underpay me. The administration doesn't give us any support. I used to fight against all that because of the kids, but even the kids are hell now. Go into private practice while you can.

> JUNE
> I'm going to stay on you. I just want to tell you up front.

> ANN
> Great.

INT. EDDIE'S KITCHEN - NIGHT

SOUNDTRACK – JAMES ANDREWS – SWEET EMMA

June, Eddie, and EMMA are in Eddie's kitchen cooking. Lynn, Jim, and Claire are in the adjoining room at the table.

Emma is a pretty college student wearing jeans and a T-shirt. She is being extremely affectionate to Eddie.

JUNE
So how did you two meet?

Eddie and Emma start to speak. Eddie lets Emma go.

EMMA
I just walked up to him and declared my intention to get
to know him.

JUNE
Really?

EDDIE
Really!

EMMA
I'd seen him everywhere, and I just decided to force an
intro. I'm so glad I did.
(she kisses Eddie on the cheek)
It's not like me at all.

Jim enters the room looking at his beeper. He uses the phone.

CU – JIM

JIM
Yes, this is Dr. John…Okay, and what's the pressure? On the rise…Good…If it falls again beep me
right away…I understand the rules, but sometimes following the rules is bad…Put 9-1-1 in the page and I'll
come right away…Okay, thanks.
(He hangs up)
Is dinner almost ready?

JUNE
Yes, Mr. Dr. Man.

Eddie Tebbe

INT. EDDIE'S SMALL LIVING ROOM – MOMENTS LATER

SOUNDTRACK – JAMES ANDREWS – SWEET EMMA (continues)

A few card tables have been put together.

Eddie and Jim go to the table. Eddie sits by his mom, and Jim sits on the other side of him.

Lynn has less coordination and moves around a lot.

> LYNN
> (to Eddie)
> I really like her.

> EDDIE
> (to Lynn)
> Me too. We've been spending a lot of time together.

> LYNN
> (to Eddie)
> I think she's the one.

> EDDIE
> (to Lynn)
> It really seems like that. We'll find out soon enough.

June and Emma enter with the steaks, mashed potatoes, and broccoli.

Emma makes Jim move so she can sit by Eddie.

June goes to cut Eddie's steak, but Emma beats her to it.

INT. EDDIE'S - LATER

SOUNDTRACK – NEVILLE BROTHERS – YELLOW MOON

Jim gets beeped and rushes out.

Everybody starts to leave.

Eddie is saying good-bye to Claire at the door.

                    CLAIRE
I know we've talked about how at times it's hard for you
to gauge a woman's intentions because they are all so
loving towards you, and I've seen it, but this is different. Don't let this one pass by without making a move.

                    EDDIE
I have things in the works.

                    CLAIRE
Does your mom need a ride?

                    EDDIE
June's giving her a ride.

Claire leaves. Eddie sits on the couch.

                    LYNN
I'm going to do the dishes.

                    EDDIE
Mom, sit down. I'll do the dishes tomorrow.

                    LYNN
That's what you used to say as a kid.

                    EDDIE
Well, it's my place and I'll leave the dishes as long as I
want.

June and Emma enter from the kitchen.

                    EMMA
The dishes are done.

                    EDDIE
See Mom? I know how to get the dishes done.

                    JUNE
                 (to Eddie)
What are you doing tonight?

                    EMMA
We were going to go to Tip's to see the Subdudes, but I
have that test to study for.

                    EDDIE
I guess I'm soloing tonight. I might just
get to bed early.

                    JUNE
The great Eddie not going out on a Saturday night?

                    EDDIE
I can't remember such a thing, but she has me wore
down.

                    EMMA
Don't blame me, Mr.

Eddie and Emma tussle a lot.

JUNE
(to Lynn)
Are you ready?

LYNN
Sure dear.

Emma, June, and Lynn leave at the same time.

Emma and Eddie hug tightly but are hesitant about the kiss and end up kissing on half of the mouth.

Eddie Tebbe

INT. HOWLING WOLF MUSIC CLUB – NIGHT

SOUNDTRACK – GEORGE PORTER JR. & RUNNIN' PARDNERS
– NO MORE OKEY DOKE

Eddie and Emma are dancing. They are dancing side by side at first but
start dancing together. Eddie makes a slow dancing motion to
GEORGE who winks back. The band plays Fever. Eddie and Emma
start to slow dance. It gets very hot between them.

EXT. OUTSIDE THE CLUB – LATER

SOUNDTRACK – VAN MORRISON – MOONDANCE

Eddie and Emma go out of the club and down the street. They are in
each other's arms. Eddie leans in and they kiss. It starts slow and gets
more passionate. Emma breaks off.

EMMA

I can't.

She runs off.

EDDIE
Emma, wait! Where are you going?

SOUNDTRACK – SUBDUDES – ANOTHER HEARTBREAK NOW

Emma disappears around the corner. Eddie leans against the building sliding down to the ground and puts his head in his hands.

George walks by.

                    GEORGE
        Eddie, where'd that fine young thing go?

                    EDDIE
        She ran off, and I have...

                    GEORGE
        You always have the ladies around you.

                    EDDIE
              (rolling his eyes.)
        This was different.

Eddie Tebbe

INT. R BAR – NIGHT

SOUNDTRACK – U2 – STILL HAVEN'T FOUND WHAT I'M
LOOKING FOR

Claire and Eddie are sitting at the bar.

> EDDIE
> …And I had her money and keys in my pocket. She
> didn't answer my calls for a week. Finally, I had to just
> show up at her door. I didn't even need to knock if I
> didn't want to. I gave her her stuff back and asked for
> an explanation.

> CLAIRE
> What could she possibly say?

> EDDIE
> Not much at first. Well, the first thing she said is she
> missed me. Then she went down the list of stupid ex-
> cuses. I kept saying, "You need to do better." She fi-
> nally admitted my CP might have had something to do
> with it. I have to give her a little credit there. Every
> other girl has steadfastly denied that obvious fact. She
> wasn't challenging herself though. She admitted to hav-
> ing very strong feelings, including sexually, but…
> (beats his fist on the bar)
> I thought that finding a girl that saw me sexually was
> going to be hard, but when I found her that would be
> it. Now I realize it is going to be so much harder. Act-
> ing on those feelings is a much bigger leap. I'm heart-
> broken, yeah, but I'm also disillusioned, and that's bad.

> CLAIRE
> Now what?

EDDIE

As far as she goes, I told her I couldn't be around her at all. She wanted to still be friends. I told her that if we were the only two people in an elevator, I wouldn't speak to her.

CLAIRE

That sounds a bit mean.

EDDIE

It was. I'm hurt. I want her to hurt.

CLAIRE

When you stop hurting, you'll regret being hurtful.

EDDIE

Very true, but even when I stop hurting, I'll still need to protect myself. I can't have any contact with...that woman because of my emotional state. I'm too on edge. There's been no outlet for my emotional needs and desires. Until there is I have to move on completely from a situation like this. Self-preservation is my only goal right now.

CLAIRE

Could she change her mind?

EDDIE

I fantasize about her just knocking on my door and throwing herself at me. But come on.

CLAIRE

Are you going to be okay?

                              EDDIE
I'm worried about my balance. I've always liked the
Yin and Yang symbol. My life has great things and horrible things, but there has been balance. I've been able
to deal with that. I'm feeling less and less in balance.
For the first time I don't know how to get something
done.

                              CLAIRE
I have faith in you.

Jim comes in happy. Eddie puts his finger over his lips.

INT. EDDIE'S APARTMENT – NIGHT – 1995

Eddie and June are watching a movie, Roxanne.

CU – EDDIE'S FACE

Tears are rolling down his face.

There is a knock on the door. It's Jim and Claire. They are excited.

SOUNDTRACK – PAUL MCCARTNEY – BABY I'M AMAZED

                         JIM
         Guess what?

                         EDDIE
         What?

                         JIM
         Guess what I did?

                         EDDIE
         Bought a vase at Pottery Barn.

JIM

I proposed.

EDDIE

Thank you for that, but I'm not a church member.

CLAIRE

And I said yes.

EDDIE

Congrats.

They all hug.

JUNE

That's great. When's the wedding?

CLAIRE

We don't know, but it was so romantic. We had a wonderful dinner at Bella Luna on the river. The scene was beautiful. The stars were out. He had the ring on a white rose, he got on one knee, and recited a poem. I was crying so hard.

JIM
(mouths to Eddie)

Thank you.

Eddie winks at Jim.

INT. WAREHOUSE - DAY

SOUNDTRACK – SNOOKS EAGLIN – BOOGIE ON REGGAE WOMAN

June is at a food bank packing boxes. HEATHER comes up to help.

Heather is in her early thirties and plain.

Eddie Tebbe

HEATHER
The man in there told me to ask you what I can do.

JUNE
Pack each box with a variety of the food.
HEATHER
Sounds simple enough.

JUNE
Yes, it is, but also back breaking. I need a rest.

HEATHER
I'm Heather.

JUNE
Hi, I'm June.

HEATHER
How long have you been doing this?

JUNE
Since seven.

HEATHER
No, I meant years.

JUNE
Since I was a junior in high school. I don't understand
why there is hunger and homelessness. There are more
than enough resources. When I was young, I thought
this problem was going to be fixed. Now I know I'll be
doing this my whole life. It's sad.

HEATHER
That's so true. I think I've seen you before.

> JUNE
> I've been seen before. Where?

> HEATHER
> (winks)

Charlene's?

> JUNE
> (winks)
> Yes, I've been there in my day.

> HEATHER
> Good. Should we load this stuff onto a truck?

> JUNE
> That's what I'm waiting for. Here he comes finally.

Eddie pulls up in a truck.

CU - BUMPER STICKER THAT READS "THINK GLOBALLY, ACT LOCALLY"

> JUNE
> Where have you been?

> EDDIE
> I'm late once in my life. I didn't get to bed until 5am. You're lucky I'm here at all.

> JUNE
> Eddie, this is Heather.

> HEATHER
> Nice to meet you.

> EDDIE

Hi.

                          JUNE
So let's get this truck loaded. Do you have the
addresses for delivery?

                          EDDIE
Yes dear.

                          JUNE
Don't forget that place where we did that that day.

                          EDDIE
It will be my first stop.
                    (They load the truck)
So this is what Sunday morning looks like. Have a nice
day, ladies.

Eddie drives off.

                          HEATHER
May I treat you to brunch?

                          JUNE
Sure, that sounds great.

EXT. PJ'S COFFEE – DAY

SOUNDTRACK – ERIC CLAPTON – WONDERFUL TONIGHT

June and Heather talking, gazing into each other's eyes.

INT. JUNE'S BEDROOM – MORNING - STORMY

SOUNDTRACK – ARETHA FRANKLIN – NATURAL WOMAN

June and Heather are cuddling in bed.

JUNE

So, what brought you here?

HEATHER

Friends kept telling me to visit New Orleans. I came for a three-day weekend and never left. I had somebody ship my stuff.

JUNE

This town does something to you.

HEATHER

So, tell my something about yourself.

JUNE

Like what?

HEATHER

Who's your rock?

JUNE

My rock?

HEATHER

Yes, the one person in your life you couldn't do without. Mine is my younger sister Natalie. She has helped me in so many ways. I'm trying to talk her into moving here. I think she's close.

JUNE

Eddie. We have been side by side since we were babies. I can't imagine him not being in my life. He's the music of my life. Whenever I was upset, he used to tell me these great stories. I used to crawl into bed with him to feel safe. He made me not be afraid of stormy weather.

                    HEATHER
He's a great guy. I can tell.

                    JUNE
Did you always know you were gay?

                    HEATHER
No. It wasn't until a few years ago. I was never happy.
Now I am. How about you?

                    JUNE
I pretty much always knew.

EXT. IN FRONT OF HEATHER'S HOUSE - DAY

SOUNDTRACK – SLY & THE FAMILY STONE – STAND

Eddie and Jim are pulling up with June's stuff in the truck.

                    EDDIE
And all that sounds great. The Republicans' philosophies sound great. If the playing field was even, which
it isn't. If everybody was smart and righteous, which
they aren't. If big business cared about more than making their stock go up, which it doesn't. So the actual effect of Republican policies is to keep the rich, rich and
the poor, poor.

June and Heather meet them to unload.

                    HEATHER
        Hi.

                    JUNE
They're at each other again. What's the topic today?

                    ◀ 228 ▶

EDDIE

Politics.

JIM

Hi. And the Democrats have all the answers. More taxes, that's the answer? Bigger government, that's better?

EDDIE

Not all the time. First, we have to agree that the whole political system sucks. After that I just pick the best of the evils and hope for the best. A lot of what the Democrats do isn't helpful.

JIM

So you support things you don't believe in. How is that good?

EDDIE

It's not good. It's the way things are. I'm a realist.

HEATHER

I don't vote at all.

EDDIE

I still vote.

HEATHER

Thanks for helping do this.

JIM

You'll have to stay together for at least two years now.

JUNE

Is that all?

Eddie Tebbe

INT. HOSPITAL ROOM - DAY

SOUNDTRACK – JON CLEARY – GROOVE ME

Jim and a NURSE II are by a hospital bed. The male patient is asleep.

NURSE II
I don't know doctor. I could get in trouble for that.

JIM
I'm sure you could, but I'm also sure you won't. This is a friend of mine and it would really help him. I'll take the heat if comes to that, but it won't, trust me.

NURSE II
I guess so.

JIM
(winks)
I'll owe you one.

NURSE II
(smiles)
Okay.

The patient awakes. The nurse leaves.

JIM
How are you feeling?

PATIENT
(rubs his chest)
Sore.

JIM
Good.

                    PATIENT
Some friend you are.

                      JIM
I'd rather you sore than dead. I had to bang on your
chest and shock you. Be happy you're sore.

                    PATIENT
I almost died?

                      JIM
You were dead.

                    PATIENT
Thank you.

                      JIM
Anything for a friend.

INT. LYNN'S KITCHEN - EVENING

SOUNDTRACK – LINDA RONSTADT & AARON NEVILLE –
WHEN SOMETHING IS WRONG WITH MY BABY

Eddie walks in on his mother trying to cook. The kitchen is a mess.
Eddie looks at the food, which is not cooked enough.

Lynn is very unbalanced physically and emotionally.

                    EDDIE
Mom, go sit down I'll finish up in here.

                    LYNN
Why? I have it.

                    EDDIE
Let me help you.

                    LYNN
I said I have it.

                    EDDIE
Come on, Mom.

                    LYNN
Leave me alone.

                    EDDIE
Mom, you need help.

                    LYNN
No, I don't.

                    EDDIE
Yes, you do.

                    LYNN
What do you know about it?

                    EDDIE
I know a lot. You taught me to fight against my CP, but
you also taught me to be reasonable and practical. Let
me help you like you helped me.

                    LYNN
No, no, no!

Eddie steps back in awe and sadness as Lynn throws a fit. Finally, she
collapses. Eddie gets on the floor with her and holds her.

INT. THE R BAR - NIGHT

SOUNDTRACK – ERIC CLAPTON – RUNNING ON FATE

Eddie is sitting at the bar. There is a couple at the other end of the bar. They are being touchy. Eddie watches them. He fights back his tears.

INT. AT JIM'S FRONT DOOR – NIGHT - 1996

SOUNDTRACK – PAUL SIMON – 50 WAYS TO LEAVE YOUR LOVER

Jim is getting home from work. He is making noise. Claire shushes him.

> CLAIRE
> I just got the baby asleep.

> JIM
> I called and asked you to wait for me.

> CLAIRE
> That was three hours ago. It's past ten o'clock.
> JIM
> I never get to put her asleep.

> CLAIRE
> There are a lot of things you don't get to do
> lately. You're never home.

> JIM
> Not this again.

> CLAIRE
> Yes, this again. You called three hours ago to tell me
> you here coming home. It's a twenty-minute drive.

JIM

I got sidetracked.

CLAIRE

How?

JIM

I stopped for one cocktail. Dr. Smith was there. I had to socialize a little.

CLAIRE

Three hours?

JIM

I didn't realize…

CLAIRE

You never realize. Do you love your daughter?

JIM

Yes.

CLAIRE

Do you love me?

JIM

Yes.

CLAIRE

What else is there to realize?

JIM

I am thinking about you and Elly. I'm trying to advance my career. I'm driven, remember? That's one of the things you love about me.

CLAIRE

You have other responsibilities. I'm not complaining about long hours, but when you leave that hospital Elly and I have to come first. You're missing so much of Elly's life. You can't get these moments back. You haven't touched me in so long.

JIM

When I try you reject me.

CLAIRE

Crawling into bed at three in the morning, drunk and smelling of another woman, trying to stick your dick into my ass is not trying to make love to me. You're right though, I don't feel like making love when you are fucking other women.

She starts crying.

JIM

Christ, Claire, I don't know what you're taking about.

CLAIRE

You do remember that I'm intelligent. Well, don't act stupid with me.
          (Jim tries to pull her close)
Leave.

Eddie Tebbe

INT. EDDIE'S LIVING ROOM – LATER THAT NIGHT

SOUNDTRACK – SINEAD O'CONNOR – NOTHING COMPARES 2U

Jim and Eddie are on the sofa.

>   JIM
> Thanks for letting me stay here. Claire will calm down.

>   EDDIE
> What's the problem?

>   JIM
> She's gone crazy since the baby. When I try to be with her she gets mad. When I don't try she gets mad. I go out for a drink, she freaks. What am I supposed to do?

>   EDDIE
> And that's it?

>   JIM
> Well, sure.

>   EDDIE
> What is she going to tell me?

>   JIM
> She thinks I'm having an affair.

>   EDDIE
> Are you?
>   JIM
> I'm not having an affair. I'm not in love with another woman.

EDDIE

But.

JIM

But what?

EDDIE

Have you had sex, gotten blowjobs, or made out with another female since your wedding day?

JIM

You don't trust me.

EDDIE

I know how you are. You can tell me.

JIM

I have had some flings, that's all.

EDDIE

That's all!

JIM

I should go.

EDDIE

No, I'm not letting you get away that easy. Cheating is
wrong. Period. I don't care what Claire has
done. There is no reason, no excuse, and no justification
for being unfaithful. Now it doesn't have to kill your
marriage. It can be forgiven, but you have to want
it. You're my friend and I love you, but you're a jah-
muke. You stumble through life never knowing a thing
about the bigger picture. You're good at stuff and suc-
cessful with never understanding what life's about. The
world hands you everything. You let impulses and desires control you. In the end money, power, stuff, and
how many girls you banged won't matter. Relationship,
connections, and love is what you are going to be thinking about.

JIM

So why do you love me? Why does Claire love me?

EDDIE

I don't know. That's another subject though. Do you
love Claire?

JIM

Yes.

EDDIE

Do you want to save your marriage?

JIM

Yes.

EDDIE

Then you go home right now…

JIM

And confess…

> EDDIE
> No, no, no, no, never confess when she's still mad. Women might know, but when you confess, they freak out. Tell her that you love her. Tell her you want to save your marriage. Suggest y'all go to marriage counseling. When you are in counseling tell the truth about everything.

INT. MATERNITY WARD - DAY

SOUNDTRACK – CRANBERRIES - LINGER

June is looking at the babies. She is trying not to cry. Jim walks up.

> JIM
> I thought you left.

> JUNE
> I just wanted to take a gander. Look how beautiful they all are.

> JIM
> You've been volunteering a lot here lately.

> JUNE
> Yeah. How's Elly?

> JIM
> A little angel she is. I put her to sleep last night. Her little head was resting on my arm. It was something.

> JUNE
> (wiping tears away)
> That's wonderful.

> JIM
> You really want one.

                    JUNE
More than anything.

                    JIM
How about you come over tonight? Elly loves her aunt
June.

                    JUNE
Thanks.

INT. EDDIE'S BEDROOM – NIGHT

SOUNDTRACK – STEVE WINWOOD – ROLL WITH IT

Eddie is asleep in bed. The clock reads 3:30 am. The phone rings. After taking a while Eddie answers.

> EDDIE
>
> Yeah.

> JUNE
>
> Did I wake you?

> EDDIE
>
> Uh, what's wrong?

> JUNE
>
> Heather and I just broke-up. Can I come stay with you?

> EDDIE
>
> Sure, sure, I'll be here.

> JUNE
>
> Can you come get me?

> EDDIE
>
> Why? Wait, tell me later. I'm on my way.

Eddie Tebbe

INT. JUNE'S OFFICE – DAY

SOUNDTRACK – TOM PETTY – FREE FALLING

June is getting ready to leave her office. A teenage girl, BETTY,
comes up.

> BETTY
> Can I talk to you?

> JUNE
> I'm already late.

> BETTY
> It's really important.

> JUNE
> Okay.

Betty shuts the door and sits.

> BETTY
> My boyfriend, Mike, is really pressuring me to have sex,
> and well, you're the only person I trust enough to talk to
> about this.

> JUNE
> You can't talk to your parents?

> BETTY
> My parents? No way.

JUNE

So, you don't want to have sex?

BETTY

You've said we aren't mature enough.

JUNE

I'm glad to hear somebody has listened. What is Mike saying?

BETTY

He's telling me that if I don't have sex with him he'll break up with me. I love him. He can't leave me.

JUNE

Something in you knows that he's wrong to put you in this situation or you wouldn't be here.

BETTY

My body wants to have sex, and I love him. So why do I feel it's wrong?

JUNE

Because you're a very smart and mature teenager. It is never right for one person to pressure another into sex.

BETTY

But if I don't, he'll leave me.

JUNE

Maybe, but maybe not. Teenage boys say a lot that they never follow up on.

BETTY

I don't know if I can take that chance.

Eddie Tebbe

> JUNE
>
> I can promise you that if you are pressured into having sex you will regret it and resent him.

They sit for a while. Betty gives June a hug.

> BETTY
>
> Thank you.

> JUNE
>
> What are you going to do?

> BETTY
>
> I don't know.

> JUNE
> (sternly)
>
> If you have sex, make him wear a condom. That is non-negotiable.

> BETTY
> (leaving)
>
> I know. No glove, no shove.

June tries not to smile but does.

EXT. JIM AND CLAIRE'S PATIO – DAY

SOUNDTRACK – NEVILLE BROTHERS – 30 X 90

Claire is sitting on the patio.

> JUNE
> (VO)
>
> Hello.

CLAIRE

I'm out here.

June comes out from the kitchen door.

JUNE

Sorry I'm late. A student had a minor life crisis when I was walking out. You know, to do it or not.

CLAIRE

And the answer is? Homemade daiquiri?

JUNE

Sure. This girl is pretty smart. Most talk to me after the fact. She might say no.

CLAIRE

Is that why you seem in a good mood? I thought it might be your pending Paris trip with Eddie for his graduation.

JUNE

That's part of it, but this girl said a few things that let me know I am making an impact. It's hard to see that sometimes. Plus, with all the shit that went down with Heather...

CLAIRE

Did she ever explain why she cheated on you?

JUNE

Just that she was sorry.

CLAIRE

Can you forgive her?

JUNE

She doesn't want to be with me. She fell in love.

CLAIRE

I thought it might have been just a fling.

JUNE

No. I probably could have forgiven her, after seeing
what you did with Jim and how good it turned out.

CLAIRE

I thought that once that trust was gone that was it. I was
so close to walking out.

JUNE

What stopped you?

CLAIRE

A lot of things. First, I'm a fighter. I don't like to walk
away. Second, I still love him. Third was Eddie. I used
to think everything had to be perfect or else it wasn't
worth having. Eddie deals with problems I can't come
close to comprehending every minute and still finds a
way to enjoy life. Now, I didn't realize all this until re-
cently. Have you met anyone?

JUNE

I have some defect in my radar. Five of my girl couples
friends have children or have them on the way. They all
want children. Everybody I fall for won't even talk
about the possibility. The only thing that I ever wanted
is children.

CLAIRE

How do you plan to father your future
children?

JUNE
I'd like it to be Eddie, but he has Huntington's hanging
over his head.
CLAIRE
You'll figure it out. You always do.

INT. FILLED AUDITORIUM – NIGHT - 1997

SOUNDTRACK – QUEEN – WE WILL ROCK YOU / WE ARE THE
CHAMPIONS

Eddie's UNO graduation. The diplomas are being passed out. When
they get to Eddie the Chancellor steps to the microphone.

CHANCELLOR
I have never stopped to speak at this interval. I feel
compelled to comment this one time. This next student
has been working toward this day for a long time. I had
the pleasure of teaching him, while learning from him,
years ago when I still taught. He had an effect on me
like no other student. I feel proud and inspired to witness the completion of this journey and send him on his
next.

Earning a bachelor's in psychology, Eddie Perry.

The audience stands in ovation. The Chancellor hands Eddie his di-
ploma. They embrace.

Eddie Tebbe

EXT. EIFFEL TOWER – SUNSET

SOUNDTRACK – NEVILLE BROTHERS – ARIANNE

Eddie and June are on the top level. They're looking out over Paris.

> EDDIE
> This is absolutely amazing.
> JUNE
> I can't believe we are here.

> EDDIE
> This was a great idea. I didn't think I'd like Paris,
> but…wow.

Eddie's eyes are welling up.

> JUNE
> What's wrong?

Eddie looks at June then back at the sunset.

> EDDIE
> This is the most beautiful sight I'll ever witness.

> JUNE
> What is it about a sunset that gets you so much?

> EDDIE
> There's meaning in them. Somewhere?

> JUNE
> It's so romantic.

> EDDIE
> (to himself)
> There's always bitter with the sweet.

INT. EDDIE'S LIVING ROOM - DAY

SOUNDTRACK – JOE COCKER – YOU CAN LEAVE YOUR HAT ON

Eddie is watching TV in his house clothes. The doorbell rings. He answers it. It is Emma.

> EDDIE
>
> Emma?

> EMMA
>
> Hi, Eddie. It's been a long time.

> EDDIE
>
> Well, yeah.

> EMMA
>
> Can I come in?

INT. JUNE'S LIVING ROOM – THAT NIGHT

SOUNDTRACK – THE METERS – JUST KISSED MY BABY

Eddie is telling June about the evening.

> JUNE
>
> She did what?

> EDDIE
>
> She threw herself at me.

> JUNE
>
> Like how?

EDDIE

At first, we just talked about nothing much. She kept hinting that she was open to me making a move on her, but I wasn't biting. Finally, she just said, "Do you want to have sex with me?" I would have loved to have seen my reaction. I was in shock. I said, "Sure."

JUNE

No shit, that is…so great. And?

EDDIE

And what?

JUNE

How was it, shithead?

EDDIE

I enjoyed myself. I don't think I gave her the best lay possible. I was just trying not to faint. The most amazing thing was how natural it felt.

JUNE

Did she say why?

EDDIE

Not exactly. She's engaged and living in St. Louis. She tried to make it sound like she was doing it for me, and I don't doubt that was part of it. There were moments though that made clear to me that she wanted to be there. I think she was just finding out what being with me was like. She came close before and it may have been on her mind. At the same time, she didn't want to enjoy it too much.

JUNE

Now what?

                    EDDIE
She'll go get married, and I feel like a great weight has
been lifted off my shoulders. I've been sleepwalking the
last couple of years. Now I feel like I've broken
through. I haven't been this excited in a long time.

EXT. BALCONY – DAY

SOUNDTRACK – JAMES TAYLOR – FIRE AND RAIN

At the reception after Eddie's mom's funeral. Eddie is on a balcony
looking over a beautiful garden. Aunt Maggie comes out and stands
next to Eddie putting her arm around him.

                    EDDIE
You gave a good speech.

                    MAGGIE
What you wrote was beautiful. Claire did a great job
reading it.

                    EDDIE
I couldn't.

                    MAGGIE
I looked up to your mom from the moment I met her. I
get so angry that she had Huntington's. It's the most un-
fair thing I've seen.
                    (cries)
She handled all her trials and tribulations
with such grace. She raised you into a
fine young man. Not right now, but
soon, I want to talk to you about Huntington's testing. They have developed
an accurate test.

> **EDDIE**
> I know. I know.

> **MAGGIE**
> This thing is winding down. Do you need anything?

> **EDDIE**
> Lots of things, but…none that you can provide.

> **MAGGIE**
> I know.
> (She kisses Eddie and starts to go back inside but hesitates)
> I'm positive it was an accident.

She goes in. After a minute June and her father come out holding each other. June is crying.

> **JOHN**
> Your mom was an impressive lady. She taught me a thing or two in the years I've known her. It's a great loss. If there's anything you need, well you know.
> (He pats Eddie on the shoulder)
> I'm sure it was an accident.
> (to June)
> You take care of him.

John goes in. Eddie and June embrace. June is crying. Eddie is trying not to but relents. They calm down after a while.

> **JUNE**
> You needed some air?

> **EDDIE**
> And some peace.

JUNE

Yeah. I used to wish your mom was my mom.

EDDIE

Really?

JUNE

Did you ever wish my mom was yours?

EDDIE

No, I don't think I did.
JUNE
I'm not surprised. I felt like she was my mom a lot.

EDDIE

I know she loved you like a daughter.

JUNE

Good.

EDDIE

Do you think her fall was an accident?

JUNE

Well, I guess, why?

EDDIE

So many people have reassured me that they think it was
an accident.

JUNE

Isn't that what people do? Nobody wants to consider
otherwise.

                    EDDIE
I don't mind. She didn't have anything to look forward
to. She was about to be put in a home. There's no treatment much less a cure. Are there not situations when
suicide is okay? Most people who think of killing themselves don't. Most people who do actually end their
lives just needed help. Ever since we saw the "Elephant
Man" when we were kids, I've intellectually pondered
suicide. I think everybody has the ability to want to die,
but where is the point? What's the breaking point? I
wonder that about myself. It's a tricky subject, but if
Mom threw herself down those stairs, I wouldn't think
less of her.

                    JUNE
So, you think she did it on purpose?

                    EDDIE
Actually no, I think it was an accident.

                    JUNE
Me too.

                    EDDIE
            (pulls June to him)
Don't go anywhere. I feel so alone. You are all I have
left in this world.

                    JUNE
That's not true.

                    EDDIE
It's pretty damn close.

INT. DARK ROOM

SOUNDTRACK – TOM PETTY – YOU DIDN'T KNOW HOW IT FEELS

Show time passing by flipping through a photo album. The first pictures show Eddie grieving, then they show different combinations of the four enjoying life, then they show Eddie alone and depressed.

INT. EDDIE'S APARTMENT – DAY - 1999

SOUNDTRACK – STEVIE RAY VAUGHAN – LITTLE WING

Eddie has a scruffy beard. The place is a mess. Eddie is playing solitaire on the computer. The phone rings, but he doesn't answer it. It's June. She leaves a message.

> JUNE
> (VO)
> Hi Eddie. Are you there? Give me a call. We're going to the R Bar if you want to meet us.

Eddie just continues playing for a while. He looks at his watch. He turns the computer off, grabs his coat, and heads for the door. At the door he takes a deep breath and smiles.

> EDDIE
> Showtime.

He leaves.

Eddie Tebbe

INT. BAR ROOM - EVENING

SOUNDTRACK – GEORGE PORTER JR. & RUNNIN' PARDNERS
– LET'S GET IT

Jim is at a bar sitting next to a WOMAN. Jim looks at his watch.

                    JIM
          I have to be leaving.

                    WOMAN
          You don't need to leave alone you know.

                    JIM
                 (laughing)
          Actually, I do. I'm a happily married man and I want to
          stay that way.

                    WOMAN
          I won't tell.

                    JIM
          But I'll know.

                    WOMAN
          Then why did you sit here and talk me up?

                    JIM
          I was just being friendly. I'm sorry if you got the wrong
          impression. Good luck in your hunting.

INT. TEACHER'S LUNCHROOM AT SCHOOL - DAY

SOUNDTRACK – THE METERS – FIYO ON THE BAYOU

Ann's retirement party at June's work. They have just toasted Ann.
Ann pulls June outside.

TWO SHOT

> ANN
> I wanted to thank you.

> JUNE
> For what?

> ANN
> For saving me. Without you I'd have retired six years
> ago bitter and mean. Because of you my six best years
> were my last. I did more good than in all the previous
> time.

They hug.

Eddie Tebbe

INT. R BAR - DAY

SOUNDTRACK – SUBDUDES – TIRED OF BEING ALONE

Eddie is throwing darts at the board as hard as he can. Claire enters.

> CLAIRE
> I thought I might find you here.
> EDDIE
> Are you looking for me?

> CLAIRE
> Yes. We're worried about you.

> EDDIE
> I'm going through a bad time.

> CLAIRE
> What can I do to help?

> EDDIE
> Not to be mean, but it's not something
> you'll understand.

> CLAIRE
> Try me, I'm pretty smart.

> EDDIE
> It has nothing to do with brains. It has to do with being
> able to relate to what I'm saying. The meanings of the
> words are different.

> CLAIRE
> Like what?

> EDDIE
> If I say I'm lonely, you'd say…

CLAIRE
We've all been lonely.

EDDIE
Exactly, which is insulting to me. You have no idea the
level of loneliness I'm talking about because you've
never experienced it. It's like me trying to relate a paper
cut with you giving birth. Would you like that?

CLAIRE
No, I wouldn't.

EDDIE
People mean well, and I take that into account. The first
reaction is for people to relate themselves to your problem, and between people with similar experiences
maybe it's okay, but with me it's not. People subcon-
sciously believe their suffering is the worst, but that's
not actually true. Within their own lives nobody should
minimize somebody's problems, but on the larger scale
isn't it obvious that not having any romantic relationship
in their life is lonelier than something that has had the
normal ups and downs?

CLAIRE
I see what you mean, and I won't say anything like
that. I'm here as a friend who loves you. Just try to explain, please.

EDDIE
(pause)
How much do you know about psychology?

CLAIRE
A normal amount, I guess.

EDDIE

Everybody needs good emotional energy to live. Some of it is internally produced, some comes from achievement, some from friends and family, and a big part comes from love. Each is distinctive and can't substitute for another. In all lives the fulfillment of these fluctuates, and it throws a wrench into the mix, but it smooths out easily. When need for love, intimacy, sex, and to be connected with another person goes totally unfulfilled it's like a vacuum sucking all the other energies out. Think about all you have gained from Elly, Jim, from your first boyfriend, and everything in-between. Imagine you had none of that. Where would you be?

CLAIRE

I don't know.

EDDIE

I feel like a starving man that has to sit at the dinner table of the greatest feast who doesn't get to eat. I get to see it, I get to smell it, sometimes I get to feel it, and one time I got to taste it, but I never get to eat. Would that not drive anyone crazy?

CLAIRE

If I say there are worse things, is that stupid?

EDDIE

No. There are a lot of worse things. At least I get to be at the table. More people than you think are on the outside looking in. I've never felt that, but I figure it would be worse. I think my situation is more complicated. I have to deal with conflicting issues. Life gives me contradictory input. I'd rather be at the table than outside looking in. The thing is knowing other people are worse off doesn't help me. Well, it is important to have perspective, but it doesn't make me less alone.

CLAIRE
Where does your love for June fit into this?

EDDIE
It's hard to be around her. I know that that love will always be unrequited, and that would be fine if I was stronger, or I had somebody else, but in my state the pull towards her takes so much energy to fight I've been avoiding her.

CLAIRE
You've been so strong up to now. I guess I took it for granted. Why haven't you expressed these feelings before?

EDDIE
I've always tried to keep my dark side hidden from people. I have been, but I'm running out of energy. I don't even cry anymore. A major change has to come soon.

CLAIRE
I can't believe you won't get what you need.
(kisses Eddie on the forehead)
I never thanked you for saving my marriage. I know it was your idea for marriage counseling.

Eddie Tebbe

EXT. CITY PARK – BEAUTIFUL DAY

SOUNDTRACK – BEATLES – GOOD DAY SUNSHINE

Eddie and June are walking in the park.

JUNE

I want to know what's wrong.

EDDIE

I know, but this is the first good day I've had in a long
time. I don't want to think about my problems.

June gets out of breath, so they sit. Eddie is watching June watching
the kids.

JUNE

I've almost made a major decision.

EDDIE

What?

JUNE

I'm going to have a baby.

EDDIE

Good. You should have for a long time.

JUNE

It's going to be hard.

EDDIE

No shit. But do it.

JUNE

I wish you could be that father.

◀ 262 ▶

EDDIE
I can't do that right now.

JUNE
I know. I have a doctor's appointment tomorrow.

EDDIE
Good, good, get that ball rolling.

JUNE
I feel exhausted. I think I need to go.

EDDIE
Are you all right?

JUNE
I'm fine.

EDDIE
Do you need a ride home?

JUNE
I live two blocks. I'm fine. You stay and enjoy the day.

Eddie watches June as she leaves. He puts his face in his hands.

Eddie Tebbe

INT. DOCTOR'S OFFICE - DAY

SOUNDTRACK – OTIS REDDING – PAIN IN MY HEART

June is in the examining room of her gynecologist. The DOCTOR
comes back in.

> DOCTOR
> Sorry that took so long. Have you been feeling fatigued
> lately?

> JUNE
> I've been tired.

> DOCTOR
> Out of breath?

> JUNE
> Yeah, is there something wrong?

> DOCTOR
> These are vague symptoms, but yes, I would like your
> primary physician to do some tests. That's...

> JUNE
> Dr. Smith.

> DOCTOR
> He's an excellent physician.

INT. EDDIE'S APARTMENT – DAY

SOUNDTRACK – JIM CLIFF – MANY RIVERS TO CROSS

Eddie is alone in his apartment. It and him are a complete mess. The phone rings, but Eddie doesn't answer it. It's Jim.

> JIM
> (VO)
> Hey Eddie, I haven't seen you in a while. I've left some messages. Call me or I'll have to send out a search party.

The TV is on, but Eddie is staring through it, not at it. He has a bottle of sleeping pills in his hand. He throws the bottle across the room.

> EDDIE
> Fuck. I can't. Now what?

The phone rings again. It's June. She sounds funny.

> JUNE
> (VO)
> Eddie, please call me as soon as you can.

INT. JUNE'S APARTMENT – NIGHT

SOUNDTRACK – JOE COCKER – WITH A LITTLE HELP FROM MY FRIENDS

Eddie shows up at June's.

> EDDIE
> What's wrong?

> **JUNE**
> Sit down.

> **EDDIE**
> What's wrong?

> **JUNE**
> I have a heart problem.

> **EDDIE**
> And...

> **JUNE**
> It's very bad. I need a transplant.

Eddie is shocked. After it sinks in he starts to cry. They cry and hold each other. Eddie holds her head against his chest. Later they talk.

> **EDDIE**
> What needs to be done?

> **JUNE**
> There's not much. I'm wrapping up a few details and I'll be checking into the hospital.

> **EDDIE**
> Why?

> **JUNE**
> They need to monitor me, plus I have no strength. It took me all day just to do some dishes.

> **EDDIE**
> Fuck the dishes.
> (slamming his hands on the table)

EDDIE
I mean, I'll take care of your place. How can this happen so fast?

June comes behind Eddie and puts her arms around him.

JUNE
Something like this really slaps you into understanding what's important.

EDDIE
It sure does. I always said you had too big of a heart.

INT. HOSPITAL ROOM – DAY

SOUNDTRACK – BEATLES – IN MY LIFE

June is asleep. Eddie is sitting facing her, leaning against her.

EDDIE
Jim has been very straight with me. He really doesn't have a choice. You need a new heart soon, and your rare blood type... I can't see you die, I won't see you die.

June wakes up.

JUNE
Have you been here all night?

EDDIE
Yes, where else should I be?

JUNE
You still need to live your life.

                              EDDIE
I need to save you. If I could save you, would you want
me to?

                              JUNE
Ah, yes. Why? Have you been a superhero all this time
and I didn't know it?

                              EDDIE
Kind of. I need to go do some things.

                              JUNE
                    (June takes Eddie's hand)
Thank you for being here. When you come back we
need to have a heart to heart. I didn't want to die without telling you a few things. Then you can tell me a
story.

                              EDDIE
You're not going to die.

Eddie walks to the door, pauses, goes back to June. He leans over and
kisses her. It's a long, feelings filled kiss.

INT. EDDIE'S APARTMENT - DAY

SOUNDTRACK – FRANK SINATRA – MY WAY

Eddie is picking up all his possessions. He has all the boxes labeled with people's names and Goodwill. He is in a great mood. He writes a letter, but all that is seen is the envelope that reads "June".

EXT. RIVERSIDE BEHIND AUDUBON PARK – SUNSET

SOUNDTRACK – NEVILLE BROTHERS – A CHANGE IS GONNA COME

Eddie watches the sunset.

Eddie Tebbe

INT. HOSPITAL ROOM - DAY

SOUNDTRACK – FIFTH DIMENSION – LET THE SUNSHINE IN
Eddie is standing by June's bed as she sleeps.

> EDDIE
> My only regret is that I don't get to say goodbye to
> you. You've been the love of my life. You're beyond
> beauty. I do love you more than life. Be safe in all your
> endeavors and open to the world. Once upon a time…

Eddie gently kisses her lips. June wakes up, but Eddie is gone. She
puts her fingers to her lips.

INT. JIM'S OFFICE – DAY

SOUNDTRACK – BEETHOVEN – PIANO SONATA # 14

Jim is sitting at his desk in his office working on some charts. Eddie
walks in, sits down, and puts a large manila envelope beside him. Jim
smiles.

> JIM
> They never warned me about the paperwork. They
> made us go to school for eight years, then trained us for
> four more, but they never showed us how to do paper-
> work or deal with hospital administration. That might
> have changed my life.
> (looking at his watch)
> Sorry I can't stay long. I have a staff
> meeting in five minutes.

> EDDIE
> I think you may want to cancel.

JIM

I always want to cancel. They're a waste of my time. Is something up?

EDDIE

If I shoot myself in the head right now could my heart be put in June?

(Jim waits for the punch line)

I'm serious.

JIM

It physically can be done, but…. What are we talking about?

EDDIE

How long does she have?

JIM

Well, that's hard to…

EDDIE

Jim, man. A day or two, right?

JIM

Ah, right.

EDDIE

Well then this is it.

Eddie walks to the window. He looks out the window talking with his back towards Jim.

JIM

What?

EDDIE

It's a beautiful fall day. I've always loved fall days when it just starts cooling off. It always makes me giddy. It's a good day to die.

JIM

What?

EDDIE
(not turning around)
I'm going to kill myself and I want my heart to go to June.

JIM

That's not funny.

EDDIE

I'm not trying to be funny.

JIM

You can't just kill yourself.

EDDIE

Sure, I can.

JIM

You might not be a match.

EDDIE

I've had all the tests.

JIM

I know you love June, but killing yourself for her is insane. Plus, it might not work.

Eddie sits sideways in the window. He mostly looks out the window as he talks, occasionally looking at Jim.

EDDIE

I'm betting it will, and I'm not insane. What if I was going to do it anyway?

JIM

Why would you want to do it anyway?

EDDIE
(laughs)
You normal people kill me. What makes you think I haven't considered suicide every day?

JIM

You have a great life.

EDDIE

There are many great things in my life.

JIM

Well!

EDDIE

Well, do I have to explain it to you? Can't you figure things out?

JIM

Maybe I can't, maybe I can, but I'm not letting you off the hook. So sit there and explain away.

EDDIE

I'm losing it. I'm tired and I can't deal with anything anymore. I knew it was coming. I've always wondered when I'd hit the wall. Humans have needs, and when those needs go unfulfilled long enough life becomes unnatural. There are ways to deal with that for a certain time, but then there's nothing to be done. From that point there are only two basic ways to go. First you end your life or second you go crazy. I'm starting to go crazy. I've found no evidence that anybody can live their life alone without suffering one of those fates. The need to be with someone, to connect physically, emotionally, and psychologically, to have them say I want to be with you, and you share everything with them, is only second to the need to eat. When a need goes unfulfilled it creates a black hole inside you. That black hole sucks in the surroundings' energies trying to be fulfilled. That causes an imbalance and you have to build up your other energies to feed the hole. If, like me, that need goes completely unfulfilled that black hole enlarges until it sucks in every remnant of energy, and nothing that is in you or given to you can offset that black hole except that single thing that fulfills the need. Nobody would expect me to survive without food. Why do they expect me to survive without love?

Jim's SECRETARY enters.

SECRETARY

You're late for your meeting.

Jim gets up and takes her by the arm and guides her to the door.

JIM

You tell them I'm tied up and cancel everything else. I'm locking the door. If you knock on it or call me, you'll be fired.

SECRETARY

What's wrong?

JIM

Not now.
(shutting and locking the door.)
Okay, I understand you're not happy. I understand that because of your feelings for June it's hard to see her sick. But you can't just end your life. There are so many good things in your life.

EDDIE

You're right, but nothing is more important than what I'm talking about. Think about humans. At no time in history have humans liked being alone. Listen to people, look at books and poems, movies and music, everything in us needs love. The lengths people go to not to be alone, it's astounding.

JIM

But you're not going to live your life alone. There's somebody out there for you I know it.

EDDIE

I don't doubt that possibility.

JIM

Well, why give up?

EDDIE

It's not a given. Even if it was, I couldn't handle the situation anyway. Last week I took my car in because of a noise. When I picked it up it still made the noise. Take it back, right? I couldn't. I took it to another mechanic. I still heard the noise, so I took it to a third mechanic. Five days, three mechanics, and a hundred dollars later the noise was gone, but it should have been one day, one mechanic, and twenty-five dollars. I couldn't just say I still hear the noise. Any situation that might turn slightly tense, not even close to conflictive, but just cause me to assert myself, is beyond my capability to deal with.

JIM

That doesn't make sense.

EDDIE

You said it, but it's my life. How can I possibly conquer my biggest challenge if I can't handle any simple situation?

JIM

You don't seem distraught by this.

EDDIE

I'm not. I've never been happier or more at peace. You're not looking on the bright side. June will be saved. That's the important part.

JIM

You love her enough to end your life for her?

EDDIE

Yes. Even if I was in perfect condition.

                    JIM
Has she approved this plan?

                   EDDIE
No.

                    JIM
Can you imagine what she will feel like?

                   EDDIE
She'll be able to feel. She'll be alive.

                    JIM
Do you understand how important you are? I need you.

                   EDDIE
It's not fair, Jim.

                    JIM
                  (pause)
There are other things to be done to get you back on
track. There's psychological help. There are happy
drugs. I can help. We can get you through this. I know
you've been through a lot, but the second half of your
life will be the pay off. It will be so good.
          (Eddie shakes his head)
Why not?
          (Eddie points to the envelope.)

                   EDDIE
It's the HD test. I have it. I don't have a second half of
my life.
          (Jim exhales and falls back in his chair)
Do you see where I'm coming from now? June is too
special of a human to die this young. For me, this is my
life. Maybe this is why I have existed.

Eddie Tebbe

> JIM
> I can't sit here and say it's okay.

> EDDIE
> I didn't come here for your permission.

> JIM
> (gets up and walks to the door.)
> I need to take a walk.

> EDDIE
> (smiles)
> I understand perfectly well that this isn't fair to you.

> JIM
> Don't worry about me. Let's concentrate on you.

Jim leaves the room then shuts the door behind him.

INT. OUTSIDE OFFICE – MOMENTS LATER

SOUNDTRACK – NONE

Jim starts giving his secretary instructions quietly.

> JIM
> Get on the phone and get the head of Psych. down here
> right now. He's probably still in the meeting.

> SECRETARY
> (starts dialing)
> What's…

There's a gunshot from Jim's office.

CU- ON JIM'S SHOCKED FACE

EXT. CEMETERY – DAY

SOUNDTRACK – BILL WITHERS – AIN'T NO SUNSHINE

Jim stands at Eddie's grave as the crowd leaves. Claire is holding on to his arm. Jim doesn't cry.

> JIM
> I need a moment. Can you wait in the car?
> (Claire kisses him as she leaves)
> Now what, man? Do you think this is all right? If you had given me time maybe I'd been able to figure out a better solution than this. You were always so self-right-eous. Well, damn you, damn you.

INT. JUNE'S KITCHEN - DAY

SOUNDTRACK – JOHN BOUTTE – SOMEONE TO WATCH OVER ME

June is in her apartment washing dishes. The window over the sink faces the street where Jim and Claire park. He has an envelope in his hand. June meets them at the door.

> CLAIRE
> How are you doing?

> JUNE
> I told you to stop making house calls. I'm doing fine. It's been three months. I was contemplating getting back to work.

> JIM
> Not yet, but soon. You are doing great though. I came about this.

He holds up the envelope.

JUNE

Are those my test results? I really don't want bad news right now.

CLAIRE

No, no indeed.

JIM

I'm not sure what kind of news this is. This is a letter from Eddie. He wanted us to read it together. I was instructed to give it to you when you had recovered.

June bites her lip and holds her heart

JIM

I thought you were strong enough. I could...

JUNE

No, I want to read it. Maybe it will give me some clo sure. Have you...

JIM

I think I'm moving on from my anger. I was so mad and hurt I didn't know how to act and he wasn't there to tell me.
(laughs)
I miss him. I keep waiting for him to walk through my office door and cheer me up. He'll never do that again.

June takes the envelope and sits between Claire and Jim. She opens the envelope, there's a letter and a second envelope with "Test Results" on it. She takes the letter and starts to read it.

JUNE

My Dearest June,

I know that you are reading this with Jim and Claire by your side. It has worked. I don't want for my last thoughts to be same lame explanation of why I decided to end my life. I gave Jim those, and hopefully he can relay them. You three are the most important people in my life. You three are the only ones I hope can understand and forgive me.

Jim, I know I'm not your favorite person right now. I know that I used you and our friendship. In time those feelings will pass, and you'll remember me fondly. You made my life better. Claire, what you brought to my life was unmistakable. Now I leave Jim in your hands. You take it easy, thank you.

June, in my final act of my life I was able to accomplish the only thing that was important, to give of myself completely to someone, to be one with someone. I got to do it with my only true love. I can't predict what might have happened, but at my lowest moment life gave me what I needed. The answer to everything was right there.

It's hard for a person to understand if their life meant something. Did I make a difference? If you have love, a family, and you've treated them right, then that's making a difference. I don't doubt I've been loved by friends and family. I don't doubt that I've affected my world. Unfortunately, those things do not fulfill all the needs inside. I never fit into this world. Although my life has been amazing, I never found peace.

Eddie Tebbe

> Maybe I would have had the strength to carry on, to find
> these things in the second half of my life, but the second
> half has been taken away by the copy of the test results in
> that envelope. I must confess I did not look at the results,
> but I know (but if I'm wrong, I left a deposit for you at the
> hospital's sperm bank. Use them if you can.)

They look at the envelope.

                              JIM
>   Open it.

June hands it to Jim. He opens it, reads it, then shakes his head no.

CU – ON JIM GRIMACING

CU – ON CLAIRE CLOSING HER EYES

CU – ON JUNE BITING HER LIP

JUNE
(continues reading)
It won't have mattered anyway. My mind was made up.
The thing is I would have given my life for yours in any
situation. Remember I owe you one. We were put on
this world to save each other. The only drawback that I
see is guilt. How can I avoid causing the feelings of
guilt you will feel? Everything I'm writing is to that effect. I'm not sure it will work but I rather you alive with
guilt, than dead without. I'd like to assure you that I die
happy and satisfied. That's because of you, June.
You're more beautiful than a sunset. You made my life
mean something, and now you gave my life meaning,
the meaning that allows a person to pass with peace.
Thank you.

My Final Time To Say I Love You.
Eddie

P. S. Once upon a time...

June breaks down crying. Jim and Claire hold her.

Eddie Tebbe

EXT. CEMETERY – DAY

SOUNDTRACK – ERIC CLAPTON – TEARS IN HEAVEN

June is standing at Eddie's grave eight months pregnant. It has just finished raining. The sun is shining bright. She is crying as she puts
flowers on the grave.

> JUNE
>
> I'm sorry I haven't been to visit you. I'm still mad at
> you, you bastard. I don't like this life. I don't like it
> without you. What made you think you could make
> those decisions without talking to me? I wouldn't have
> let you do it, but you knew that. I was your best friend
> so why couldn't you tell me how bad things were? I
> would have done anything for you. You gave me your
> heart, but in the same moment you broke it in a million
> pieces. It's been four years and I still feel this gulf. It's
> worse than any breakup I ever had. You were my sun,
> but I didn't know you'd be a shooting star. Who's going
> to tell me stories?
>
> (cries)
>
> Well, I came here for another reason. As you can see,
> I'm about to have a baby. It's the most incredible feel-
> ing to have a life forming inside me. I'm doing it alone.
> I know it's going to be hard, but it's already been worth
> it. Although I did meet someone a month ago and I feel
> good about it. I know it's a boy, and I've already cho-
> sen his name, Eddie Louis Perry Jr. He's your son dear.
> He's going to be a beautiful boy. I'm going to tell him
> all about his father. I'm going to make sure he under-
> stands how special, strong, and wonderful you were.

JUNE

How amazingly blessed I was to know you, and you not only saved my life you made me live. When he asks me where his father is I'll put his hand on my heart, and say "Right here."

        (holds her heart)

I love you with everything in me. I hope you have found peace.

        (leaning over and kissing the tombstone)

        You're my heart.

Eddie Tebbe

Good-Bye Lovely Linda

Good-bye lovely Linda
You are going away
We sure will miss you
We wish you could stay

Good-bye lovely Linda
With your calming effect
When you are gone
Will things be a hectic mess

Good-bye lovely Linda
We've always relied on you
When you're not here
Who will we turn to

Good-bye lovely Linda
The knowledge you possess
And your experience
Can't just be imparted to the rest

Good-bye lovely Linda
Life moves in funny ways
But never forget
The connections you've made

Good-bye lovely Linda
We understand why
But it will be hard
To say a final good-bye

Good-bye lovely Linda
No matter where you roam
Always remember
Here is always home

Eddie Tebbe

Coping

Chorus:
The ghost in your head
Keeps going around your brain
You can't sleep
Cause of the pouring rain

Verse 1:
You feel like a mouse
That got caught by the cat
You look around the house
But don't know where you're at
Things go slow, things go fast
You think nothing will last

The body of anger comes through the door
You try to run, you try to hide
Nothing will help any more
It comes from inside

Verse 2:
The breath of God comes down
Trying to give you hope
You ignore the signs
You think you can cope
But the beast inside your heart
Can tear you apart

The eyes of forgiveness
Must come into your head
Look at the world with happiness
Before you end up dead

Verse 3:
The hand of life will give you feeling
A bird will sit on your shoulder
It will sing and show you the way
To make it through another day

Let's Get It

Listen up now
World is around
Listen up now
I'll tell you how

Band is grooving but where the song will go
Just is something I don't know
The beat can take us where it wants to
Help out, we're doing the best we can
Late at night alone in my room
Playing with my toys
All those nights on the third floor
Building a groove to make your dreams come true

Chorus:
Trying to take you to a place
I want to get it
Where nobody hurts a thing
I want to get it
There's peace, love, and fun
I want to get it
Open your eyes it can be done
We have to get it

Wake up to the news the world's gone nuts
It really hurt my heart, killing all they want
The leaders playing games, come on
This is serious stuff not one move
Just where are we going
Where will we end up
Intelligence we aren't showing
Stop this slide into oblivion

                    Chorus

Eddie Tebbe

Imagine there's a place we can get to
Across the night sky, pretty sight
Come let's ride everybody, feels right
You will never get there alone, let's get it
Why don't you open your mind
Let some new ideas in
Let the groove take your soul
The funk will teach you a thing or two
Chorus

Fourth Verse:
Imagine there's a man walking his dog alone
Across the levee at sunset, pretty sight
A woman comes the other way, they speak
Before long it becomes a daily thing
They go out on one date
Sparks fly from the start
Never before has he been relaxed
But this is different must be the thing, true love
Chorus

Purest Moment

When I was a kid
Running with the boys
Playing good vs. bad
With imaginary guns
Everything a possible toy
Filthy dirty every day
Feelings were in the second
Pain forgotten within a moment
Able to experience complete joy
The whole world was right there
I knew my place
Whatever else there was
I didn't care

Then one summer day
Everything changed
My world turned upside down
There she was
Visiting for a week
Her aunt and uncle
From down the street
I had known many girls
But in one look I knew
She was unique
Feelings I'd never felt
Sprung to life
The intensity terrified me

As we caught our breath
From racing down the street
Our shirts wet mounds on the
ground
The sun beating our little bodies
She walked around the corner

Strawberry blond hair to her
shoulders
Waving in the light breeze
I stopped dead, memorized
Hypnotized
By her emerald green eyes
Then she smiled at me
Her luminescence radiated
It made me wobbly
I don't understand
What was going on
It took a while to realize
I wasn't going to die
Having to adjust to this new
world
Somehow I made it through the
week
Or though I thought
Following her around
Like a little puppy
Got in a few fights
When the boys teased me
It was definitely
My first true love

Eddie Tebbe

We played all week
Barely left each other's side
There was nothing else
In the world
We fit together
Like nothing I've ever felt
As young as we were
The difference was known
Why couldn't it last forever
I didn't want to think of her
leaving
But she would the next morning
I woke up early
Just to see her off

As we said good-bye
I tried not to cry
Then she leaned in
Putting her lips on mine
They were moist
Soft as a cloud looks
And tasted simply sweet
My world imploded
Exploded
As I stood there watching her
leave
Unable to move
Electricity raced through me
Body, mind, and soul

Now I have lived
A life worth living
Traveling the world
Seen the greatest places
I've loved the deepest
I've made love
Have had buck-wild sex
Until dawn's breaking
I've savored the finest food
I've encountered extraordinary
people
Experiencing the highest
And the lowest
It has all been grand

Yet I'm still searching
And know I'll never find
A moment that pure
A moment where
Innocence collides with
knowledge
Where all possibilities open up
When you know what life is
about
Some discover early
Some discover late
It only happens once
But we chase it the rest of our
lives
So I still search
For that purest moment

It's Me

You're looking to the east
You're looking to the west
I don't know what you're
looking for
You already found the best
I'm not conceited
I don't play that game
But you'll be hard pressed to find
A man quite the same

It's me
Oh baby it's me
It's me it's me
Why can't you see

You're looking left
You're looking right
You're looking for a man
To stay with you all night
I'm the man
The one for you
No other man
Can do what I do

You're looking to the north
You're looking to the south
I'm right in front of your face

Do I have to knock you out?
I'm an original
Can't you see
Ain't nobody around
Anything like me

You're looking far
You're looking near
What you're looking for
Is already here
I'm unique
From head to feet
Compare me to any man
And I'll have him beat

You're looking up
You're looking down
You're looking for something
That can't be found
I'm the one
One of a kind
Make love to me once
And I know you'll be mine
So come to bad
That's how it should go
And for God's sake stop looking
out that window

Eddie Tebbe

Tomorrow's Too Late for Me

Hold your breath, please turn away
Don't you say a word to me
I wanted you yesterday
Tomorrow's too late for me

With your eyes, you took my heart
Tore it apart, hurting me
I wanted you yesterday
Tomorrow's too late for me

You turned your back, made me wait
Another date, passed by me
I wanted you yesterday
Tomorrow's too late for me

You stopped smiling, love passed by
I had to cry, could it be
I wanted you yesterday
Tomorrow's too late for me

Crying eyes, you're feeling bad
A little sad, over me
I wanted you yesterday
Tomorrow's too late for me

Now you want another chance
But don't do that to me
I wanted you yesterday
Tomorrow's too late for me

Hold your breath, please turn away
Don't you say a word to me
I wanted you yesterday
Tomorrow's too late for me

Funk Emergency

Call the doctor
Call the nurse
Better call someone
It might get worse
We're coming in
At full speed
So get ready
It's a funk emergency

It's an overdose
She's exhausted
Dripping with sweat
She almost lost it
Her body aches
From head to toe
Dancing all night
At the show

He's in withdrawal
I can tell
White and clammy
Looks like hell

He needs some music
It has been too long
He needs to hear
A good funky song

Call the doctor
Call the nurse
Better call someone
It might get worse
We're coming in
At full speed
So get ready
It's a funk emergency

We're back we're back
What's right is right
We'll solve some problems
For you tonight
Some will be caused
We can't help that
Just have some fun
That's where it's at

Eddie Tebbe

The Feeling

Kelly Smits saw the place from a block away. She drove her twenty-year old, '96 model, Mazda 626, with New York plates, straight up to the building, parking in the first spot available. She was on the corner of Napoleon and Tchoupitoulas looking at Tipitina's, a place she had dreamed about, and had tried to get to for years.

Tipitina's, known locally as Tip's, was the grand dame of New Orleans' music clubs. It had been in the same building, a big two-story house renovated into a bar, since the seventies. It did close for a few years in the early eighties but reopened bigger and better. There were other hard times because of the economy, other bars with better locations and more money for bigger names, and bad management. Tip's survived it all. There was an intangible feeling that Tip's had that other places didn't. Bands sounded better even though the sound system wasn't the best. The place wasn't comfortable, the air conditioner didn't cool things off, there were few stools and no tables, and the place was dirty. When bands played at Tip's it was about the music. The bands felt it, and so did the people.

For five years Kelly listened to anybody who had been to New Orleans and heard wonderful stories. The most frequent recommendation was to go to Tip's. So that's what she did. It was only three in the afternoon and Kelly didn't know if the place was open. It was hard to tell from the outside. She walked up, pushed one of the double glass doors which opened, and went inside. The place was dark, not because the lights weren't on, but they were dim. The light coming in through the glass doors was the brightest light in the place. The sunbeam shone directly on the bronzed bust of Henry Roeland Byrd, known as Professor Longhair or just Fess, the patron saint of Tip's. The bar got its name from a Fess song. The bust and gigantic portrait of him over the stage were there to guard Tipitina's soul.

Kelly's eyes adjusted to the darkness and she walked to the bar along the far-right wall. The bartender and a person reading the paper, at the far end of the bar, were the only people in the place. The bartender was busy cleaning. He hadn't noticed that someone had entered. The other person didn't care. Kelly walked slowly taking a good look around. The place was bigger than she pictured. People gave her the impression that Tip's was small. Kelly found it very spacious, with a big stage, and a second story balcony.

The bartender noticed Kelly while she was looking the other way. She turned quickly sending her dark brown hair, that came halfway down her back, airborne when he spoke, not expecting the silence to be broken.

"Can I help you?" the bartender said with a smile. He was in his fifties with gray hair and a beard.

"I guess I'll take a beer." She paused, "A local beer."

"Abita?"

"No, I've had that."

"Dixie? You probably haven't had that."

"No, is it good?"

"Depends on you. Some people love it and others think it's piss. Want one?"

"Yeah, why not."

He handed her the bottle; she took a sip but said nothing.

"I take it you're not from here. I'm Rich."

"I'm Kelly." She reached her hand out, but he was washing dishes. Instead he winked at her.

"Are you here for a visit or for good?"

"I don't know yet. I'm here for a while at least. I'm here to learn about good guitar playing."

"You've come to the right place. Do you play?"

"I've had some success playing guitar in New York. I also play a little piano, and I sing."

When she was five, her parents made her take piano lessons. She was very talented but didn't like being forced to play, so she stopped. The dreams of money and fame caused her to start playing guitar as a teenager. At eighteen her technique was good. She moved from a small town in Michigan to New York City and started her career.

"Would you like the numbers of some teachers?" Rich asked.

"No, no, I'm very confident about my playing. I'm looking for the feeling I got when I heard a boot-leg tape of Ryan Jones. I'd been playing in New York for ten years with local success, but something wasn't right. I thought it was because I hadn't hit it big. Then one night at someone's party they played that tape. It was like an epiphany. That was what I wanted. To make people feel like he made me feel. That was how to hit it big, get that feeling. I tried to find more recordings, but only found three poorly produced CDs that were twenty years old. While looking for Ryan's music I found out there were more great guitar players from New Orleans, and I fell in love with it all. So finally, I'm here. Do you know anything about Ryan Jones?"

Rich looked around. The man at the end of the bar only moved to turn the pages of the paper. Rich smiled looking into Kelly's dark brown eyes.

"Ryan 'Little King' Jones. You were right to get an amazing feeling listening to him. I've been around Tip's since it opened in one form or another and seen some incredible, unbelievable music, but he was the best. He played with more emotion than anybody. Every song, every note had feeling. I miss his playing."

Kelly was interested in everything she could find out about Ryan. In her research she wasn't able to find out much about Ryan and what had happened to him. She was hoping he was still around.

"So what happened to him?"

"At seventeen he exploded onto the music scene. After five years he was the biggest thing going. Then he got a recording deal and moved to L.A. His playing was still great, but the emotion was gone. His three CDs didn't do well so he came back. When he came back, he played with a vengeance. For three years he took music where it had never been. Then he just disappeared and hasn't played since." Rich cracked his neck.

"Is he around? I would love to talk to him."

"He's around, but he only pops up now and then."

The man at the end of the bar turned slightly and motioned for another beer. Rich took him another. Kelly saw the man's profile. He had very beautiful skin, smooth and clear, but there was a deep gash-like scar that came across the corner of his right eye that caught her attention. "That must have hurt," she thought.

Rich returned and continued the conversation with Kelly. She needed some information about a place to stay and a job. Rich did his best to help her out, giving her names and numbers. She was tired after her long drive.

"I'm beat. I think I'll go find a hotel." Kelly got up and put three dollars on the bar.

Rich gave the money back. "It's on me. See that stack of magazines by the door? That's the 'Wavelength', the local music magazine. Take one. It's a good way to learn what's going on around town."

"Thanks," Kelly walked towards the door.

The man at the end of the bar walked to where Rich was and smiled at him.

"Nice body," the man said.

"She wants to talk to you."

"I can hear just fine, thank you."

"You think she has it?"

"How can I tell?"

"But you're intrigued, aren't you?"

Ryan walked to the door. "We'll see, my friend, we'll see," he said without turning around.

It took Kelly only a week to settle in. She found an apartment uptown, which was the hotbed of the music scene, and got a job bartending days at F & M's Patio Bar. She was astonished by how nice people were and how willing they were to help a stranger. People wanted to be friends upon first meeting. Four days into her stay she already had a handful of numbers as well as invitations to meet and do stuff. With only three shifts a week money wouldn't be flowing, but the bills would be paid. She could work more, but she wanted as much free time as possible for music, to learn and play.

Every Monday night was open mic at The Maple Leaf. Kelly wanted to jump in with both feet. She didn't have much original material so covers would have to do for now. Trying not to put too much pressure on herself or let her expectations run high, she couldn't help getting nervous while setting up her equipment. She looked around the bar at the fifty or so people. Few were looking at her, but she felt everyone staring. Stage fright had never been a problem, but she felt like so much was riding on this performance. Rich caught her eye giving her a wink, a smile, and a thumbs-up. It made her feel better that he had come.

It was time to start. Kelly kept things simple. It was only her and her guitar. She played some folk and blues, focusing on her playing, not singing. Once comfortable she started looking around. A few people danced, some talked, but most listened. One person in the audience struck her as being familiar, but she couldn't place him until he turned, showing the scar across his right eye. He was studying her. For a moment she forgot about the song she was playing, then recovered quickly. That was "him" something told her.

The vibe from the crowd was good. As Kelly studied the crowd, she saw smiles and wide eyes. Nobody had their eyes closed. She wanted their eyes closed, to make the audience be drawn into the sound, overwhelming them. Nobody was feeling the music enough to close their eyes. She wouldn't hit it big unless they felt it.

After the show she received words of encouragement from Rich and some other people. She didn't hear what they said because she was trying to find the scar man in the crowd. He was headed for the door. Kelly caught up to him outside.

"Wait up," she said loudly.

Ryan turned knowing it was he she wanted even though there were many other people outside.

"Yes?" Ryan said with irritation.

"What did you think?" Kelly was afraid to ask if he was Ryan Jones.

He looked bewildered. "You ran out here to ask my opinion? Who am I to you?"

"Well----I just thought----never mind. Sorry to bother you."

She wanted to ask, but it wouldn't come out, plus this guy was too young. He turned with a knowing what you're thinking smile and started to walk away.

Kelly said really quickly, "You're Ryan 'Little King' Jones, aren't you?"

Ryan turned slowly. "What would ever give you that idea?"

"No real reason, just my gut feeling."

"Gut feeling?"

"Yeah, gut feeling. I'm right, right?" Kelly was more confident.

Ryan thought for a minute rubbing his hand over the scar.

"Yeah, yeah right." He turned again and walked away without stopping.

Kelly didn't know what to say, "Wait, wait, I want to talk to you."

"I know what you want. If I feel like talking, you'll see me again," he said without turning around.

A month had gone by and Kelly hadn't seen Ryan again. Disappointed, she tried not to dwell on it. Things were still going well. She was still playing at The Maple Leaf on Monday nights, and some other open mic nights at other bars. A bass player and drummer were now accompanying her. With a keyboard player joining soon she was on the verge of having a band. Their first paying gig was in three weeks. She was off to a fast start and that made her feel good. There was much practicing to be done, and, with Kelly playing on her own daily, her fingers were sore.

F & M's was slow. Kelly sat daydreaming about the roar of the crowd. She was going to play for the people.

"Can I have a Dixie, please?"

Kelly awoke from the daydream. "Sure, that's two fifty." It took her a few seconds to realize who it was.

"So, I'm here. What you want to talk about?" Ryan said.

It took her a little time to gather her thoughts. "Well, I guess it's simple. I want you to teach me about how you do what you do... or did."

"You think it's that simple?" Ryan took a big swig of his beer.

"I doubt it's simple, but I'm willing to learn and work hard." She was put off by his attitude but was hoping it was temporary.

"What have you been doing since you got here?"

"I've been practicing like crazy. Also trying to get a band together, and going to see, and talking to some of the other good local guitar players. Not getting much sleep, that's for sure."

He cleared his throat, "I like your desire and your playing, so maybe I'll teach you a thing or two."

She was so excited she wanted to start right then. She tried to keep cool but not very successfully. Her reaction caused him to laugh.

"Have you heard of The Mermaid Lounge?" Ryan asked.

"No."

"Get the address from the *Wavelength* and meet me there tomorrow at ten."

"Okay."

Ryan finished his beer, put three dollars on the bar, and walked out.

Kelly was fifteen minutes late getting to The Mermaid Lounge. Even with directions she got lost. Ryan saw her parking. As she got out of the car, she took her guitar out of the trunk. Ryan walked over and told her to put the guitar back. She was confused but complied. He explained to her that they were there to observe. She understood the value of learning other guitar players' techniques. She just wished he would have told her his plan. She felt a little stupid bringing her guitar. Ryan didn't seem to care so she relaxed.

The band was really good, and Kelly watched the guitar player all night. She hoped Ryan would sit in with the band; he didn't. He didn't pay much attention to the band or Kelly. He socialized most of the time leaving her to watch the band.

After the show Kelly expected they would sit down and talk about what she should have learned from this experience. She sat and watched Ryan walk towards her anticipating his words of wisdom.

"Do you want another lesson?" Ryan said with a slur.

Kelly took a second to collect her thoughts before answering, suppressing her New York attitude. Patience was never her strong suit, but she gave him the benefit of the doubt.

"Sure. When?"

"Tomorrow around two at Benny's."

"I'm working until eight."

Ryan was already walking out the door. "No, two A.M."

For the next week and a half Kelly didn't get much sleep. She was going out every night, seeing some great bands, but not always great guitar playing. She was trying to keep an open mind. He would tell her to observe, and then would barely stay with her, much less talk or explain what she was supposed to be learning.

Kelly sat more disgusted than any other night. They were at Donna's seeing the Mark Mullins Band. The band sounded great, but it was a brass band with no guitar or piano.

Kelly was tired and wanted to go home. At the set break she decided to leave. Ryan was close behind her.

"Are you going?" he said, unaware anything was wrong.

"I'm tired, and I'm going home," she snapped.

"It's very important to watch Mark play."

"He plays great, but he plays trombone, not guitar." She sat on some steps nearby and wiped her face.

"You still don't get it. Do you?"

Kelly didn't like his patronizing tone of voice. The New York attitude took over for the first time since she came to New Orleans.

"I guess I don't. Why don't you tell me? Maybe you can't. Maybe you quit playing because you lost it. Maybe you can't teach me shit." She was now standing face to face with Ryan who was taken aback from this show of aggression but liked that it was there.

He gave her a charming look and said, "Okay, okay. I was hoping you would realize what I was trying to show you. I like your desire to learn. Moving here from New York shows me something special but the motivation behind the move is wrong. Why do you want to learn to do what I used to do?"

"Well." She knew why. "Because you touched me when I listened to your music. I want to do that."

"Why?"

"Why do I want to touch people?"

"Why?"

She hesitated. "Because I want to make people feel good."

"Why?"

She thought for longer this time. "To make it big," she said waiting for another why.

"That's the problem. Your goal can never be to make it big. You have to play for the music and yourself. Some of the best musicians starve to death, and some of the worst make it big. Some of the best make it big, and some of the worst starve. It doesn't matter. Make the music in your heart. It sounds like a cliché, but it's true."

Kelly didn't say anything. She sat back down and was absorbing his comment. She had heard it before, but now it meant something.

Ryan sat next to her putting his hand on her shoulder, "Think about what Mark is doing when he's playing, when he's in that moment. It's only him and his trombone. He's not performing. There's no money, no audience, no worries, and sometimes no other band members. Being a good performer is important. Making money and pleasing the audience are important, but if it's that musical place you're trying to get to you have to try to become the music. It's that moment you need to strive for. You're good, real good, but you need to open your mind and heart."

"Okay, then can you help me?" she asked.

He smiled. "From now on I'll be more helpful."

"That would be nice."

"Okay then, let's go back inside." They got up and walked back inside. "You have to watch and listen to Mark at the same time, but separately. No matter whether he gets into that place or not he sounds great, but when he gets into it you can hear, feel, and see the difference. He goes from moving and looking around to having his head down and eyes closed. The sound gets better, and the people listening can feel it. It's magical."

They took two seats in the front. Neither drank any more until after the show. Ryan sat with Kelly and pointed out things to her. She was now getting something from the experience. She was starting to learn what she needed to grow musically.

"How ya feeling?" Ryan asked looking down at Kelly, who was sitting on the couch with her eyes closed. She slowly opened her eyes.

"I'm doing okay. A little nervous though," she answered.

"There's a pretty good crowd for your first real gig."

"I thought I wasn't supposed to worry about stuff like that," she said with a smirk.

He sat next to her and patted her leg, "You're not, but I can."

They sat in silence for a few minutes.

"Don't expect too much at first. You have a lot of old habits that will take a while to break. Give yourself time."

Eddie Tebbe

It was weird for Kelly to play and not think about how she sounded, how the audience reacted, or how many people were there. She was changing. She only studied the audience's reactions five times the whole night.

For the next six months Kelly and Ryan spent an abundant amount of time together. Without playing she was learning more about how to make good music than ever before. It was a great teacher student relationship. She was also becoming attached to him. She wanted to know more about him. She wanted to be friends. Ryan only talked about music. Kelly knew nothing about his life, where he lived, what he did for a living, or anything like that, and every time she tried to inquire he would avoid answering. She was afraid to push because it might have a negative effect on their teacher student relationship. She figured their relationship would change in time, as soon as she had learned enough.

With Ryan's help, Kelly's band got a gig at Tip's. She had made enormous strides in her playing, and she was happy about that. She thought less about other things and was coming closer to that place she wanted to achieve. But she didn't feel that she had truly gotten there yet. If there was a gig that she felt could help her make that leap to the next level, it was the Tip's gig.

The whole band was excited to be playing Tip's. If they made a good impression there it meant something. At sound check Kelly rubbed the bust of Fess like Ryan said he did before every gig.

As the band members peeked up front to see the turnout, which was very good for a first gig at Tip's, Kelly and Ryan sat holding hands. She was much calmer than she ever thought she would be. All of Ryan's talk about not pushing things, about letting things flow, had made a difference.

"You'll do great," he said.

"I'm not even worried," she answered.

"Okay then. Do it." He leaned over and gave her a light kiss.

She paused just before going on stage. There was something in the air. The excitement, the energy, the power, the feelings were there. She could feel it. It was almost tangible. Her heart started beating faster and she ran out on stage in a blur.

The show went by so fast Kelly couldn't believe it was time for the encore. She knew she had played better than ever before. There were a few times during the show that she looked around. People were getting into it. Their eyes were closed. She knew it before she looked. She could feel it.

She played the encore with all her heart. This was what the next level felt like. Kelly loved it, and she didn't want it to end. In the middle of the encore she took her solo. Everything else ceased being. It was just her and the music. Her eyes were shut, her mind was closed to distractions, and her heart poured out through the music. When the song was over, she slowly opened her eyes. The sound of the cheering came back, the reality of where she was and what she was doing came back, and she looked around. Ryan was standing by the bar. Kelly could see him clear as day. He was glowing. His eyes were closed and there was a glimmer from the tears on his cheeks.

After the show it took Kelly five minutes to start wondering where Ryan was. Wasn't he going to celebrate this moment with her? He was the reason she had gotten here. She went out front to look for him, but he was nowhere to be seen. She caught the eye of Rich who was halfway down the bar serving drinks.

"Have you seen Ryan?" she asked loudly, trying to speak over the music.

Rich was trying to deal with his customers and gave her a signal to wait a minute. As soon as he could, he walked over.

"What?"

"Have you seen Ryan?"

"Yeah he was just here. I think he went home."

"Home----Why----I thought----Home?"

"He just left. Maybe you can catch him," he said trying to relieve her confusion.

"What way did he go?"

"He lives on Constance and Jena."

"Where's that?"

"Three blocks up, one over, in the old fire station."

"Thanks." She patted his hand and started to run through the crowd.

"Hey," Rich yelled to stop her.

She turned around.

"You were great tonight," he said softly, and she understood.

"Thank you," she mouthed back, then turned around and headed out the door.

She walked quickly down Napoleon towards Constance. Off in the distance she saw a man's figure turn the corner onto Constance. She picked up her pace to try to gain ground. As she turned the corner onto Constance she saw Ryan entering his house, and she slowed down, getting more nervous the closer she got to his front door. She rang the doorbell hoping it wasn't the wrong thing to do. Ryan answered the door.

"Kelly, what are you doing here?" he said genuinely surprised

"I'm not sure. Why did you leave?"

Ryan sat down on the top step. He didn't say anything for a while. She sat on the step below and looked up at him.

"What's wrong?" she asked.

"You did great tonight. Just remember, to keep that feeling, you have to work on it. It can slip away. Never get sidetracked."

"Thank you and okay, but why did you leave without talking to me?" She put her hand on his knee.

"You don't need me anymore. Take what you've learned, but I can't help you anymore."

She grabbed his hands. "I don't believe that. I know you can teach me more, and what if you can't? We can't be friends? I've grown very attached to you. I want to know what's wrong."

He pulled away. "Look, I can't deal with this right now or even at all. You have all I can give. I can't be around you anymore..."

"I don't understand." She had a mixture of hurt and anger in her voice.

"And you won't," he said as he got up to go inside.

"Did I do something wrong?"

He stopped, and without turning around said softly. "You reminded me of me." He continued inside and shut the door.

Kelly lost track of time sitting on the steps. So many thoughts ran through her brain, so many feelings ran through her heart, that it took a long time just to get herself centered.

As she wiped the tears out of her eyes and stood to leave, she heard a faint sound coming from inside. Even though not clear it moved her. Instead of walking away she walked to the door. Without thinking she put her hand on the doorknob, turned it, and the door opened. The faint sound turned into clearer music. It was the strumming of an acoustic guitar. Even at a low and muffled volume it was the most beautiful song she had ever heard. She followed the music to another door. When she opened it, a flood of bottled up music flowed over her like a river. The emotion behind the music made her weak. She leaned against the door for support.

Kelly made her way up the stairs. As she entered the large room at the top, she saw a fully equipped recording studio, but everything was covered with sheets and dusty. She saw an almost translucent figure of Ryan facing the corner of the room. Very weak she fell on her knees and slumped forward. The music was playing games with her soul. It was reopening old emotional wounds then healing them again. It felt like she was a jigsaw puzzle that the music blew apart then put back together, but this time the pieces fit. Kelly looked up, Ryan was gone, and there was a sphere of light and colors trilling around. The music was coming out of it. The beauty of it drew her towards it. She crawled to the light, towards the music. The closer she got, the more peaceful she felt. She reached out to touch the light, to feel the music, and as her finger made contact there was a shearing sound and a force that blew her back causing her to lose consciousness.

As Kelly regained consciousness she was disoriented. The first clear vision was Ryan looking down at her.

"Where-----------What------I--I--I--." She rubbed her forehead.

"Take it easy." He was holding her hands.

She tried to sit up. "You, you, became the music?"

He laid her back down. "Calm down. You've been through an--ah--unusual experience. Don't try to think about it."

"You became the music."

He looked away and she saw a new scar across the back of his neck.

"Did I do that?" she asked as she rubbed his neck.

"Yes, yes."

"I don't know what to say." She was a little stronger. "I've never heard music so pure, so soft and hard, so sad and happy. I've never had such strong feelings. You have a power unheard of. Why do you keep it to yourself?"

He didn't answer. She turned his head around to look him in the eye.

"Why hide it? You can change things with your gift."

"You don't understand. You can't understand."

There was a long pause. She let go of his face.

"The world isn't ready to understand. It's much more complicated than you think. It doesn't work like you may think."

"I heard you for a few minutes and I'll never be the same. You can change people."

She had lost her burst of strength.

"You need some rest. I need some too. We'll talk about this later."

It didn't take her long to fall asleep. He pulled a cover up to her neck. He rubbed her sleeping face. "You'll understand, and maybe you can do better with it than I have." He left the room.

Kenneth Johnson felt a rush of excitement when he saw Tip's. He parked his twenty-year old, 2016 Mazda 626 in the first place he saw. It was a hot summer's day, and he had driven for eight hours. He hoped the place was open. There was nobody around, but the doors were open. It wasn't any cooler inside, just darker. Kenneth's eyes adjusted to the light change right before bumping into the bust of Fess. He looked around. The place was bigger than he pictured. The first person he saw was an ancient bartender reading the newspaper.

"Can I get a cold one?" Kenneth said as he walked up to the bar. He then noticed a woman sitting at the end of the bar. She faced the other way, but from his angle she was very pretty with beautiful skin, except for three scars, one on her neck, and two on her arm. They were unusual looking. They must have hurt.

"Tap or bottle?" the bartender asked.

"Whatever is colder and make it local."

The bartender gave him a bottle of Dixie.

"Are you here for a visit or to stay?"

"Just four days."

"Nice to meet you. I'm Rich."

"Hi, I'm Kenneth." They shook hands. "I'm trying to find someone. Have you been around here long?"

"Almost sixty years. Long enough."

"I heard a tape done here about fifteen years ago. It was a guitar player named Kelly 'The Queen' Smits. It made such an impression on me. I play, but I want to play like her. That's my ticket. I found other stuff of hers, and it's all great, but nothing in the last ten years. Do you know if she's still around?"

Rich glanced towards the woman at the end of the bar. "Ya, she's still around. She doesn't play anymore. I miss her playing. She was the best I had ever heard. She could play so emotionally it would make a rock cry and then smile."

"Do you know how I can find her?"

"She'll pop up now and then. Maybe you can catch her."

"I only have four days."

"You'll stay."

"I'll stay?"

"I can tell. Believe me, you'll stay. You may be one of the ones that doesn't even go home to get their stuff. That I can't tell, but you'll stay, take my word on it." Rich gave Kenneth a big grin and a wink.

"How much for the beer? I have to get checked into my hotel before six."

"It's on me. Grab one of them magazines by the door. It gives all the information about what's going on, and in the back there's ads for apartments."

"Thanks, you crazy old man. I already love this place," Kenneth said as he left.

Kelly took the last swig of her Dixie. She walked to where Rich is standing.

"He wants to talk to you," Rich said.

"I can hear, you know."

"You think he has it?"

"I don't know yet."

Eddie Tebbe

"Are you going to find out?"

She walked towards the door. "We'll see, my friend, we'll see," Kelly said turning and giving Rich a wink.

Tricky Friend

Verse one:
Oh, it's that old feeling again
Creeping up from deep inside
Lord knows it's not a sin
To want to take a long ride
Loud music, wind blowing
Leaving your cares behind
Not sure where you're going
Feeling good as you pass the signs

Chorus:
I love my home
But I want to go
The road is calling
I want you to know
There's good and bad
I've seen the show
There's happy and sad
Dancing in the front row

Verse two:
The road sings its song
Drawing people in
It does not take long
To forget where you've been
It sounds so romantic
To be out on the road
It's not so fantastic
If you bring a heavy load

Eddie Tebbe

Verse three:
Having that freedom
Can be a big help
Getting caught in the dope
Won't solve your self
The road's a tricky friend
Use it wise, use it well
I hope that in the end
There's a good story to tell

Got Fess

(Inspired by The Fess Heads)
He enchants your heart
He infects your soul
That's why he's called
The Bach of rock 'n roll
The one question to ask
The answer must be yes
I know I have
But do you got fess?

9th Ward Jonny

Verse one:
9th ward Jonny, he's a cool cat I say
9th ward Jonny, comes strolling down the way
People part like the Red Sea
Nobody wants to take responsibility
For making him late he gots to go
He's rolling on to the next show

Chorus:
9th ward Jonny, he rolls, he rolls
9th ward Jonny is rolling
9th ward Jonny, he rolls, he rolls
9th ward Jonny is rolling
9th ward Jonny, he rolls, he rolls
9th ward Jonny is rolling

Verse two:
He's not a pimp, gangster, or thug
He's not a dealer of any drug
He's not flashy by any means
But he's chilling on the scene
He's a player of the highest kind
He's an ivory twinkler divine

Verse three:
It's like Jekyll and Hyde at first sight
Off stage mild mannered and nice
On stage he becomes a madman
Pounding those keys into sand
On stage he doesn't say a word
His fingers are the best I've heard

Eddie Tebbe

Bone Funk

Chorus:
It's a bone funk
Going to funk you to the bone
It's a bone funk
Ain't going to leave you alone
It's a bone funk
Going to funk you to the bone
It's a bone funk
There is no reason to stay home

Verse 1:
Pay homage to
The God of funk
Try to get through
All of this junk
Everyday
Every time
Every way
Every rhyme

Verse 2:
This bad funk goes
Straight through the skin
Your head and toes
Will let it in
Reaches the bone
It takes a hold
Leave it alone
It's much too bold

Verse 3:
Nobody wants
To get too old
A person's haunts
Will turn them cold
The funk will keep
People alive
Won't get too deep
With all the jive

Old Man with One Glove

I play the devil's music in devilish time
That's what they say about rock and roll
But it's the only thing that is mine
And it just may save my soul
That's why I play rock and roll

I was born by the devil's hand
I've been on the road since I was five
Somewhere along the line I joined a band
I had to stay alive
To get through the bullshit and jive

It was a small bar in New Orleans
Where I found my love
It was there on the scene
It must have come from up above
Came through an old man with one glove

He played the guitar like a God
I couldn't keep my eyes off him
For the first time I didn't feel odd
That was when I picked up a guitar
And I finally fit in

Eddie Tebbe

Chasing Love from New Orleans to Seattle

Chorus:
Chasing love from New Orleans to Seattle
With a stop in Dallas just to change planes
Flying into the night not knowing what to expect
Fears and hopes collide within me
Not being able to eat the meal in front of me
I'm thinking, wishing, praying, and hoping
Staring out on the dark night sky

I still remember how we first met
She seemed so interested to know me better
But I was shy and waited too long
She was seeing another guy
I was still picking up on certain vibes
Could I be wrong about what I was feeling
I was waiting around for my chance to find out
Then she went home leaving me wondering
                                        Chorus
With nothing said and nothing done
Except some looks and a slow dance
What makes me think there's something
It's the feeling I have deep in my heart
It's the feeling I have only had a few times
It's the feeling I have to follow no matter what
Are her feelings even close to mine?
She was very excited to hear I was coming
                                        Chorus
Fate has never been kind to me in love
My heart has been broken in many ways
There are basic needs that go unfulfilled
But I still believe fate will come through
Across the country in Seattle she lives her life
Can I become a part of it almost overnight?
There are so many obstacles that keep me from love
I'm not going to let geography be another one
                                        Chorus

Smell the Funk

Chorus:
You have to smell the funk
With your olfactory nerve
You have to smell the funk
It's something you deserve
You have to smell the funk
It should penetrate your nose
You have to smell the funk
Feel it in your toes

Verse 1:
Some people think
Music is in the ear
They've never been
Way, way down here
In New Orleans
Music is alive
It walks and talks
And never dies

Verse 2:
The kind of music
We call funk
Can't be heard
By any punk

Using your senses
You hear, see, and feel
But if you can't smell
Funk has no appeal

Verse 3:
Walking down the street
There's a smell in the air
It pulls you in
You better beware
It comes from a bar
Where the funk is played
Although you try
You can't stay away

Verse 4:
Some smells are good
Some smells are bad
Funk smells the best
That you ever had
You go home stinky
Smelling like sweat
You know you had fun
When your shirt's all wet

Eddie Tebbe

Stumbling Joe

Chorus:
Stumbling Joe, he's tripping, wobbling, bumbling
Out of the bar late at night
Stumbling Joe, he's windering, wondering, pundering
What has happened to his life

Verse one:
Stumbling Joe grew up dirty, dirt poor
Stumbling Joe's family couldn't afford any doors
Stumbling Joe only had a third-grade education
Stumbling Joe moved across the nation

Verse two:
Stumbling Joe knocked-up Maria at fifteen
Stumbling Joe never was too keen
Stumbling Joe went to that war, I don't know the name
Stumbling Joe if you ask me has never been the same

Verse three:
Stumbling Joe knew he didn't father all those kids
Stumbling Joe never asked Maria what she did
Stumbling Joe worked in the factory all his life
Stumbling Joe is a hard-worn leathery sight

I Was Born to Drum

I was born to drum
It is in my soul
It never gets old
My body looks like drumsticks

I was born to drum
From an early age
I could not be caged
I needed to get a fix

I was born to drum
It's in my heartbeat
The way I walk streets
It's how I get my kicks

I was born to drum
To earn a living
With no misgivings
I take a little pride

I was born to drum
Demons had me
So hard to break free
The drums always a guide

I was born to drum
I have led a life
Wonderful insight
The journey's quite a ride

Eddie Tebbe

Fantasies

Eugene waited for the elevator in One Shell Square. A lady with long black hair, wearing a long flowing wrap around skirt and a loose blouse, was the only other person waiting. When the elevator came, they got in. Eugene pressed the 44th floor and the lady pressed the 50th. He watched the lady intently. She looked at him, and they looked in each other's eyes for a few seconds before the lady looked away. He couldn't believe his luck. He moved closer to the lady.

"I know what you want," he whispered.

He put his hands on her arms and started rubbing. He rubbed down her arms and onto her legs. Then one of his hands found the break in the skirt. The hand worked its way under the skirt and rubbed the lady over her panties. The other hand found its way under the blouse and rubbed her breast over her bra. The lady closed her eyes, opened her legs a little, and started moaning. He kept rubbing. The elevator stopped at the 44th floor. When the door opened, he stepped out in the lobby with a big grin. The elevator's door closed behind him.

Eugene entered Cooter Brown's. It was his favorite hangout. He had been there most of the day but left to go home and get ready for Friday night. The whole place seemed different. The night crew was now working, and the night people were now out. He carried himself with the attitude and bravado of Casanova. He knew he could get any woman in the room at any time and had a reputation for doing so. All the men wanted to know his secret.

Eugene sat at the bar and ordered a beer. Before the beer got there some of his admirers were already around him. He loved the attention and reputation. He went to great lengths to perpetuate it. He drank the beer and told of his latest encounter. All the guys were amazed. They wanted to hear more, but he was called away by Windgate, the owner of the bar, who was his oldest friend.

"What's up, bro?" Windgate said as they hugged.

"Same old thing," Eugene replied as they sat down at Windgate's table.

Eddie Tebbe

They talked for a while about what had happened while Windgate was on vacation, about sports, movies, whatever came up, but then the conversation turned serious.

"Well, I did it," Windgate said.

"Did what?"

"I proposed to Susan."

"You did? Congratulations." Eugene grabbed Windgate's shoulder. "That's great, really great. When?"

"We're going to wait a year."

They sat there smiling at each other.

"What about you? When are you going to stop messing around? You're the last one. You're next."

Eugene took a swig of his beer. "I'm having a great time. I'm hoping I never get the sign."

"You still believe in that voodoo stuff?"

"When we went downtown that night and went into that voodoo shop, when we each got one wish, I wished to know when a girl was my true love. The woman did that hocus pocus and told me I now had the ability to know when a woman loved me. I didn't believe, but ever since then I've been able to read women's fantasies. I just look into their eyes and I know what they want. Maybe she did the wrong hocus pocus, but I wouldn't have dreamed of asking for this power." Eugene laughed. "I mean, please."

"What a night that was. If I would have halfway believed those wishes would come true I would have asked for something long term. To get laid that night, what a waste of a wish. And you, what a fucking lucky break." Windgate shook his head and took a sip of beer. "So what's the bet for tonight?"

"I don't know. You tell me," Eugene said.

Windgate thought for a minute. "Three new women, separately, on the premises."

"That might be a bit much. There may not be three women who fantasize about having sex in public here."

"Chicken."

"Okay, but don't spend all your money."

They talked for a while more. Then Windgate got called away to deal with a problem.

From across the room Vern yelled for Eugene to come over. Vern was a nice enough guy, but Vern took to Eugene a million times more than Eugene took to Vern. Eugene walked over, hoping he wouldn't get stuck all night.

"Hey man, come over here and meet someone," Vern said walking towards him.

They shook hands, walked to Vern's table, and sat down. He was introducing Eugene to his date. Eugene looked at the woman but saw nothing special. He was busy scoping out the bar for his conquests.

"I'm sorry. What was your name?" Eugene asked.

"Dominique."

"Dominique, very beautiful. Nice to meet you."

"Maybe I shouldn't introduce y'all. Eugene here is the biggest lady killer in town." Vern laughed. "Can you believe that? Short, chubby, balding, with glasses, and can get any woman any time."

"Shut up, Vern," Eugene said.

"No, no, I'm intrigued," Dominique said. "Is that an inside joke or are you a lady killer?"

"No joke," Vern said before Eugene could reply.

"Yo Vernmeister," a deep voice said from a few tables away. It was some of Vern's old frat brothers.

"Excuse me for a sec," Vern said. "I haven't seen those guys for a while. I'll be back."

Eugene watched the interaction between the frat brothers with wonder. His attention was pulled back to Dominique when she spoke.

"Why are you a lady killer?"

"I don't think of it like that."

"Then how do you think of it?"

"I have a gift of being able to give women what they want. It's what I do."

"What does that mean?"

Eugene hesitated. Dominique smiled patiently waiting for an answer. He looked into her eyes waiting to know her fantasies. Nothing was coming. Every time he looked into a woman's eyes, he knew their fantasies, but this woman was like a blank slate. He didn't know what to say or what to do. A life shaking fear overcame him. He nervously excused himself and went outside. What was happening? Was his power gone? He grabbed the first woman he saw, looking straight into her eyes. A flood of fantasies entered his brain. He calmed down a little, but still went home disturbed.

It took two weeks of reading every woman's fantasies for him to accept that there was nothing wrong with him. Dominique was the only woman he had met that didn't have fantasies.

"Hello, lady killer," Dominique said to Eugene's back.

He turned around from the frozen steaks. He was surprised to see her. "Oh, hi."

"Lady killers usually don't run away from ladies." She playfully punched his shoulder.

"Yeah, I'm sorry about that. Something just came over me. I hope I didn't look too stupid."

"Not too much." She laughed.

"Well, I'm just here getting something to cook for dinner. So, maybe I'll see you around." He smiled, grabbed the closest steaks, and started to walk away.

"Wait. I don't feel like cooking. Do you? Why don't we get a bite somewhere?"

He turned around. "I don't think Vern would appreciate that, given my reputation."

"Vern? That was just a date and neither of us wants a second."

He was on the spot. He didn't know what he wanted to do. This woman was a bit forward and definitely weird. He was about to make up an excuse, but then realized this woman presented a challenge he hadn't had in a long time, to get a female in bed without knowing her fantasies. Plus, it wouldn't be good if word got out that he refused a woman, so Eugene accepted her offer.

They went to Joey K's. It was a neighborhood restaurant that was friendly without being too cozy. Eugene felt uncomfortable at first. He was unused to this situation. The conversation was controlled by Dominique. Just get to know you stuff at first. He relaxed as he forgot about the situation and started enjoying her company. They had a lot in common. They laughed about things they've both done in the past as if they had done them together. Before they knew it, they had finished the meal and four cups of coffee. Eugene looked at his watch.

"I really do have to go. I had a lot of fun. Thanks."

"We should do this again. I'll give you my card."

Dominique handed him a card. He kissed her on the cheek and left. As he drove home, he looked at the card. He had a good time with her. Maybe too good. He put the card in his pocket, not knowing if he would call her.

Having decided two days earlier not to call Dominique, Eugene wondered why he was listening to her phone ring. It was an uncontrollable compulsion. After seven rings he went to hang up the phone. At the last moment before the phone was on the hook, he heard a faint hello. He put the phone back to his ear. Dominique was out of breath.

"Hello."

"Hey, Dominique, it's Eugene."

"Eugene, hey, hold on one minute. I was in the shower."

He heard the phone hit the tabletop, and then the sound of wet feet pattering across the floor. He pictured her scurrying through her apartment nude and dripping wet. She was back on the phone in no time. She must have only put a towel around her.

Eugene paced while on the phone. He was nervous with the situation he had put himself in. He was going to ask her to dinner and get off the phone quickly. Talking on the phone wasn't his favorite thing to do.

"Eugene, how are you doing?"

"Pretty good. How about you?"

"Better now."

There was a pause.

"Well, I thought we might go to dinner again." He was wondering where his confidence had gone.

"That sounds nice. When?"

"Is Tuesday night okay?"

"Fine."

Eugene was lying on the couch by the end of the phone call. An hour phone conversation. It was the longest he had ever had.

The dinner and the next two dates went wonderfully, but nothing sexual, except a few kisses, had happened yet. They had such a good time being with each other the sexual side wasn't as important to him. He thought about how odd that was, how odd the whole situation was, as he cooked dinner. Dominique was to arrive in ten minutes. Everything was in place. He had his best serving set out, including brass candle holders, an antique vase with flowers, and a beautiful tablecloth. A romantic setting, his good cooking, and his charm would find out where this relationship was going.

Dominique showed up on time. She was looking sexier than Eugene had ever noticed. He was happy to have a physical reaction to her because it was her personality that he thought about most. Now he could make some serious moves.

She handed him a loaf of French bread and a bottle of wine. "I hope this is okay? I don't know much about wines."

He looked at the label. "It's just the kind I would have bought."

As they talked over a glass of wine he found himself more and more attracted to her. He had to ask her to repeat some of the things she said.

"Is there something on your mind?" she asked.

"Sorry I'm a little distracted."

He got up to check on dinner.

"By what?"

"You," he said, turning his head to see her reaction.

She smiled and took a sip of wine while looking at him.

"That was a wonderful dinner."

"Thanks."

They left the dining room and moved to the living room. She sat on the leather couch rubbing it with her hands. He put on a Theresa Andersson CD. He then joined her on the couch. They finished the last of the wine and the conversation.

He took her hand and kissed her palm. He had always had the power of knowledge. Knowing exactly what the woman wanted made him a great lover. Now he had to go on instinct. He hoped he was doing the right thing. She took the hint and returned the favor. They moved together mutually, and started kissing, going from hard and deep to softer then hard again. She pulled away looking relieved.

"I was afraid this was never going to happen," she said.

Eugene smiled then moved back in to continue kissing. Dominique then took the initiative. She unbuttoned his shirt and pulled it off. She rubbed his hairy chest. His hands were finding their way to her zipper. The dress was on the floor with the shirt, quickly followed by pants, underwear, and bra. He kept condoms handy at all times so there was no time wasted. They had intercourse on the couch. Everything happened so fast he didn't have time to think. He was halfway sitting up, and she was lying back on him. He kissed her ear while she lightly rubbed his legs. They were both silent. He was trying to figure out what the difference was between knowing every move to make and not knowing.

"Want to take a bath?" she asked.

"Sure, let's go upstairs."

They spent the next two hours in the tub exploring each other's bodies. There was some oral sex, but mainly massaging, sucking, and kissing. They moved to the bedroom and started having intercourse again. This time it was slower and more deliberate. He had time to think how different it felt not knowing what she was thinking. It added to the excitement of the moment. He liked it. He was on top holding himself away from her and looked her in the eyes. All he saw was her desire for him. He kissed her.

Eugene sat on his back porch looking at the stars and drinking iced tea. He had just experienced the best sex of his life. What was next? There were feelings inside him he never knew he had. Dominique came up behind him, put her arms around him, and kissed his neck.

"That was great," she said.

He turned around and put his arms around her waist. He noticed that she was wearing one of his T-shirts.

"Now I know why you are a lady killer. I was beginning to think your reputation was undeserved."

"What have you heard about me?"

"From other guys it's that you can get any woman you want. From other women it's that you know exactly what to say and do, like you're reading their thoughts."

"Did I do everything right tonight?"

"Everything." She grinned. "What's your secret?"

He hesitated. He had never told his secret to a woman before. "I can read women's fantasies."

She laughed. "Very funny."

He didn't laugh. He wished he hadn't said it, but he decided not to play it off.

"You're serious?"

"Yes."

"Are you psychic in general or ...?"

"No, just women's fantasies."

"How would that be?"

He took a breath. "You won't believe me."

"But I'll believe the result."

"Okay. I asked a voodoo woman to make me be able to know when a woman was my true love. I guess she messed up because ever since I can read women's fantasies."

"Hey there, stranger," Windgate said with a hug.

"Man, oh man," Eugene said.

"What's up. What have you been up to?"

"Nothing much."

"I heard you've been seeing someone."

"Well, I guess I have," Eugene struggled.

"Is it serious?"

"I don't know."

"Are y'all monogamous?"

"I don't know. We haven't talked about it."

"Do you love her?"

Eugene looked straight at Windgate. "I don't know. I've never felt like this before. I know that. We made love a few nights ago for the first time. It was the best sex I ever had. I can't read her fantasies, and it makes everything better. Last night we talked on the phone for three hours. We had phone sex. That was great."

"Well, it sounds like you're in love." Windgate laughed. "You're going to have to hang up your wild ways. Your fans are going to be upset."

"Wait, wait, wait, we aren't that far yet. I still have my gift. I don't know if I'm ready to give that up. Maybe I can't. I told her about it."

"Why?" Windgate shook his head.

"I have no idea."

Eugene and Windgate drank hard. They talked about sports, old times, and women. They were still going strong as the sun came up. They ate breakfast at Camellia Grill. Eugene was talking to a beautiful woman. He looked into her eyes and smiled, then leaned over and whispered in her ear. Twenty minutes later they were in his bedroom.

He looked into her eyes. He stopped unbuttoning her blouse.

"I'm sorry. I can't do this," Eugene said while getting up.

The woman got up and dressed quickly. He tried to apologize, explaining the situation with Dominique.

"Look." The woman stopped him. "It's okay. I'm just going to leave."

He walked her to the door. He opened the door at the same time that Dominique was ringing the doorbell. She saw the other woman and dropped a bag of groceries that was in her arms. The sound of eggs breaking and the milk pouring out of the bag attended little reaction. The woman stepped through Eugene, Dominique, and the mess, and walked away without a word. Dominique started crying and Eugene stood there not knowing what to do. She walked past him and sat down in the closest chair she could find. He left the mess to pay attention to her.

"Dominique, I'm sorry. It's not what you..."

"I was afraid of this." She tried to compose herself.

"Nothing happened."

"I'm not upset about that. I realize we haven't committed to this relationship, but that is what I want." She took a breath. "Because I'm in love with you."

"I think I'm in love with you too," he said quickly.

"I'm afraid that won't be enough." She caressed his cheek.

"What does that mean?"

"I've been thinking about the power that you have, and no matter how strong your feelings are for me you won't be able to resist the temptations. I don't know if I can take a broken heart." She leaned over and gave him a kiss, got up, and walked out.

"Wait, wait, Dominique, wait!"

She didn't turn back.

Eugene was exhausted, but too restless to sleep. There had to be a way to keep Dominique. His thoughts went from one extreme to another. He couldn't look in women's eyes if he blinded himself, or maybe they could live in the middle of nowhere. Sometime later in the day he decided to try to hunt down the voodoo lady that gave him his power.

He drove downtown to the French Quarter and found the voodoo shop. The first room looked exactly the same as it did years ago. Before he could ask to see the fortune teller the man behind the counter pointed. Following where the man was pointing, he entered a side room. The lady in the room offered him a seat.

"Hello, Eugene, welcome back."

"You remember me?"

"I remember everybody."

"Do you know why I'm here?"

"I'm a voodoo lady, not a psychic. Why are you here?"

"When I was here years ago you offered me a wish. I said I want to be able to know who my true love is. I don't know what went wrong, but ever since then I've been..."

The lady interrupted. "Reading women's fantasies, and now you've met a woman that you can't do that with."

"Yes, but how did you know?" Eugene said leaning forward.

"That's how you're supposed to tell."

He sat back to take everything in. "She's my true love?"

"Do you love her?"

"Yes."

"Then what more do you need to know?"

"I don't think she'll be with me as long as I can read women's fantasies. Can you take that back?"

"Commit to her mind, body, and soul, and you'll never again be able to read women's fantasies."

"It's that easy?"

"A lot of life's problems are easily solved," the lady said with a laugh.

He thanked her and started to leave.

"May you and Dominique be happy forever."

He turned. He thought about asking how she knew Dominique's name, but decided not to. He turned back and left the shop.

Windgate stood up and raised his glass. "To the happy couple. May life show them a good time," he said with a wink towards Eugene.

Eugene, Dominique, and Susan raised their glasses. They were celebrating Eugene and Dominique's engagement, and the plans to have a double wedding, with a fine dinner at Gautreaux's. Everybody was happy and having a good time. They were the loudest people in the restaurant but couldn't care less.

The young and adorable bus girl asked Eugene if he wanted more water. He looked into her eyes. She had beautiful blue eyes. That was all he got out of it. No fantasies.

Eugene leaned over to Dominique. "I love you." They kissed.

Eddie Tebbe

My World

I live in my own world
A land hard to get to
People come to visit
But they can't stay
They go away

To the visitor it's magnificently beautiful
But the beauty can turn to grossest ugliness
Some people see some
When they come

The mountains are as high as any
But the valleys grow deeper
As time goes by
It makes me cry

The brightness of the light can blind
But it can't penetrate the darkness
The darkness grows
Does my face show?

Visitors get to see the wonder and uniqueness
But when they leave the horror creeps out
They see the best
I feel the rest

I would like to banish the ugliness
But the beauty and horror go together
They don't separate
How long can I wait?

Eddie Tebbe

What Won't Be Will Be

What will be won't be
Can't you see
The world is funny
Let's be free
What's wrong is right
Understand
What's in the night
Can't be planned
What's big is small
Open your eyes
Any costume
Can't disguise
What won't be will be
Can't you see
The world is funny
Let's be free

What will be won't be
Can't you see
The world is funny
Let's be free
What's loud is quiet
Take a listen
All is heard
When we pitch in

What's hard is soft
Touch your hand
It's important
That you understand
What won't be will be
Can't you see
The world is funny
Let's be free

What will be won't be
Can't you see
The world is funny
Let's be free
What we see we don't
Perceptions aren't kind
Illusions live
In your mind
What's true is false
It works that way
Confusion hits
Let us pray
What won't be will be
Can't you see
The world is funny
Let's be free

New Year's Poem

The year is done
And what should I say
Let's us keep hope
For a brighter day

The year was good
But wasn't great
The search goes on
For a love and mate

Until I find
Endless love for me
I never know
How the sky will be

Last year I saw
Sunlight in the sky
Shine through the clouds
May it never die

For years before
Darkness took control
It's always there
Playing a big role

I hope the best
Will happen next year
For you and me
Is happiness near?

Future poems
Whether bad or best
All my hopes are
May darkness be less

Happy New Years
To everyone
When life clouds up
Believe in the sun

Eddie Tebbe

Hopeless Night

It's these moments late at night
That hurt the worst
Afraid to go to bed
Wanting to hold someone
Wondering what passion feels like
Wonder if I will ever know

Wanting to cry but it doesn't help
Tears can't fill the void
I've tried to fill the void with everything
Nothing works, not even for a moment
Superficial things can be more harmful
I know what I need but can't find it

Hopelessness is a horrible feeling
The worst I have ever felt
Worse than fear, worse than faithlessness
Worse than pain, even worse than the worst broken heart
I fight within myself to keep my spirit up
I'm losing the fight more and more I need someone's help

I can keep myself going, doing quite well from the outside
I can face my fears, find a faith, ease my pain, and mend my heart
I can't give myself hope someone needs to do that
Waiting for a miracle is hard
When will it come, will it come?
I'm waiting and waiting, waiting and waiting

If I can borrow a few lines
See me
Hear me
Touch me
Feel me
That will give me hope

Toothsome

Verse one:
See that woman walking down the street
Looking so fine, looking so neat
Boy, I'd like to sink my teeth into her
I would tell her if I could
She's toothsome
Toothsome's real good

Chorus:
Toothsome
That's what I said
Say toothsome
When they blow your head
It's toothsome
When it's so good
Toothsome
You know you should

Verse two:
What is nicer than big ripe fruit
Succulent and tasty teeming with juice
The minute you see one
Your mouth waters
It's toothsome
Toothsome's what ya oughta

Verse three:
Aren't you sick of the same words
Compliments are old everyone has heard
We need something new
Something real fresh
Say toothsome
Toothsome stands out from the rest

Eddie Tebbe

Jane (The Beginning)

You're a mystery to me
A maze to figure out
Charming and alluring
And I have no doubt

You could warm my soul
Or break my heart
Build me up
Or tear me apart

The direction we take
I can't predict
Friends, lovers, soul mates
Or lots of conflicts

I'm willing to take a chance
But you need an open mind
I hope we can go forward
I hope it won't take time

I Saw the Girl

Chorus:
I saw the girl that broke my heart tonight
All the memories came back into sight
I thought I was going to be all right
But I saw the girl that broke my heart tonight

Verse 1:
Four o'clock driving home from Tip's
Had fun everything was hip
Hanging backstage with the singer's wife
You would think I had the time of my life
But

Verse 2:
We were friends for a long, long time
From the beginning I thought she was fine
The way she acted it seems like she wanted me
But when I asked her out, she said it wouldn't be

Verse 3:
We were closer than the feathers on a bird
She was mine, I was hers
Everyone said we should be together
It wasn't up to me, it was up to her

Verse 4:
She didn't see things the way I did
Sometimes she treated me like a kid
Thinking she could lead me on
She thought I would never be gone

Verse 5:
She wanted to treat me like a boyfriend
Thinking I would always be there in the end
I shocked her when I walked away
I wonder what she has to say

Eddie Tebbe

Paradox

Verse one:
As I look back at my life
Experiences I've had
Adventures I've been on
The stories I could tell
If you never lose sight
Of the good and bad
The things you learn
Might keep you from hell

Chorus:
The more things change
The more they stay the same
This I know is true
This I'm telling you
The more things change
The more they stay the same

Verse two:
Last year things were so bad
I packed up my stuff and left
I drove away trying to find
Reasons for all the madness
A year later and things change
New job, car, house, and friends
And I have a much clearer mind
So why can't I shake this sadness

Verse three:
Politicians since the start
Smile and promise the world
Easy to believe words from their mouths
This time things will be different
But once in office they get bought
They forget about the boys and girls
And through their smiles and white teeth
Their lies become evident

If I Was Strong

If I was strong
I'd stand as a friend
With you 'til the end
If I was strong

If I was strong
I'd change your mind
By always being kind
If I was strong

If I was strong
The right words would come
My heart is where they're from
If I was strong

If I was strong
When you held my hand
You would understand
If I was strong

If I was strong
I'd have the world on a string

And have it put on a ring
If I was strong

If I was strong
The difference would be great
What a future I'd create
If I was strong

If I was strong
I'd make the world know
The difficulty life shows
If I was strong

If I was strong
What I needed I'd get
But I can't get it without it
If I was strong

If I was strong
I'd figure out the trick
The irony is so thick
If I was strong

Eddie Tebbe

What's You Doing

Baby, baby, baby, baby
What's ya doing, what's ya doing
Baby what's ya doing
Baby, baby, baby, baby
What's ya doing, what's ya doing
Baby what's ya doing
O, I'm gonna leave
Baby baby gonna leave
Baby baby what's ya going what's
ya doing
Baby what's ya doing
I'm working hard
You're sitting at the bar
I pay them bills
You're taking them pills
What's ya doing to yaself
Cause I know what ya doing to me
I'm gonna leave
Baby I'm going to leave

Baby, baby, what's ya doing
What's ya doing, what's ya doing
Baby what's ya doing
Baby, baby, what's ya doing
What's ya doing, what's ya doing
Baby what's ya doing
O, I'm gonna leave
Baby baby gonna leave
Baby baby what's ya going what's
ya doing
Baby what's ya doing

O, I work so hard
You drink at the bar
Making money to pay bills
You just pop those pills
What's ya doing to yourself
Cause I know what ya doing to me
I'm gonna leave
Baby I'm going to leave

Baby, baby, baby, baby
What's ya doing, what's ya doing
Baby what's ya doing
Baby, baby, what's ya doing
What's ya doing, what's ya doing
Baby what's ya doing
O, I'm gonna leave
Baby baby gonna leave
Baby baby what's ya doing what's
ya doing
Baby what's you doing
I break my back, my work's hard
All day long ya drinking at the bar
I'm making money I'm paying the
bills
Red, blue, pink you'll take any
pills
What's ya doing to yourself
Cause I know what ya doing to me
I'm gonna leave
Baby I'm going to leave

Doing the Dirty Do

Doing the do, doing the dirty do
Doing the do, doing the dirty do
Doing the do, doing the dirty do
Doing the do, doing the dirty do

Tell me what you want to do
Dance dance dance the whole
night through
How nasty do you want to be
Let's see if you can keep
up with me
You have to slide up
way up close
You have to feel the motion
coast to coast
You have to move your hips
round and round
You have to bend your knees to
the ground
Doing the do, doing the dirty do

Doing the do, doing the dirty do
Doing the do, doing the dirty do
Doing the do, doing the dirty do
Doing the do, doing the dirty do

Spread your legs just a little bit
Just enough for my leg to fit
Our hands will go where it
feels best
No more talking, looks will
do the rest
Rub rub rub rub a-dub a-dub

I want to make our sweat
fill a tub
Doing the do, doing the dirty do

Doing the do, doing the dirty do
Doing the do, doing the dirty do

We have to move as one,
not as two
We have to move tonight as
lovers do

Doing the do, doing the dirty do
Doing the do, doing the dirty do
Doing the do, doing the dirty do
Doing the do, doing the dirty do

Now that this groove is
going strong
Generating the friction
makes me long
Let's take this off the dance floor
Go somewhere I can give
you more

Doing the do, doing the dirty do
Doing the do, doing the dirty do
Doing the do, doing the dirty do
Doing the do, doing the dirty do
Doing the do, doing the dirty do
Doing the do, doing the dirty do
Doing the do, doing the dirty do

Eddie Tebbe

Fate's View, Story Two

At 331 March Street, in New Orleans, Louisiana, there is a house. It's two stories, has three bedrooms, two bathrooms, a double living room/dining room combination, kitchen, and breakfast nook. From the outside it looks like any other house on that block, except it is kept up better than the other houses. It's freshly painted light blue with the window frames and other woodwork their natural color. The upstairs balcony has a beautiful wood railing while the front porch has a swing and two rocking chairs all handcrafted cedar, I think. The small grassy area in front, and alongside, the house is neatly trimmed, and lined with small flowers. I don't know much about flowers, some are purple, some are yellow, but I don't know their names. The front door is mainly stained glass. Very beautiful. Before people enter the house, they can tell that a lot of time, energy, love, and money has gone into the house.

The inside is a work in progress. The first room is the living room that is completed. It's a big room with a high ceiling and a hardwood floor. It's big enough to fit a large sofa, love seat, a recliner, two other chairs, a coffee table, two end tables, an entertainment center, and a CD holder. In addition, there are built-in wood bookshelves, a fireplace and a wood mantel, and both are filled with books, antiques, and knick-knacks. The walls are painted violet, and there are well-framed pictures hung nicely. Everything in the room is light colored, with two big windows emitting light. The room is cheery. There are sliding doors between the living room and dining room, but they are rarely shut. The dining room has a totally different mood. It's a little smaller than the front room. It has a large glass top table in the middle of the room. At the moment it has two chairs on each side, and one at each end, but two more chairs could fit with ease. On the dark blue walls are paintings, and around the edges of the room are sculptures. All are made by one of the occupants of the house. On the other side of a small unpainted hallway there is a mess that will be the kitchen. It's about halfway finished. It has...

Wait a minute. I'm sorry. I'm being very descriptive about stuff that doesn't matter. This story isn't even about the people who live here. Sometimes I get into a descriptive mood, but I'm over it now. So I'll stick to what is important.

In the back of the house there is an oversized two car garage. The few little windows along the back are painted black, and it has more locks on it than anyone feels necessary. Those few people who have asked why so many locks are needed receive the same answer. That is where the expensive woodworking equipment is kept. This is not a lie, but the equipment takes up little space. The rest of the space is taken up by the stuff that gives income to the occupants of the house.

In this nice middleclass neighborhood, in this, paid for, house occupied by three nice people who are friendly, community oriented, helpful, and wonderful neighbors are burglars. They are very professional, and good at what they do. None of them have come close to being caught. They work as a team. They take advantage of opportunity. They can be in and out of a house in ten minutes with people sleeping. They are very good, and make good money, money that lets them live an easy life. No drugs, no low life connections, just easy money with low risk. Tonight is a work night.

* * *

Fifteen minutes before I get there this is what happens.

Maureen Davis drives up to her house and parks. She drives a twenty-five year old green VW bug, the kind you can hear from two blocks away, that brings a smile to all ex-hippies. The car is overloaded with paper bags full of food, but Maureen feels like she has room because there are usually three kids in the car as well.

Maureen gets out of the car. At first glimpse it's easy to tell that she was once a very attractive woman. A seven year bad marriage, three kids, six, eight, and ten, and three years of being a single mother has worn on her. Where she was once a hundred and twenty-five pounds, she is now a hundred and seventy. Where she once had wavy blond hair, she now has uncontrollable stringy hair with some premature gray. Everything about her was messy because she didn't have time to worry about her appearance. Working as a waitress in a cafe and raising three kids was all she could handle at the moment.

Her once bouncy step had turned into a sluggish drag. Her feet and back hurt from her long working hours of serving low priced food, but she kept telling herself it was easier to do the chores without the kids. It was close to a miracle when their almost non existent father took all three kids for a three day weekend. Once they were gone Maureen had a choice. Do nothing or do everything even though this was supposed to be a choreless weekend. She decided to do everything first then do nothing. She could do all the chores, well, so much faster without three kids. It was almost like doing nothing. She could read while at the laundromat instead of chasing the kids. Grocery shopping was almost fun without three kids all wanting everything. Cleaning the house was simple when she didn't have to clean after kids who made messes right where she had just cleaned. Even work was nicer knowing a quiet house awaited. It was now about noon on Saturday. On Friday she had worked a little overtime and then did laundry. Today the groceries were already done. She could thoroughly clean the shotgun house the rest of the day, take an extremely long hot bath, go to bed early, and get a wonderful night's sleep. First, she had to bring in and put away the food, and that is where she makes her mistake. I would like to add that if the kids were here they would catch the mistake. They aren't here. So I am.

There are fifteen bags of food. On Maureen's first trip she carries three, leaving one hand free to open the door. Like in most shotgun houses the kitchen is all the way in the back. It takes Maureen five trips. The first two are the hardest because she can't see her feet. Three times she almost falls because of the toys in the house. When coming through the door on the last trip Maureen uses her foot to shut the door. The door automatically locks. She has no idea that she left her keys in the lock on the outside. They don't stand out too much, but if you know what you are looking for they say "Welcome."

The shotgun has three rooms in the front of the house with a hallway connecting to the kitchen. An undersized bathroom is off the hallway. After Maureen cleans up the place will look better, but it will still be a rundown house that the landlord cares little about. It's a good thing that Maureen is handy. She is also good with money. Between her income, a little child support, and some food stamps she has been able to make the most of it. The kids are fed well. Everything they have looks pretty new but is pretty old. The kids have most of the toys they want including a Sega and a computer, both used. The kids have no idea how close things are to bad. The way Maureen figures it, with a few more years, a better income after a promotion, older kids, and financial aid she will be able to take some business classes at the University of New Orleans. For now it was payday to payday. If everything stayed normal things would be good, but any bad luck like medical problems, a robbery, or natural disaster would crush her family. Maureen has fought so hard for three years. Any bad luck would send her right back.

Now that I'm here there are many ways I can handle this situation. Right now, inside, Maureen, a woman I admire, is enjoying listening to her music while she puts away her groceries.

I have decided to break this Coke bottle. That is all I have to do this time. Inside she hears the bottle break. She takes a walk through the house, opens the door, and steps outside. Seeing nothing she turns to go back. She sees her keys in the lock. She thinks that it was lucky that someone broke that bottle. The keys could have been there all night. Anybody could have taken them, taken the car, or come inside.

Fickle Finger Of Fate

Is there a higher meaning
And what's in control
From the beginning
We have needed to know
The search continues each day
Each individual finds their way
There are infinite choices
To fulfill those needs

In my life I've chosen fate
It has significance, but no
structure
It has purpose without being ab-
solute
It doesn't have the power to cre-
ate
Fate and freewill hold hands
But how to make you
understand
In my mind it's quite clear
At least for myself

When most people thank God
I thank fate
What a person thinks as coinci-
dence
I think as fate
But I'm not trying to persuade
you
You'll have to decide what to do
I'm pondering one question here

What controls the fickle finger of
fate

Is it predestined
From the beginning of time
Is it random, like a tornado
With no reason nor rhyme
Is it a cosmic karma effect
Feeding off your efforts
Could it be a combination
Or something beyond our
thoughts

Raging against it
Can be a waste of energy
Just accepting it
Isn't right either
There's a trick to this fight
That's hard to get right
Maybe it doesn't matter
However we act

I think we'll never know
Are we not supposed to
We just have to deal with life
Not understanding every detail
Make as much as you can
positive
Don't concentrate on the negative
And hope that that fickle finger
Points goodness your way

Eddie Tebbe

The Stranger I've Always Known

Chorus:
He's in me, he's in you
What are we to do
The stranger I've always known
He knows me to the bone
It's a constant battle for control
Who will win is who is bold
The truth will be shown
The stranger I've always known

Verse one:
Everything's fine day by day
With a friend as you play
Seeing his toys makes you sad
Without worry you get mad
Lashing out with so much anger
Puts everything in danger
Watch for the signs or be a pawn
The first glimpses come early on

Verse two:
Everybody lives side by side
The world's problem can't hide
Life hasn't given you a
nice result
Surely it must be their fault
I hate those people over there
If they all died, I wouldn't care
With them all gone I'd be better
Why are differences
such a bother

Verse three:
Every personality builds
step by step
Dark things happened
while you slept
Your subconscious played
out in dreams
Never can tell what it all means
But can you see them
in the mirror
Deep in your own eyes
can't be clearer
The dark side nobody talks about
The dark side we can't live
without

A Week in New Orleans

On what day of the week should we start
This little story about New Orleans nights
What we do and how we think
Sweet rationalizations make everything right

Hump day a.k.a. Wednesday, our favorite by name
It's the middle of the week
A break is badly needed
Relax, have fun, sleep is for the meek

Thursday is practically a weekend night
We only have eight hours of work to go
That can be done on no sleep
Just have to do enough to make some dough

T. G. I. F. That's what people say
Maybe we do have to wake up early
But Friday only comes once a week
So to hell if tomorrow we feel surly

Surely we can't stay home on Saturday night
There's too much fun to be had
Take what we have to take to keep up
Believing tomorrow we'll be glad

Sunday we may be feeling tired
An afternoon nap does so much good
We don't want the weekend to end
Let's go out whether or not we should

Eddie Tebbe

Blue Monday hits really hard
We have to blow off some steam
Call someone to bitch and whine
Let's go out for one shot of Beam

Tuesday now is it necessary to go anywhere
Well isn't that the point after all
So why stop now it's our way of life
We just keep having a ball

Power Tool Packing Mama

(Inspired by and dedicated to Jeffrey West)

Chorus:
I'm a power tool packing mama
I'll fix anything you need
I'm a power tool packing mama
I'll do anything I please
With my tools by my side
I'll bring any task to its knees

Verse 1:
You need your nail driven
I can do that
You need your screw screwed
I can do that
I'll fix anything you want me to fix
And I don't waste time I do it quick

Verse 2:
You need some wood sanded
I can do that
You need some cabinets built
I can do that
I'm good with my hands and have every tool
Whatever problem comes I keep my cool

Verse 3:
When people say power tool
They think of a man
That's a bunch of bullshit
I'm doing all I can
I fix this I fix that
While my man sits on the couch no better than a rat

Eddie Tebbe

New Sounds

New sounds what's it going to be like
People ask me why you want to do that
I say because it's my way
I just want to play

Change can be a good thing
New grooves play in an old tune
Making the old sound new
That is what we do

So come take a listen
Don't judge 'til we finish
Listen with an open mind
You'll have a good time

Decisions don't come easy
Contemplating over time
Held my breath took a chance
Hope people still come to dance

I'm Vicious

You betta jump back jack
When I walk down the street
You betta bend right over
And start kissing my feet
You betta open the door
Or you might get beat
You betta do what I want
When I take my seat

Chorus:
Because I'm vicious
O,o,o, I'm vicious
The baddest in town
The best around
I'm vicious

People respect
My ability
Providing the groove
The possibilities
Inventing the beat
Handing it down
Not selling out
My hometown
                    Chorus

You betta listen up
When I play tonight
You betta listen close
And get it right
You betta understand
Or get out of sight
You betta feel the groove
When the band's so tight
                    Chorus
People love it
When I play bass
I've been around
But still set the pace
Following me
Should be done
I don't imitate
I'm number one
                    Chorus
I don't know if it's right
To sing about myself
But when you play like me
Ego doesn't stay shelved
So indulge my whim
And enjoy the song
Everybody is welcome
To sing a long
                    Chorus

Eddie Tebbe

Coffee with Lou

"April showers bring May flowers." In New Orleans April showers bring more showers in May. The rain has been falling heavily since early on the morning of May 28th. It's now 2:00 p.m. on the 30th, and the rain hasn't stopped. Nobody expected this kind of rain. The forecast was for a slight chance of showers. Up until a half hour before the rain started it was a crystal-clear night. The sky shone bright with an almost full moon and stars galore. Then the clouds tumbled in from the South, no thunder, no lighting, no warning, just a complete cloud cover that turned the city black. The rain started falling shortly afterwards. The sun has risen, set, rose again, is still up, and without a clock nobody would have known. The city has been in complete darkness since the rain started.

The city is working hard to fight the rising water. Cars are pulled up on the neutral grounds, sandbags and other homemade barriers surround houses, and the city's water pumps are running at maximum. It's hard to pump water out of a place that is below sea level. Some parts of New Orleans are under water, but some parts can be gotten around in, barely.

The continuous sheets of big and heavy raindrops beating on the large windows of the cafe is the only sound in the place. The radio has been turned off because of lack of new information. The thickness of the rain made the big pink neon sign that flashed 'Mary's Cafe Open 24 hours' unseeable from the cafe. Inside, Mary's Cafe is bright with white fluorescent light that bounces off the white tile floor and walls, the white Formica counter and table-tops, and the white cushions on the seats. It's the cleanest looking twenty-four-hour diner around. Everything sparkles. Most of the city is in a blackout, but Mary's Cafe happens to be lucky. So it stays open, not because it expects business, but because it is senseless to go anywhere. The short elderly man named Danny with short white hair is usually the cook. For the last twenty-four hours he manned the cafe by himself, which isn't hard because no one has come in until just an hour ago.

Danny is sleeping in the back when the man comes in causing the bell attached to the door to jingle. By the time Danny makes it to the front the man is sitting at the counter, in the seat closest to the kitchen door that is farthest from the front door, reading the local paper. The man orders a cup of black coffee in a deep voice then leaves a twenty on the counter. The man makes Danny feel odd. Something is weird about this man. He isn't wet, and there are no signs of a raincoat or umbrella. He is dressed in a custom-made silk Italian suit. His shoes alone could pay Danny's rent for a few months. He doesn't take off his fedora or his sunglasses, and that makes Danny wonder. As far as he can see the man's face has character that only comes with age and experience, but he isn't old looking. He is very tall and overbearing even sitting down. Everything about this guy is perfectly in place, but he isn't. He reads the paper, drinks his black coffee, and says nothing for an hour.

The door opens, the bell rings, and Danny turns to see who is coming in, but the man doesn't. He just reads his paper, never looking up. Out of the dark rain a young man steps into the light and dryness of the cafe. The floor around the door isn't dry for long. The young man has a raincoat on, but it doesn't matter. He is soaked to the bone. It's a dismal sight. The young man's attitude is as soaked as his body. He stands there, not knowing what to do.

"I've got some towels in the back. Wait a sec," Danny says already walking towards the back.

There's no movement or even acknowledgment. Danny is back quickly with four white towels. He hands them to the young man.

"What in the world are you doing walking around, boy?" asks Danny.

The young man is a little confused, "I, I, ah, ah, I."

"Boy, you just dry off, and I'll get you some hot coffee before you catch your death."

The young man dries off as much as possible while Danny pours some coffee. With a towel over his head and one over his shoulder it is hard not to laugh at the young man. His long blond hair is fussed dry. His wet clothes hang heavy on his five foot seven not very built body. His face is young looking with acne. He squints his eyes as if he's missing his glasses, but he makes it to the seat at the counter where his coffee waits. It feels good to hold the hot cup in his hands, but his shaking makes it hard to drink. Danny stands nearby, ready to help, but the man on the other side of the counter still doesn't look up.

It is a while before anything is said. The small lake that the young man made when he came in is mopped up by Danny. The young man sits at the counter sipping his coffee and staring into space. He is a man with something on his mind. Danny wonders what could make him walk around in this weather.

The young man's mind is like a whirlwind in which feelings, images, and memories fly around. Dealing with the emotions caused by what he saw was going to be hard enough. In addition, emotions from a horrible childhood, that the young man foolishly thought were gone, deep seated fears, and core emotions were resurfacing. His childhood was lonely, being an only child and having no real friends. His parents made a good living, but they both had to work hard and weren't around. He wasn't unusually smart, but turned to books and his computer, making him the best student in school. He dreamed about what he didn't have, friends, playing sports, going to dances, and most of all a girlfriend. If he only had a girlfriend. If he was only wanted.

Danny walked up to him.

"What's your name? We'll be here a while. Might as well know each other's name. I'm Danny."

"Hi, I'm Jude. Thanks for the towels."

"No prob."

They shake hands.

"This is some weird weather."

Danny walks towards one of the windows, looking into the dark rain.

"I've lived my whole life in this town, and we get some odd weather here, but I've never seen this. There's no thunder, no lightning, no wind, just straight constant rain which is good because if this is a regular storm, with this much rain, the whole town would be underwater. Don't get me wrong. Most of the city is flooded, but the worst floods always involve the river and lake overflowing. That isn't going to happen with this rain, and the flooded parts will clear quickly. Did you hear any warning? I didn't. These young weathermen rely too much on computers. I'd bet you Nash knew. You probably don't remember Nash Roberts. The best weatherman ever. He could smell a storm."

"I remember him from when I was a kid," Jude says not knowing what else to say.

The conversation revolves around the weather for some time, not out of a lack of other subjects, like usual, but because it is an interesting subject at the moment. Jude doesn't have as much to say as Danny. He could barely get a word in even if he did. Danny is an old New Orleanian. He likes to talk about anything, and within a conversation he will tell, no matter what the subject, his family history in detail. An answer to a yes or no question can take ten minutes. So Jude sips his coffee and listens. He doesn't pay attention, but Danny would have never known or cared. Danny knows what he is doing. He is nosy and wants to know what is disturbing Jude. It is hard not to be pushy. So, Danny keeps talking until he feels the time is right. The time is right.

"So, what in the world were you doing out there?"

Jude thought at first. Does he want to talk about it? Finally, he decides it couldn't hurt.

"I didn't know what else to do. I walked in on my wife doing it with my upstairs neighbor. I couldn't stay there, I was already wet from walking home, so I just walked back out."

"Man, that's a tough thing to take. How long were you walking out there?"

"About forty-five minutes maybe, it's hard to tell."

"Good thing I was open."

"You're telling me. I didn't even know this place was here. I could hardly see the lights. It's almost an accident, or something, that I'm here." Jude shakes his head.

"How long you've been married?"

"Two years."

"Two years?" Danny is surprised. "How old are you anyway?"

"Twenty-three."

"And her?"

"Twenty-two"

"You got married early for nowadays. I married my Littia when we were seventeen, but in those days that's what you did, and there was none of this divorce. We stuck it out. You'll probably get divorced?"

Jude takes a deep breath. "I don't know. I haven't gotten that far yet. I can't think straight, my feelings are all confused, and I would do anything to stop these feelings. I haven't had these feeling in years. As a kid, especially a teenager, I was always confused, and doubted myself. I had no friends. I was the typical nerd, bony, pimply face, glasses, the clothes, and everything. It took me until I was twenty to look halfway like a grownup. Then I met the girl of my dreams, and she liked me. Me. Since then I've felt like a new man. I don't want to go back. I need her. I believed she wanted me. I need that. I don't know what I'm going to do. I can't think of the future. I have to figure out what went wrong."

There is a long pause.

"Well," Danny says.

"I don't know. Life has been hectic lately. I'm trying to finish up my electrical engineering degree at Tulane, and she's working. We haven't fought much. On the other hand, we don't see each other much."

There is another pause.

"I love her with all my heart. I thought she loved me. We fell in love quickly and got married within a year of our first date. She's not from here. She was going to Tulane but has stopped until I finish. I know she doesn't like living here, and I've told her I'll move. She didn't tell me anything was wrong, and we've had good communication. I've been looking back over the past couple of months, and even looking back I don't see any weird actions. The only thing I can think is she doesn't love me, and I've been a fool." Jude wipes tears off his cheeks.

"That's not always true. Me and Littia love each other, and we've been married fifty years. A lot of good times, but some bad too. More when we were young. We almost broke up countless times. We didn't communicate. Nobody even talked like that. I had affairs, and she had affairs. We were young and stupid, both of us, and maybe we should have broken up, but we didn't, thank God. Now that's just me. I've seen people who should break up. I've also seen a lot of Oprah because of my wife, and I don't tell her, but I've learned a lot. You've got to talk to her and find out why she did it. You've got to realize y'all are so young, even if you don't think so, and y'all will make mistakes. All and all be ready to forgive her."

The man at the end of the counter looks over his sunglasses towards the kitchen door. Seconds later there is a noise in the back.

"I'll be back. Think about that." Danny goes in the back to see what made the noise. Jude starts staring into space again thinking about what Danny said. He doesn't notice the man following Danny into the back. Danny doesn't even notice until he is all the way in the kitchen. After he notices he turns to ask how he can help. The man reaches over and puts his hand on Danny's shoulder. Danny faints. The man turns, walks back to the front, and takes his seat without Jude even knowing he moved.

"That old man doesn't know what he's talking about," says the man putting his paper down. He has a very deep voice.

Jude is startled by the voice, and the fact that the man spoke.

"Listen to me for a while," the man says motioning towards a table. They both get up, walk to a table, and sit across from each other.

"Hi, I'm Jude,' he says reaching out a hand.

"You can call me Lou if you must," the man responds not wanting to shake hands.

"Kinda bright out. Wish I had sunglasses," Jude says with a nervous smile. It is a stupid thing to say, but this man intimidates Jude.

Lou is not amused. "I have very sensitive eyes. I'm not here to talk about me. I'm here to give you an opportunity."

"What kind of opportunity?"

"For a better life, one with no guilt, no remorse, and no self-doubt. Decisions would be easy. This situation you're in would mean nothing. I can give you what you think your wife gives you and more, much, much more, always knowing exactly what you want, and how to get it, a life of never feeling unwanted." Lou leans back and smiles a smile of sinister confidence.

"Sounds good. Too good to be true."

"Maybe it is, but it's too good to pass up. Are you willing to listen?"

Jude thinks for a few moments, "Yes."

Lou speaks with eloquence and confidence. He is a great salesman. Everything he says sounds great, not only great, but right. If listened to closely it is selfishness he is talking about, and if just anybody lived like this they would be seen as selfish, but Lou could give Jude a gift. It isn't just about an attitude or way of life. Lou can give Jude the gift he has. Jude listens, and is hypnotized. Lou doesn't have to do any extra pushing. Jude wants the gift. He wants it so badly that he doesn't think or ask the cost.

Lou puts his hands over Jude's eyes making him fall asleep. Then Lou gently lays Jude's head on the table, and steps back.

A shadow in the corner starts to move, slowly forming three little mounds. The mounds grow until they are three feet tall. The extra blackness starts to melt away leaving three boyish figures that barely have facial features. Each figure has a tool in their hand. The first one has a special drill. The second has a tube and a fancy ten-ounce bottle. The bottle is dark green with detailed engravings of people being attacked by snakes. The third has a black leather case.

After a short conference they go to work. They move like shadows working as a team. The first climbs on the booth next to the sleeping Jude. It marks its spot and drills a tiny hole at the base of his skull. There is no blood. The second figure takes over immediately putting one end of the tube to the hole and the other end to the bottle. The bottle slowly changes color from dark green to a glowing golden color. The third figure takes the bottle and corks it, places the case on the table, and opens it. It is custom made to hold six of the bottles. Currently three bottles are dark green, and two are glowing golden. With the inclusion of the bottle just used there are three glowing golden. The case is closed, the three figures go back to the corner, and they melt away.

It is completely silent except for the falling rain. Lou smiles at his handiwork. This was easier than he thought it would be. He takes a notepad and pen from his inside coat pocket, and flips to the last page with writing on it. The page has a list of six names. The first two names have checks by them, while the third name has a line through it. Lou proceeds to put a check by the fourth name, Jude Hebert. The notepad and pen are put back, and he pulls out a Band-Aid, placing it on the hole left by the drill. He starts towards the door when he hears

Eddie Tebbe

Danny awakening in the back. Without turning around he takes a hundred dollar bill out of his pocket and tosses it on the counter. As he opens the door, and steps outside, the rain parts only enough for him to walk out. After he walks a few steps the rain continues around him, but he stays perfectly dry.

Eight hours later the rain stops.

The Circle

A young man makes a promise to his child
Watching him in the nursery for a while
He says things will be different this time
I'll treat you right
I won't treat you like my father treated me
He beat me every night
I'll get a job and we'll get out of this place
I don't want to see any sadness come over your face

For a while everything goes good and they are happy
Then the jobs get hard to find and they run out of money
But good intentions don't pay the bills
And it's hard for a young man to keep his will
He breaks down and he starts to drink
Everything the family does starts to stink
Before you know it, the fists are flying
All the little boy feels like doing is crying

Growing up on the streets is hard
When your mom and dad hang out in bars
The little boy grows up with anger and pain
Like a wild horse you can't hold the reins
He tries to do good but he feels hated by the world
He does some bad things and finds himself a girl
So he takes comfort with his girl in the back room
And you know she is pregnant way, way too soon

Eddie Tebbe

The children are the future, but we don't care
Stand up to the problems if you dare
The girl goes into labor and has a baby
Another child in this world that's so crazy
A young man makes a promise to his child
Watching him in the nursery for a while
He says things will be different this time
I'll treat you right

I won't treat you like my father treated me
He beat me every night
I'll get a job and we'll get out of this place
I don't want to see any sadness come over your face

The Journey

Chorus:
We come to play
We come to play good for you
We come to say
We come to say here's
something new
It's all in the same mind set
The pieces are just changed
Maybe it's a better puzzle
Let's find out all the same
We come to play
We come to play good for you
We come to say
We come to say here's
something new

Verse one:
It's no slap on the old
We reached greatness
It was a real fun ride
A band is a musical journey
Every journey must end
It's both sad and happy
It's now time to say goodbye

Verse two:
I'll always look back
With many fond memories
At all the changes
We went through
There is lots of confusion
But my mind is focused
On the future and something
new

Verse three:
So join with me
As we start anew
And begin down a different
road
The feeling is right
The players are on
We still need your energy
To complete this journey

Eddie Tebbe

The Gris Gris Man

Chorus:
I'm the gris gris man
Ain't got no degrees
I'm the gris gris man
Learnt it from my family
Talking bout the old way
Like generations have done
Following the old rules
Come inside at once
Listen to my voice
Do what I say
But you must believe
For your hurt to go away

Verse 1:
I was born with the gift
Got it from my mother
Like her father had
And his father's brother
Tested through time
The tradition runs deep
It an honor to serve
The gris gris man belief
It's an important role
To where I live
People count on me
And all that I give

Verse 2:
I don't practice voodoo
The theatrics are made up
To sell to tourists
So they'll buy stuff
People of New Orleans
Who know the truth
Line up at my door
For my words, herbs, and roots
Physical ailments
Are easily solved
I work on the soul
To deepen a person's resolve

Verse 3:
The medical profession
Has passed healing by
H.M.O.s and doctor bills
Frustration runs high
Let's step back a moment
Technology's too advanced
Keeping people alive
Isn't always the best chance
To improve their being
It comes back to the soul
Let the docs laugh at me
I know the wisdom of the old

Go Round

Chorus:
Things in this world do go round
Sometimes when you're feeling down
Hold on to your faith
You'll be happy like a clown
Things in this life do go round

Verse 1:
Be good to all mankind
Or you'll know in your mind
That you've been bad
Then you'll be sad
Things in this world do go round

Verse 2:
So you say you love that girl
She's the only one in the world
Then she broke your heart
But don't get mad, get smart
Things in this life do go round

Verse 3:
I'm old and seen all there is to see
So please, please take it from me
I've seen people come and go
This is one thing they all show
Things in this world do go round.

Eddie Tebbe

Thank You

Just how can I ever show
The gratitude within me
Words are the less effective way
But all I have today
If you could see through my eyes
And into my soul
If you could get in my mind
Or feel my heart
You'd know what it meant
The care and understanding
The love I felt
Was immense help
To see me through
Thank you

Da Medicine Man

First verse:
Go and look him up
When you got the ills
It's his specialty
He'll cure the rhythm chills
It doesn't take a lot
He doesn't give you pills
Just put some music on, he'll say
So you can't sit still

Chorus:
He's a guy doing what he can
He's all right, he's da medicine man
If it's a musical ailment that you have
Music lovers use da medicine man

Second verse:
So you have funky fungus
I've had it myself
It's a problem he sees a lot
He knows the answer well
Just use the ointment
That he has to sell
Rest is not needed
Get up off the shelf

Third verse:
Whether it's the groovy pains
Or the achy shakes
Working hard day and night
What he lacks he will make
When something goes wrong
Or the music world brakes
They all go to him
Cause he got what it takes

Eddie Tebbe

Thank You Friends

Chorus:
Thank you for saving my life
Sheltering me during the storm
Filling me with your warmth
Thank you
Thank you for your shining light
Wrapping me in your love
Holding me like a glove
Thank you

Verse one:
In the Gulf, Katrina turned
But I wasn't really scared
Riding her was like a dare
You phoned
Your voice was so concerned
You said leaving was right
That choice changed my life
Couldn't have known

Verse two:
The hurricane was a mighty force
The levees let us down
Still too many people around
Heartbreak
Human nature exposed was worst
From comfort and safety
I watched on tv
Heartbreak

Verse three:
The destruction was immense
Pain in the core of my soul
In days I grew very old
Limbo
My life was in suspense
My hometown in ruins
The lost was unknowing
Limbo

This Is All I Have

Verse 1:
This is my purpose
A curse and a blessing
That's what life's about
This is my purpose
So I willfully commit
This is all I have
Our symbiotic relationship
The energy that we share
This is all I have
We both need the fix

Chorus:
This moment in time is
all we share
It's all I have to give you
To do with as you will
This moment in time I stand bare

Verse 2:
This is my purpose
What knowledge can I part
I've seen the worst, the best
This is my purpose
May it be of benefit
This is all I have
The pain deep in my eyes
From so much heartbreak
This is all I have
Am I such a misfit

Verse 3:
This is my purpose
I know no other way
The path's been strange
This is my purpose
What is left to admit
This is all I have
My soul ripped open
Bleeding on the floor
This is all I have
To you I gladly give it

Eddie Tebbe

Lafayette Blues

Chorus:

I got the blues since my baby went to Lafayette
I got the blues since she went home
She left me stinky
And she ain't coming back

Verse 1:

I thought I knew now to be a real man
I thought I had to get in all the girls' pants
I thought I had to look up all their skirts
I just didn't know who it would hurt

Verse 2:

She said she was sick of all my messing around
She was packing her bags and leaving town
I begged and begged her not to walk out that door
But she went home and ain't coming back no more

Verse 3:

In Lafayette she has a big brother
He found out what happen from their mother
He came all the way to New Orleans
Just to break both my knees

Verse 4:

I got the blues since my baby went home
I got more blues since her brother broke my bones
I won't fool around no more baby can we talk
You know I won't fool around cause I can't walk

Little Bitty Party Town

(The Jazz Fest Song)

End of April beginning of May
The people come out and play
Transforming the fairgrounds
Into a little bitty party town
Where you can dance
on the grass
Where you can really
shake your ass

Chorus

Little bitty party town
Little bitty party town
You better come to get down
Everybody is welcome
So come, come, come
To the fair grounds
To a little bitty party town

It is what we call Jazz Fest
For two weekends there's no rest
Shows all night fest all day
Everybody knows the way
To the fair grounds
To a little bitty party town

Chorus

People come from everywhere
Enjoying the time without a care
The feeling is really good
Just like life should
Be all year round
In the little bitty party town

Chorus

New Orleans has Jazz Fest
To show local music at its best
Plus the best music you can hear
All happens once a year
Transforming the fair grounds
Into a little bitty party town

Chorus

The food is also home grown
With every bite you will moan
Because it's so great
You'll remember what you ate
Out at the fair grounds
In our little bitty party town

Chorus

Eddie Tebbe

All I Have to Say

Time is tight so listen to me friend
While I tell you some things about Alison
She's sharp, compassionate loves Mardi Gras
Dancing, festivals, travel, dogs, bread and butter
There's few things I hope she'll understand
I try to tell her while I still can

I want her to know life lessons show you what to do and not to do
When to have a big picture view and when to have a little view
About treasuring the moment but trying to think beyond
About not repeating bad behavior just because it's fun
The mood should be light, for all of your life
That's pretty much all I have to say

The only other thing I think that matters
Is don't get caught up in all of the chatter

I want her to know life lessons show you what to do and not to do
When to have a big picture and when to have a little view
About treasuring the moment but trying to think beyond
About not repeating bad behavior or just because it's fun
The mood should be light, for all of your life
That's pretty much all I have to say

Hitting the Road

I learned to laugh like my mother
did with all of my heart
and my soul
her laugh made me
laugh when I was a kid
I miss it now that I'm old

Her love for hitting the road
and trying to do what was right
yes her love for hitting the road
has lasted me all of my life

She worked for justice
and freedom passed that
work on to me
she never cared for money and
such as long as her
spirit was free

Her love for hitting the road
and trying to do what was right
yes her love for hitting the road
has lasted me all of my life

Always she encouraged me
like most folks never would
to face the challenges that may be
and do the best I could

I remember camping
and playing darts
the kind of stuff we do
folks say she was indomitable
she passed that to me too

Her love for hitting the road
and trying to do what was right
yes her love for hitting the road
has lasted me all of my life

Made in the USA
Middletown, DE
05 January 2023

21375693R00219